Poetry
and
Privacy

Poetry and Privacy

Questioning Public Interpretations
of Contemporary British and Irish Poetry

JOHN REDMOND

SEREN

Seren is the book imprint of
Poetry Wales Press Ltd.
57 Nolton Street, Bridgend, Wales, CF31 3AE

www.serenbooks.com
facebook.com/SerenBooks
Twitter: @SerenBooks

The right of John Redmond to be identified as
the editor of this work has been asserted in accordance
with the Copyright, Designs and Patents Act, 1988.

ISBN 978-1-85411-585-0
Epub 978-1-85411-603-1
Kindle 978-1-78172-127-8

A CIP record for this title is available from the British Library.

The publisher acknowledges the financial assistance of the Welsh Books Council.

Printed by Short Run Press, Exeter

CONTENTS

Acknowledgements

Some of these chapters have been written during a period of leave from the University of Liverpool. I am grateful to the advice and support of my colleagues from that institution: Deryn Rees-Jones, Dinah Birch, and Marcus Walsh.

I especially want to thank Neil Corcoran and Stephen Burt who offered much valuable commentary on certain chapters. Jane Ford and Patrick McGuinness also offered much encouragement.

Versions of these chapters – most of them much briefer – have appeared elsewhere. A portion of the chapter on Seamus Heaney appeared in the journal, *British and Irish Contemporary Poetry* (Spring 2008). A portion of the chapter on David Jones and W.S. Graham appeared in *Poetry Wales* (Autumn 2005). The chapter on Robert Minhinnick was influenced by an interview which I carried out with him in Porthcawl – this was later published in *Gallous* (Autumn 2008). The chapters on John Burnside and Derek Mahon had their foundation in articles written for the *London Review of Books*. Some of the chapters developed out of papers delivered at the *International Association for the Study of Irish Literatures* (IASIL) and the *American Conference for Irish Studies* (ACIS).

INTRODUCTION

This book questions a set of relationships – critical, authorial, and existential – between poetry and the public sphere. Its main contention – that readings of British and Irish poetry rely too often on a thesis of public relevance – arises out of a more general conviction: that the relationship between poetry and the public sphere is negatively woven. While all seven chapters have been written with this theme in mind, they are also designed to serve as an oblique portrait of contemporary British and Irish poetry and to offer some fresh appraisals of noteworthy poets.

A decade in to the new century, it would be too theatrical to declare, like Francis Fukuyama, that history has concluded, or to compose variations on Tom Paulin's remark that "Irish history is over." Nevertheless, the mood in these islands is distinctly *fin-de-siècle*. Many of the large-scale processes of the post-war period are grinding towards completion – our economies have been globalised, our societies have been secularised, and our cultures have been Americanised. Meanwhile the oil and debris from failed local systems continues to wash ashore: the collapse of financial institutions, the implosion of New Labour, the humiliation of the Catholic Church. As the various castles dissolve in the air we are left, to adopt Ted Hughes's phrase, "in the remains".

The sense of an ending is also keenly felt in the world of poetry. It is not an accident that both Giorgio Agamben, a philosopher, and Paul Muldoon, a poet, have written books entitled *The End of the Poem*. A scan of the melancholy shelves devoted to literary criticism turns up titles like *The Death of the Critic, After the Death of Poetry,* and *Life.After.Theory*. Of course one should be sceptical. There is easy drama in the journalistic talk of endings. Yet it is undoubtedly true that poetry and criticism – these two closely intertwined arts – are bitterly aware of their marginal status. Both have lost confidence and direction. In public life as in literary life, we have entered a period of deleveraging and disavowal, of recanting and retrenchment. This moment of kenosis seems to me like a good time for emptying out some old ways of thinking about poetry.

§

To begin with a topical episode: in 2009 the British public glanced –
not once, but twice – in the direction of poetry. The population was
stirred neither by a poem nor by a book – would that it were so – but
by a pair of appointments. At Buckingham Palace, Carol Ann Duffy
was received as the first female Poet Laureate, while, at Oxford
University, Ruth Padel was elected as the first female Professor of
Poetry. In the beginning, the media viewed these developments,
which seemed so pleasingly symmetrical, through the lens of gender
equality. But that narrative did not endure. Shortly after her election,
a national newspaper claimed that Padel, as part of her 'campaign',
had reminded a journalist of some allegations of misbehaviour once
made against her main rival, Derek Walcott. At the sight of a poet
behaving like a politician, there was an immediate hue and cry.
Editors, columnists, and celebrities from literature and television lined
up to broadcast their dismay. Such was the flood of protest that, a
mere nine days after assuming the role, Padel resigned. This story
hung in the air for a little while but, after a few turns of the news-
cycle, it was barely a memory, a murky suggestion in the public mind.
Uncertain about the goodness of all publicity, British poetry resumed
its neglected corner, as misunderstood as ever.

Although it would be possible to reflect on The Oxford Affair by
resorting to the language of faction and conspiracy – a language in
which most poets are fluent – that would be a mistake. What matters
about the professorship – and also the laureateship – is not the poet
who fills the role, but the role the poet fills. The displeasing symmetry
is this: the two most desired jobs in British poetry are not jobs at all.
What is a poet laureate supposed to *do*? What is an Oxford Professor
of Poetry *for*? While the holder of the former post is under no obliga-
tion to undertake any task of substance, the holder of the latter
position need only deliver three lectures a year. Both jobs have
prestige, to be sure, but they have no point. Their sole purpose is to
sustain a fiction – curiously widely held – that poetry should hang
on some sort of public hook.

Viewed with a tolerant eye, the laureateship represents a lingering
attachment in the public mind to the value of vatic poetry. It embod-
ies the idea that bards should say wise and delphic things in the
neighbourhood of power. Viewed with a sceptical eye, the role reduces
the poet to a kind of stage-turn wheeled out for the sake of variety,
somewhere between a contortionist and a spirit medium. Tolerantly
or sceptically viewed, the effects of the laureateship on those who
accept the role have been unambiguously negative. While the most

illustrious recent holder of the position, Ted Hughes, wrote his worst poems on behalf of the monarchy (and saw his reputation decline), his successor, Andrew Motion, after stepping down from the role, complained that, "[the laureateship] made me stop paying attention to the world in a way that allowed me then to write about it."[1]

Meanwhile the fact that Britain's leading university has maintained an idiosyncratic professorship might be looked on as another lovable quirk, like the May Day habit of jumping off Magdalen Bridge. But its significance is made all the greater because, as has long been the case in the United States, the modern university is the home of modern poetry. Oxford's awkward professorship reflects the awkwardness of an arrangement which pleases no one. A poet's best chance of a viable career may be a job in Creative Writing and yet, at the same time, British and Irish universities are spiritually hostile to the teaching of poetry composition. At heart, such universities regard Creative Writing as a dubious American import, only tolerating the subject because of its popularity with students (it boosts their fees).

Little has changed since the time in 1965 when the critic David Wright dismissed contemporary American poetry, with its proliferation of Creative Writing courses, as, "an industry rather than an art ...."[2] Such sentiments have been expressed more recently in the writing of Michael Donaghy, an influential American poet who settled in Britain. Writing in 1989, Donaghy attacked the "bizarre inbreeding" of Creative Writing courses in the United States, disparaged "the unique idiom of full-time writer-teachers" and scorned the circularity of a process where, "after graduation one is expected to publish a collection and go on to teach ... creative writing."[3] Interviewed in 2003, however, he struck a revealingly different note:

> Of *course* poetry workshops are useful. No one doubts that music can be taught because there's so much quantifiable technique imparted at the conservatory. An apprenticeship in poetry requires a more oblique process, but there are so many ways a mentor can help .... it's still the best job I ever had.[4]

Introducing a selection of Donaghy's writing, Clive James noted this 'paradox' of these opposed positions, and credited the American poet with having the grace to rise above his suspicions. Probably, this is fair. But the contradiction in Donaghy's stance reflects a wider confusion in his generation about the place of poetry.

Although exceptions like the so-called 'Cambridge School' exist, the dominant culture of contemporary poetry is promotional in outlook and anti-intellectual in spirit. At least since the time of the celebrated 'New Generation', contemporary poetry has struck a sharply populist note. Hordes of apprentice poets have entered a scene where criticism, individual or collective, is discouraged. The resulting prize-giving culture, fuelled by favours and networking, has fittingly been compared by the Irish poet Dennis O'Driscoll to "insider trading".[5] Universities are therefore in the odd position of nurturing a poetic class which is not merely anti-academic but, to an alarming degree, hostile to intelligent scrutiny. At the same time, universities are themselves under pressure to justify their funding with narratives of public usefulness. As well as bringing 'customers' through the door, the presence of a poet on the payroll ticks such managerial boxes as 'outreach', 'diversification' and 'knowledge exchange'. So while universities are suspicious of poets, and poets are suspicious of universities, both sides need each other. In that context, they have opted to play down their differences, trim their expectations, and give the public what they want. It is therefore not a surprise if the associated arrangements reflect a poverty of ideas.

§

As a poet who is also an academic, specifically a lecturer in Creative Writing, the dissonant relationship between poetry and the universi-ties – and, by extension, between poetry and the public sphere – affects me directly. The figure of the poet-academic has become increasingly common, struggling along in his or her state of spiritual hyphenation. To be fair, the disharmony of all this is not solely the fault of poetry. The embrace of anti-intellectualism by recent British and Irish poetry is due in no small part to the over-intellectualism of literary theory. The vicious civil wars fought in university English departments during the 1970s and 1980s may now have abated, but their effects linger. Since my own development – and the outlook of this book – has been substantially coloured by such conflicts, I hope the reader will forgive some paragraphs of *Bildungsroman*.

I enrolled at University College Dublin in the 1980s. At that time (1986-1990) the English Department was experiencing a spring tide of literary theory, which, like numerous other things, had arrived in Ireland a little late. On campus there were some conservative presences, but the most popular and influential members of staff were left-wing, relatively theoretical academics like Seamus Deane, Declan Kiberd, and Thomas Docherty. For those eager graduates who wished to remain amidst the breeze-blocks and suburban greenery, there were two divergent literary paths. The first led to room J207, the home of the 'Modern M. A', a course devoted to Critical Theory. The second led to room J208 which housed the 'M. A. in Anglo-Irish Literature', a course devoted to novelists, playwrights, and poets.

While I set out on the latter road, I had some friends on the other course, and was soon able to reflect on their relative merits. To my surprise, I learned that many students of literary theory looked down on mere students of literature. It was apparently the settled view of the participants in J207, as they debated the merits of Habermas and Lyotard, that the goings-on in J208, where we applied ourselves to Beckett and Flann O'Brien, were 'backward' and 'primitive'. In retrospect this division may look silly, but it had concrete effects and, then and now, I regarded it as deeply unnatural. As much as I was drawn to both forms of study, and was aware of their benefits, I also had reservations about both, and these reservations were reinforced by the estrangement between the two M.A.s.

As an undergraduate my favourite area of study had been the literature of the 1930s, especially the poetry of W.H. Auden. While the poets of that low, dishonest decade had started out in famously utopian fashion, their experiences seemed to confirm that, as far as the public sphere was concerned, poetry was ineffectual. It had no special gift to speak to power. So I tended to regard the competing assumptions of the critic as hero (J207) and the writer as hero (J208) through the deflationary lens of Auden's later poetry. The hubris of deconstruction and of post-structuralism, it seemed to me, mirrored the hubris of Romanticism and of the Celtic Revival. Instead of being deeply interwoven, as they surely should have been, J207 and J208 were parted by more than a foot of concrete brutalism.

At various points in my studies, my sense of something missing in the relationship between literary criticism and literature crystallised. One such occasion occurred as I read *Warrenpoint*, the autobiography of Denis Donoghue. Dwelling on some of the books of fiction he most admired, Donoghue recorded his frustration at not being able to emulate them:

> When I read a sentence that I know I could not have written, I feel a blow of envy and direct it, in turn, upon the one who wrote it. When I read Kenneth Burke's *Towards a Better Life*, or Italo Calvino's *Mr. Palomar*, or Italo Svevo's *Confessions of Zeno*, or Primo Levi's *The Periodic Table*, I say to myself: If you only put your mind to it, you could write a book like that. I dally with that fantasy for a few moments till I realise and admit

that I could not write one sentence of any of these books.[6]

This seemed to me at the time an unusually clear and honest statement about the relationship between the writer and the critic. Donoghue's admission of a kind of competitive resentment at work in his encounters with literary texts was not something I was used to reading. Returning to this theme later in the book, he offered a memorable summary: "All I wanted was to observe a relation between myself and structures I had not invented .... Mine was the intelligence that comes after."[7]

This final phrase summed up the mostly unacknowledged position of literary critics and ultimately encouraged me towards a form of criticism which valued and admired *the intelligence which comes before.* Around this time, I came across the criticism of Harold Bloom who seemed to confront, again in unusually frank fashion, the central dilemma faced by poet, novelist, and dramatist: that of making 'something' where there was 'nothing'. Bloom was colourfully direct:

> ...the poet is condemned to learn his profoundest yearnings through an awareness of *other selves.* The poem is *within* him, yet he experiences the shame and splendour of *being found by* poems – great poems – *outside* him. To lose freedom in this fashion is never to forgive, and to learn the dread of threatened autonomy forever.[8]

What impressed me about this kind of criticism was that it considered literature from the point of view of someone *about to write* and characterised this predicament as one which includes one's relationships with others. In puncturing writerly hubris, Bloom exposed what even the most honest poets are reluctant to admit: that poems are about other poems more than they care to say.

Hubris aside, another major problem with those forms of literary criticism which were ascendant in this period was that they seem to rule out energetic activity. Against enterprise, risk, and daring, post-structuralism seemed to encourage cynicism, ennui, and fatalism. For the writer confronted with the blank page, post-structuralism seemed to offer little in the way of constructive advice. While it debunked fuzzy Romanticist notions of originality – surely a good thing – it made any form of energetic endeavour seem beside the point.

In searching for an alternative to such approaches I was led to a philosophy which was interested in concrete outcomes and which did not pretend to predict them. This was pragmatism, the loose, anti-systematic form of philosophy neatly described by Cornel West as a 'future-oriented instrumentalism'.[9] Pragmatism, as I soon discovered, was deeply sympathetic to the situation of the artist – indeed in some forms, it *aspired* to that situation – and I was gradually led on to writers who either identified with the outlook or were in some way coloured by it: William James, George Santayana, John Dewey, Richard Poirier, Giles Gunn, Frank Lentricchia, Hilary Putnam, Gianni Vattimo, Cornel West, Clifford Geertz, Charles Tilly, and Richard Rorty. Outside America, and especially in Europe, pragmatism, where it is understood at all, is not viewed so warmly. In *The American Classics*, Denis Donoghue provides a typical dismissal:

> It seems to me that the tradition is a method, not a philosophy: it has nothing to say of first or last things, and it takes pride in having nothing to say about them. [10]

But against Donoghue, I think pragmatism has much to offer the literary critic. From the defence of verbal extravagance offered by Richard Poirier, to the reflections on poetic interdependence offered by Bloom, the flexibility of pragmatism is a good antidote to the hand-me-down rhetoric so prevalent in British and Irish universities. Rather than diminish books before reading them, pragmatism encourages an open and questioning stance:

> American pragmatism, as Rorty advises, always asks of a text: what is it good for, what can I do with it, what can it do for me, what can I make it mean? I confess that I like these questions, and they are what I think strong reading is all about ...[11]

Above all, the deflationary view of poetry and of poetry criticism adopted by this book is influenced by Rorty's deflationary view of the philosophical role. Large claims have been made for poetry in the 1930s and large claims have been made for literary criticism in the 1970s, but these claims have led to no obvious outcomes in the public world. And why should they? As Rorty put it:

> It is just not the case that one has to have a Saussurian-Wittgensteinian-Derridean understanding of the nature of language in order to think clearly and usefully about politics. One does not have to be an antiessentialist in philosophy in order to be politically imaginative or politically useful. Philosophy is not *that* important for politics, nor is literature.[12]

Poets and literary critics might be taken more seriously if they had made smaller claims for what they do.

§

This book assumes that an over-reliance on public narratives is an almost universal feature of contemporary poetry criticism, detectable in lengthy analyses and in fleeting remarks. I do not claim that this is a sinister phenomenon – most of the time it is well-meaning. But it does have various kinds of distorting effect, and it is with these that the following chapters are concerned. In case this part of my argument seems too cloudy, I would like to ground it with two examples drawn from my recent reading.

In the course of her book, *Irish Pastoral*, Oona Frawley dwells on the Irish poet, Eavan Boland. At one point, she reflects on Boland's poem, 'Suburban Woman', and uses it to highlight the importance of suburban experience in the poet's work:

> The suburbs become the marginalized realm of the marginal within independent Ireland, housewives and mothers beyond the boundaries of the city, out of the reach of the countryside that governed so much of Irish ideology. The almost literal no man's land of the suburbs is made central in such poems, retrieved from the margins by metaphoric force.[13]

In such critical writing, the figure of the writer is hazily aligned with a desirable social goal – here, the liberation of the marginalized. As the language glides easily, routinely, into over-statement, the poet is depicted as a heroic player in that process. After reading the above passage, one has the vague impression of Boland striking a decisive blow, via the poem's "metaphoric force", against something dark and unspeakable called "Irish ideology." Two truths are mingled here: the social status of Irish women has greatly changed, and Boland's poetry is greatly taken up with this change. But the relationship between the truths is hugely magnified in favour of the poem's public significance.

A second example: this is from an essay by Hywel Dix on three Welsh poets, Mike Jenkins, Oliver Reynolds, and Landeg White. In his concluding remarks, Dix tries to link the value of their poetry to the waxing and waning of their political sympathies:

> Only at their very best can these poets integrate a revolutionary political ethic with the global imagination. When this happens, they produce poems capable of telling us something about the ongoing struggles of the global working class, and offering, against the dominant ideology of the day, to teach us to speak in new ways.[14]

The pattern apparent in Frawley's discussion of Boland recurs. The poets are portrayed, again, as significant actors in a momentous struggle. Again, poetry emerges victorious in the face of "ideology", and, suitably reassured, the writing gleams with moral uplift. Whereas Frawley's key word was "retrieved", here the key word is "integrated". Both terms contain a helpful mixture of vagueness and authority. The act of integrating, "a revolutionary political ethic into the global imagination" sounds impressive, but to what does it amount? From a long list of sceptical questions, one could ask the following: What is the nature and scope of the integration? What, anyway, is "the global imagination"? Why, after Marx and Lenin, does "a revolutionary political ethic" need to be integrated into it? Why exactly do we need poems – rather than newspaper articles, say, or television documentaries – to reveal to us the struggles of "the global working class"?

While the range of poets discussed in this book is diverse – there are representatives from Wales, Ireland, Scotland, and England – some emphases will become apparent. Probably more than any other public narrative, the political situation in Northern Ireland has, since the late 1960s, loomed over poetry in these islands. Hence, in the chapters which follow, I have paid a good deal of attention to Northern Irish poets. While I am keen to show the distorting magnetism of publicly-oriented interpretations, I have also chosen to look at how publicly-oriented readings of particular poems might profitably be replaced by privately-oriented ones. In some cases, I have attempted to look at how the critically-inspired positioning of a poet as a public figure prevents us from reading the private poetic influences in their work. In other cases I have attempted to interpret the poets through their movements from a public to a private stance.

A disclaimer: I will not be attempting to maintain anything but a commonsense distinction between 'public' and 'private'. This is because, as far as I can see, it is impossible to maintain a strict distinction. I am persuaded by the case, made by Raymond Geuss in his book, *Public Goods, Private Goods*, that one does well to hold a relativistic conception of the public/private distinction:

> There is no such thing as *the* public/private distinction, or, at any rate, it is a deep mistake to think that there is a single substantive distinction here that can be made to do any real philosophical or historical work. When one begins to look carefully the purported distinction between public and private begins to dissolve into a number of issues that have relatively little to do with one another.[15]

In an eminently pragmatistic manner, Geuss goes on to argue that we need to be conscious of the use to which we want to put whatever version of the public/private distinction we formulate. A second disclaimer: long ago, Edna Longley, the Northern Irish critic, argued for a definite divorce between poetry and politics.

> Poetry and politics, like church and state, should be separated. And for the same reasons: mysteries distort the rational processes which ideally prevail in social relations, while ideologies confiscate the poet's special passport to *terra incognita*.[16]

Let me be clear that I do not agree with this point of view. It is impossible to write sensibly about certain contemporary poets – Adrienne Rich and Paul Durcan spring to mind – without *some* reference to political views and events. I am hostile neither to political poems per se, nor to politically-contextualised readings of poetry. When Calvino writes that, "literature remains alive only if we set ourselves immeasurable goals, far beyond all hope of achievement," I take this to mean that we need immeasurable literary, and political, goals, not that we need to pursue political goals *through* literature.[17] When Georges Braque says, "I do not believe in things, I believe in relationships", a pragmatist can only nod in agreement.[18] Poetry and politics are related, but, given that the relationship between them is neither direct nor strong, that is the beginning rather than the end of the discussion. What this book especially opposes is the *determination* to read poetry in publicly oriented ways, the *determination* to make it fit with one kind of public program or another. In short this book opposes the excessive claims made for the public orientation of poetry.

Notes

1. *The Daily Telegraph*, March 30 2009
2. David Wright 'Introduction' to *The Mid-Century: English Poetry 1940-1960* (Middlesex: Penguin, 1965), p. 17.
3. Michael Donaghy, *The Shape of the Dance: Essays, Interviews, and Digressions* (London: Picador: 2009). p. 200.
4. Michael Donaghy, *The Shape of the Dance: Essays, Interviews, and Digressions* (London: Picador: 2009). p. 200.
5. Dennis O'Driscoll, "Pen Pals: Insider Trading in Poetry Futures" in *Troubled Thoughts, Majestic Dreams* (Oldcastle: Gallery, 2001), pp. 56-62
6. Denis Donoghue, *Warrenpoint* (New York: Knopf, 1990), p. 105

7. Denis Donoghue, *Warrenpoint* (New York: Knopf, 1990), pp. 120-121

8. Harold Bloom, *The Anxiety of Influence* first edition 1973, second edition (Oxford: OUP, 1997), p. 26.

9. Cornel West, *The American Evasion of Philosophy* (Madison: University of Wisconsin Press, 1989), p. 5.

10. Denis Donoghue, *The American Classics: A personal essay* (New Haven and London: Yale University Press, 2005), p. 49.

11. Harold Bloom, *Agon: Towards a Theory of Revisionism,* p. 19.

12. Richard Rorty, *Essays on Heidegger and others: Philosophical Papers Volume 2* (Cambridge: CUP, 1991), p. 135.

13. Oona Frawley, *Irish Pastoral: Nostalgia and Twentieth Century Irish Literature* (Dublin: Irish Academic Press, 2005), p. 151.

14. Hywel Dix, "'To Speak in New Ways': Class and Poetry in Wales since 1979" in Daniel G. Williams ed. *Slanderous Tongues: Essays on Welsh Poetry in English 1970-2005* (Bridgend: Seren, 2010) 201-225, p. 224.

15. Raymond Geuss, *Public Goods, Private Goods* (Princeton: Princeton University Press, 2001), p. 106.

16. Edna Longley, "Poetry and Politics in Northern Ireland", *The Crane Bag* 9 (1) 1985, pp. 26-40: p. 26.

17. Italo Calvino, *Six Memos for the Next Millennium* (London: Vintage, 1996), p. 112.

18. George Braque, quoted in Sanford Schwartz, *The Matrix of Modernism* (Princeton University Press, 1985), p. 103.

DEREK MAHON: THE STUDENT PRINCE

Forty years after the publication of his first collection, Derek Mahon's reputation has yet to settle. There is no reliably established view of what sort of poet he is or which parts of his canon deserve to be remembered. The causes of this uncertainty are various. Of all the Northern Irish poets who rose to prominence in the 1960s he has been the one least happy to associate his writing with the Troubles, a fact which, perversely, has made critics want to make the association for him. More damagingly, the shape of his canon has been fractured by a lengthy period of alcoholism and depression. The resulting chasm of non-publication (ten years wide) has become an obvious point of focus for critical appraisals – and a chasm is not a good place to start. On one side of this unfortunate fracture stand the brash, self-confident early poems. On the other side rear the glum later productions. Critics are almost obliged to compare and contrast these two writing phases with each other, to the likely disadvantage of the poetry's overall reputation. Furthermore, Mahon's canon has been the victim of a number of 'overshadowings' – from without – by the relatively uncontested successes of Muldoon, Heaney and Longley, and – from within – by the hypnotising excellence of 'A Disused Shed in Co. Wexford', the single poem which tends to dominate discussions of his writing, including this one.

Indeed, this unusually magical poem featured in my own personal experience of the critical friction around his reputation. In 2001, when reviewing his latest *Selected Poems* for the *London Review of Books*, I described 'A Disused Shed' as, "the best poem in his third and best collection, *The Snow Party*, the poem towards which his early work rises and from which his later work declines."[1] Although this remark was hardly disparaging, it was perceived by at least two critics as wilfully understated. It triggered two rescue missions on Mahon's behalf. The first was launched by Tom Paulin in a letter to the same journal where he dismissed my assessment of 'A Disused Shed' as, "faint negligent praise which also works to marginalise Mahon's later

work."[2] Paulin went on to supply the kind of praise which he thought
the poem was due:

> 'A Disused Shed in Co. Wexford' is a poem which is revered – revered
> and held sacred – by many writers and readers. It is a modern classic, one
> of those permanent and immortal works of art which leave one breathless
> with admiration …

The second, more downbeat, intervention was made by Hugh
Haughton, the author of the first book-length study of Mahon's
poetry. Writing in the *Cambridge Quarterly*, Haughton echoed some
of Paulin's criticisms of my review, repeating the point that I had been
unfair to Mahon's later work, and endorsing Paulin's argument that
I had overlooked the historical dimension of Mahon's writing. In his
essay Haughton described 'A Disused Shed' as, "one of the most
important modern historical poems", and wrote approvingly of
Mahon's "allusive historical intelligence", an intelligence which he
saw working as much in the later books as in Mahon's acknowledged
masterpiece.[3]

In this chapter, I belatedly resume my 'conversation' with
Haughton and Paulin, offering a more elaborate view of Mahon's
canon than the one put forward in my original review. Although
Paulin, Haughton, and I continue to differ on the strengths and
weaknesses of Mahon's work, the one thing on which we do agree is
that 'A Disused Shed' justifies the extraordinary level of attention
which it has received. Apart from its intrinsic quality, this many-
angled poem is a kind of Rosetta Stone, an interpretive key by which
the rest of his poems can be read. Accordingly, the final section of
this chapter sets out at some length my own interpretation of this
poem, and my sense that more than any of his other works it has been
badly misinterpreted. I also attempt to justify the 'controversial'
judgment I reached, many years ago now, in the *LRB* and try to show
why the pre-eminence of 'A Disused Shed' matters to Mahon's canon
as a whole. Against Paulin and Haughton, I argue Mahon's best
poems are intensely private and that they attempt, as much as possible
to diminish and deflect external influences.

It is understandable that both Paulin and Haughton want to
situate Mahon's poetry in the living stream of history, to see it ebbing
and flowing with the pressure of current events. I sympathise with
this outlook – my instincts, too, are historicist – but I think that
labelling Mahon as a 'historical poet' is, for must purposes, mislead-
ing. I had better explain why. Of course, it is true, in one sense, to say

that no poem is ever 'outside' history – history has no outside. Viewed from a certain perspective, every poem is a historical poem. But if this discussion is to be a language game worth playing, and if the term 'historical' is going to be of any use to us (whether applied to poems or not), then there must be other terms with which it can be contrasted. In characterising Mahon's canon I think that there are more relevant, contrasting descriptions which we can deploy. We might imagine these stronger terms as a kind of planetary system with the word 'privacy', at its centre, orbited by satellite terms like 'thought', 'consciousness', 'solitude', 'contemplation', and 'dream'. Mahon, both as poet and as private individual, is necessarily a part of history, but his poems, in the particular language-game I think we should play, are not so much a-historical as anti-historical.

Mahon's work defines itself so insistently against history that one is inclined to link this insistence with his ruptured pattern of publication. When Hugh Haughton loyally defends Mahon's later poetry, I think this is because he wants to see the poet's canon as a work-in-progress, as a story yet unfinished, and to see the poet himself as still calmly developing, continuing to pass through writing phases of more or less equivalent value. By contrast, I hope to show that a theme of thwarted growth not only defines Mahon's canon (as a matter of publication history) it is also one of that canon's most explicit concerns. Given that Mahon's poetry arranges itself against change, growth, evolution – even against time itself – it should not surprise us that his own development has been abridged. 'A Disused Shed' is a very fine poem, but in my view it is a terminus, the point at which Mahon stopped pushing his particular poetic envelope. Thereafter he was faced with the choice of trying to repeat a successful formula (which is what he tries in *Courtyards in Delft* [1981], *The Hunt by Night* [1982], and *Antarctica* [1985], the three collections which followed *The Snow Party*) or else of attempting to evade his more successful early style (which is what he attempts in *The Hudson Letter* [1995], *The Yellow Book* [1997], *Harbour Lights* [2005], *Life on Earth* [2008], and *An Autumn Wind* [2010], the five collections after his publication resumed.)[4]

To mention such distortions returns us to Mahon's chasm of non-publication. I believe the literary effect of this chasm was a change of attitude, on Mahon's part, to the private nature of his writing. To explain what I mean by this I want to offer a somewhat colourful analogy. One way of thinking about Mahon's poems, early and late, is suggested by the work of a fellow Ulsterman. In Brian Friel's play,

Philadelphia Here I Come, the main character, known as 'Gar public', is followed around by a shadow version of himself, 'Gar private', a character who can be seen and heard by protagonist and audience but not by other characters in the play. While 'Gar public' is timid and conformist, 'Gar private' is vital and rebellious. Bending these categories to Mahon's work, we might argue that there are two versions of the poet: a public Mahon, who is mainly visible in the late poems, and a private Mahon, who is mainly visible in the early ones. Whereas Public Mahon writes in an un-ambitious, repetitive style, in the manner of a high-class feature journalist, Private Mahon writes inwardly, apocalyptically, in the manner of a visionary ephebe. To complicate this critical picture, Public Mahon appears, at various moments, to be unhappy with Private Mahon – and while the late poet is in a position to act as his own advocate, the early poet is no longer around to defend himself.

Such a career split would not be unique and a comparison with one of Mahon's main influences, W.H. Auden, immediately suggests itself. In one of many parallels to Auden's career, we encounter, in Mahon's case, a respected poet of advanced years whose poetic identity hinges significantly on suspicions which he harbours towards his younger self. In *The Dyer's Hand,* Auden memorably divided poets into two types – the "Prospero-dominated poet" and the "Ariel-dominated poet" – thereby providing the critical language by which he hoped that he would be judged.[5] Late Auden was, according to the understandably partial late Auden, a Prospero poet – adult, truthful, sober – while early Auden was, somewhat regrettably, an Ariel poet – adolescent, unreliable, intoxicating. Mahon's revisions of his own poems invite interpretation according to this model, as attempts by a later poet who has become something of a Prospero to correct an early poet who was something of an Ariel. Indeed, if anything, Mahon's attitude to his own poetic fosterage is more troubled than Auden's. Although Mahon hypnotised others with his own brilliant beginning, it may be that the pressure of that early promise was too much for the poet himself to live with. Revealingly, he remains attracted to Cyril Connolly's line, "Whom the gods wish to destroy, they first call promising." Given the evident gaps in his poetic trajectory, it is not surprising that Mahon is sensitive to the question of his own decline. Against Hugh Haughton who makes the case for Public Mahon as the equal of Private Mahon, I want, therefore, to make the contrary case, for the latter against the former.

Since his first full collection, *Night-Crossing* published in 1968,

Mahon's books appeared with reasonable regularity, but this pattern
was broken with the ten-year gap which followed the publication of
Antarctica in 1985. In 1995, the first of his late books appeared. These
later books have had mixed reactions and while Haughton and Paulin
are inclined to defend the later style, other critics have been less kind.
Reviewing *The Yellow Book*, Peter McDonald recorded his dismay:

> The formal looseness of Mahon's new style is not unrelated to the appar-
> ent casualness of the poetry's content. If, for Robert Frost, the fun was
> in how you say a thing, for Mahon that fun has been replaced by a
> mixture of boredom and disgust. The loose form the poet adopts, with
> its often lazy rhyming and rhythmic slackness, betrays a poetry that has
> become sick of itself....[6]

McDonald's critique suggests the presence of a global fault in
Mahon's later poetry. A similar case has been made by Tim Kendall,
who saw *The Hudson Letter* as forming part of a pattern of decline in
Mahon's work, a decline that began with the collections which
appeared after *The Snow Party*:

> *The Hunt by Night* (1982) and the 'interim' pamphlet *Antarctica* (1985)
> consolidated without really advancing Mahon's reputation. Since then,
> only his translations of Jaccottet survive comparison with earlier work.
> Mahon has also channelled his energies into tinkering with old poems
> (often wrecking them in the process), and producing workmanlike
> versions of Molière and Euripides. His output suggests a poet keeping
> his hand in, waiting for the real thing.[7]

Certainly, from the technical point of view, Mahon's late poetry
lacks range and adventure – most of the poems are written in the
simple form of five-beat couplets, an extension of the four-beat
couplets of the earlier verse-letters, 'Beyond Howth Head' and 'The
Sea in Winter'. The later poetry's subject-matter represents something
of a departure, but this has not been to its advantage. There is, for
instance, a noticeable autobiographical frankness in both *The Hudson
Letter* and *The Yellow Book*. Public Mahon enters his own work as a
dramatic character in the way that Private Mahon rarely did. Whereas
the voice of an early Mahon poem might have issued from an
aluminium tin or a bump of clay, the voice of the later poetry issues,
with only a few exceptions, from Public Mahon, the ordinary citizen.
The title-poem of *The Hudson Letter* begins with the line, "Winter; a
short walk from the 10th St. Pier –" and goes on to give us glimpses
of a life based around, "A rented 'studio apartment' in New York/ five

blocks from the river,..."[8] Mahon spent some time teaching at NYU
and Barnard, and *The Hudson Letter* in particular records unresolved
trauma arising from marital breakdown and the difficulties of a long-
distance relationship with his children.

The later books are bitter, elevating exasperation with the modern
world to a key principle of composition. *The Yellow Book* is especially
grumpy: "...some of us have never known the relief/ of house and
home, being outcast in this life." ('Dusk'); "Maybe I'm finally turning
into an old fart/ but I do prefer the traditional kinds of art," ('At the
Chelsea Arts Club').[9] One could compose a long list of modern vices
from those dismissively noted in *The Yellow Book*, because substantial
parts of the poems *are* long lists of modern vices: "foreign invest-
ment", "day-trippers", "pastiche paradox of the post-modern",
"sado-monetarism", "Hugh Grant", and "the internet".

Against these repellent instances of contemporary culture,
Mahon places a surprisingly nostalgic vision of Dublin in the rare
ould times, as in section 6 of *The Yellow Book*:

> Dublin in the '60s! – Golden days
> with Clarke making a comeback, Kavanagh in his final phase;[10]

In the fourth section of *The Yellow Book* he reaches back to other
Dublin-based artists and intellectuals of the period, invoking such
names as Cathal O'Shannon and Harry Kernoff. He comments:

> Those were the days before tourism and economic growth,
> before deconstruction and the death of the author ...[11]

This highly coloured contrast of the 1960s with the 1990s leads
me on, to what I see as the heart of his poetry, and the fulcrum of this
chapter's argument, that Mahon is best seen as the student prince,
the Hamlet, of Irish poetry, and that his most successful poems are
examples of a 'student' sensibility writ large. Apart from explaining
his liking for Dublin in the 1960s (the decade during which he
attended Trinity,) this 'student' sensibility helps to explain many of
the postures in his writing: its preference for thought over action; its
recoil from the disagreeable world of work; its self-romanticisation,
its emphasis on possibility, and its quick willingness to contemplate a
general obliteration of humanity (the kind of powerful compensatory
fantasy which students are only too willing to entertain).

Mahon has not been slow to acknowledge his fondness for under-
graduate life, centrally his experiences in Trinity College Dublin. In

a passing remark which this chapter does its best to elaborate, Seamus Heaney refers to him as, "the Stephen Dedalus of Belfast."[12] To a considerable degree, the student version of Mahon is the one which his peers like to remember. Certainly it is not one they seem able to forget. Dublin in the '60s was the period when he so precociously impressed fellow students – and future poets – like Eavan Boland and Michael Longley. From his autobiographical prose we learn that Trinity very much stayed with him in adulthood. He describes, there, his state of mind on returning to Trinity, twenty years after what he calls the "trauma" of having to leave:

> ...it wasn't finals themselves that were traumatic so much as leaving Trinity, which had become for so many of us, a home from home. To be back again twenty years later, too old now to die young ... gave rise to metaphysical problems at first, to do with self-definition and a sense that, despite having lived for years in London, I'd only been away for a term or two.[13]

Elsewhere, he recalls a period when he hung out with a group of teenage writers, sipping coffee and reading Aldous Huxley, as offering, "an identity that stays with me to this day."[14] In his prose, student days are invariably bathed in a golden glow, and he is drawn to writers with similar nostalgic feelings. Writing warmly about another Trinity old boy, J.P. Donleavy, for example, Mahon notices the older writer's talent for sentimentalising the daydreams of student life:

> In many brief, transitional passages he [Donleavy] captures the fugitive quality of student life: "All those days of hope. Sitting through the golden afternoons the window open of one's room. To hear the glad carefree voices passing below. The white pop of a tennis ball."[15]

In a phrase that reflects exactly on himself, Mahon comments that "Donleavy Man isn't interested in other people. He seeks a rich repose in this life, with a sweet dream of the next. His life is a long death-wish."[16] Mahon quotes Donleavy again at the beginning of a poem which has passed through a revealing set of titles: 'Dog Days', 'Dream Days', and in the most recent *Selected*, 'J.P. Donleavy's Dublin':

> 'When you stop to consider
> The days spent dreaming of a future
> And say then, that was my life.'[17]

Although neither Public Mahon nor Private Mahon escape this special feeling for the life of students, their relationship to it is not the same. Whereas the former tends to lament his necessary distance from that youthful condition, the latter can still affect to experience it – indeed what Public Mahon appears to resent about Private Mahon is the latter's ability to linger within the sophomoric bubble. The upshot of this is that reading Mahon is like reading a Shakespeare who is all Hamlet or a Joyce who is all Stephen Dedalus. Mahon's poetry does not mature – it prefers to halt at the point where it might turn into Lear or Mark Antony, Leopold or Molly Bloom.

In the beginning of Mahon's poetry is its end. The post-Beckettian vision of general futility, which we associate with his work, was established from the start. 'Girls in Their Seasons', the first poem in Mahon's first book, does its best to sound like the last poem in his last book:

Now we are running out of light and love,
Having left far behind
By-pass and fly-over.
The moon is no longer there
And matches go out in the wind.[18]

It is easier to arrive at a vision of apocalypse than it is to move beyond one, and it is curious to see how, even if there are differences of technical approach, the tone and message of these lines closely resemble the tone and message of the later work.

In Mahon's poetry, creations have more life than their creators – an equation which also applies to the writer, usually a passive observer, and what he is writing about. Labour is absent – a key point. Whereas much Northern Irish poetry, from Heaney's *Death of a Naturalist* to Muldoon's *Hay*, has been keen to establish a close relationship between writing poetry and other kinds of work, Mahon has been happy with a clean break. Meaningful examples of manual labour are scarce in his canon. I would suggest that this is because the active working body is a natural threat to the student sensibility, an unwelcome reminder of future responsibilities. One of the major differences between Mahon's most famous poem, 'A Disused Shed in Co. Wexford', and the most famous poetic response to it, Paul Muldoon's 'Gathering Mushrooms', occurs precisely in this area. Muldoon's poem is rich with cultivation – the central image which it supplies of the poet's father tending his mushroom crop is exactly the kind of image which Mahon's poetry evades:

He'll glance back from under his peaked cap
without breaking rhythm:
his coaxing a mushroom – a flat or a cup –
the nick against his right thumb;
the bucket then, the punnet to left or right,
and so on and so forth till kingdom come.[19]

Although Muldoon's poem does contain its own minor examples
of a student sensibility, in the shape of the drug-taking narrator and
his companion, their brief, hallucinatory escape from the brute reali-
ties of Ulster is soon trumped by more obviously adult concerns. In
Mahon's poem, by contrast, the "expropriated mycologist" who was
responsible for harvesting the mushrooms is absent, presumed
kidnapped, and his activities are never depicted. True, the mushrooms
refer to their own "naïve labours", but it is entirely unclear what these
are, since their lives are drastically passive.

The one kind of work which is an exception to this negative rule
is the work of writing. Mahon's poems rarely depict labour but they
have clearly been laboured over. The question of the relationship
between poetry and work implicitly rises at every turn and a version
of another question which lingers near the centre of Mahon's writing:
is one alive when one is writing poems? The question has no definitive
answer but a clue to Mahon's attitude is provided by his poetic
revisions. In themselves a way of identifying with Auden, such
revisions invite us to see the poems as mildly interchangeable, as a
sort of structure where the furniture gets shifted around according
to mood. With the revision of lines, the migration of whole stanzas
from one poem to another, the poems appear highly glossed over –
finished rather than abandoned.

Changes of title often revolve tellingly around proper names, as
if there were an uncertainty about how much to identify the speaker
of these poems with their author. Just as 'Bruce Ismay's Soliloquy'
eventually became 'After the Titanic', so 'Knut Hamsun in Old Age'
became 'Hunger', and 'Van Gogh in the Borinage' became 'A Portrait
of the Artist'. In earlier poems, like 'Cavafy', 'Dowson and Company',
and 'Homage to Malcolm Lowry', Private Mahon appears to emerge
from his shell, extending his literary feelers towards consciousnesses
other than his own. But the feelers quickly fold backwards, and it
turns out that the artists he imagines are merely versions of himself.
Everything, even other artists, gets swallowed by Mahon's inward-
ness – at least at this self-confident stage of his career. At their most
defiant, these early poems imply, not merely that poetry is a special

form of work but that it is the only kind of work worth pursuing.

As they appear and re-appear through various *Selecteds* and *Collecteds*, many of Mahon's poems have been altered, as though the late poet could not leave the early one alone. I see Mahon's constant revisions as a mode of re-living, a way of playing out the lives we might have lived through the poems we might have written. Even Mahon's best poem can be seen in this light. Although Mahon may feel for 'A Disused Shed in Co. Wexford' some of the impatience felt by Robert Frost for 'Mending Wall' (the impatience which any poet might feel for the one poem in their canon which draws admiration at the expense of the rest), thankfully he has, since the appearance of *The Snow Party*, kept its revisions to a minimum. Instead of line-by-line alterations, Mahon has 'relived' this poem by providing it with a kind of shadow, the similarly-titled 'A Garage in Co. Cork'. The neutral reader will find it curious that Mahon appears to prefer 'A Garage in Co. Cork' to 'A Disused Shed in Co. Wexford', but this preference is consistent with the poet's general dislike for his more concentrated, visionary poems as against his more discursive and dissipated ones. Far from being the development he would like it to be, the second poem is a clear falling-off in quality which anticipates the problems of his later work.

The question of the relationship between poetry and life is also raised by the way in which Mahon tends to avoid other people in his work, or at any rate to avoid those consciousnesses which he cannot treat as extensions of himself. It is true that Public Mahon is more inclined to give other consciousnesses a try, but his attempts to commune with alterity are generally disastrous. In *The Hudson Letter*, for example, the speaker makes a desperate-sounding appeal to the homeless:

> I know you and you me, you wretched buggers,
> and I've no problem calling you my brothers
> for I too have been homeless and in detox
> with baaad niggas 'n' crack hoes on the rocks[20]

Whereas we can readily imagine Lorca or Whitman succeeding in such an address to the destitute, a literary introvert like Mahon is unlikely to get away with it. Decent and civic-minded as these expressed sentiments might be, they make for embarrassing lines of poetry. Nevertheless these lines are lauded by Hugh Haughton who, in his study of the poet, places them in an auspicious public context. Haughton notes, for example, the increase in homelessness in New

York during the period, the prevalence of HIV, and the restrictive policing of public spaces instituted by Mayor Giuliani.[21] This is helpful background, of course, but it neglects the brittle, artificial-sounding treatment adopted by the poem. Haughton quotes Mahon as saying he knew he had to take on the New York theme but he wasn't sure how, until someone said to him, "You've just been homeless yourself, why don't you write about the homeless?"[22] The lines are much too contrived and opportunistic to succeed.

Although New York may be one of the most densely populated cities in the world, *The Hudson Letter* contrives to make it seem half-deserted. By and large, Mahon is more comfortable with the city considered as a text. Given that he habitually populates his version of New York with types who seem drawn from the writing of others, we have the impression, that even as his speakers claim to be situated in Manhattan or Brooklyn, that they are actually reading of these locations from afar, that they are chiefly located on a bookshelf. While it would be unfair to criticise Mahon for not being Frank O'Hara (a writer he parodies) the differences between their styles are instructive. O'Hara, for example, usually avoids grandiose rhetoric, is positively attracted to consciousnesses other than his own, and is conspicuously at ease with the world of labour. Illustrating that last point, *Lunch Poems* frames its scenes within O'Hara's lunch hour, so that all the action leads away from, and then leads back to, a regular job. And O'Hara not only contemplates the working body, he eroticises it, whether it be in 'A Step Away from Them', with the "dirty/ glistening torsos" of its surveyed labourers, or, in 'Personal Poem', imagining himself as a construction worker in "a silver hat".[23] Such habits of thought are quite alien to a poetry like Mahon's which tries to make labour and its attendant pressures disappear. But that is exactly the kind of insulation from the world, which make the sundry boasts and protests that we generally associate with student life seem hollow.

Instead Mahon's poetry begins where labour ends – in refuse: the flotsam and jetsam of discarded articles, heaps of scrap-metal, "the terminal democracy of hatbox and crab". The adjective in Mahon's most famous title is not incidental: 'disused'. In Mahon's poetry, the ends of processes are always overwhelmingly foreseen, but the processes themselves diminish. Rome is built – and destroyed – in a day. We skip the vulgar stages of construction, the messy everyday phases of labour and organisation, and pass straight to the finished article. The great middle range of experience, so prominent in the poetry of, say, Auden, Heaney, and Muldoon, vanishes till only the lurid extremes remain. The dilations and contractions of civilisation, which Mahon likes to describe, are so implausibly massive that the best poems make them seem blackly humorous. In 'Tithonus', the eponymous god, who has been condemned to pass existence in the form of a grasshopper, imagines what it would take to depict all that he has seen:

> Not merely Golgotha
> And Krakatoa
> But the leaf-plink
>
> Of rain-drops after
> Thermopylae,
> The lizard-flick
>
> In the scrub as Genghis
> Khan entered Peking
> And the changing clouds,
>
> I would need
> Another eternity,
> Perish the thought.[24]

The poem gives the reader very little time to consider the disasters with which it is ostensibly concerned. In a period of time inversely proportional to the eternity he proposes, Tithonus takes a dismissive glance. World-disasters are dealt with as briskly as possible so that the speaker – one of Mahon's many dreamers – can return to his real interest, the realm of leaf-plinks and changing clouds. In contrast to these world-disasters, the unthreatening natural phenomena are more obviously the kind of visual and auditory accessories we associate with contemplation. They help to develop that inward continuum of thought into which the speaker drops the charged terms of history on an almost epicurean basis, as though to see how they taste. In such a context it is easier to understand the otherwise slightly absurd emphasis on maintaining tonal elegance, an elegance which would be redundant to any creature which had experienced what Tithonus has claimed to see. But then the real subject of this poem – as of many others written by Mahon – is 'thought', the word towards which this monologue creeps, and the same word *from* which 'A Disused Shed' will descend.

Mahon's easy contemplation of catastrophes such as 'Krakatoa', is a way of distancing himself from adult strife. Such thinking is

always an attempt to pre-empt the challenge of adult struggle by
depicting effort as futile – for if labour leads to obliteration why lift a
finger? The reference to 'Krakatoa' also reminds us of Mahon's
fondness for landscapes purged of human beings, a disposition which
is not confined to his poetry. In one of the prose-pieces collected in
the volume *Journalism*, for example, he has fantasised about the
provincial Ulster town of Portrush, where he lived briefly, entirely
void of people, the problems of sectarianism seemingly dissolved by
annihilation:

> I imagine a hypothetical future in which everyone has departed. The
> Catholics have all moved South or gone to the States; the Protestants have
> gone to England, or Canada, or Australia…. A light aircraft, privately
> owned, rusts on the strand. There is no sign of life. Nothing happens here,
> and maybe nothing ever happened.[25]

Nor are such imagined purges inconsistent with the student sensi-
bility. What Mahon, early and late, seems to value about the university
lifestyle is the almost limitless space it provides for undisturbed
dreaming. It is not a matter of feeling nostalgic for student japes, the
celebrated "incidents last night" of Larkin's 'Dockery and Son'.
Indeed, when Mahon looks back to student life, it is often in a manner
which seems eerily de-peopled. When he writes about the Trinity Ball,
for example, it is revealing to see what he truly missed about the
experience:

> What I really missed this year wasn't the Ball itself (at forty-five, I'm too
> old for that sort of thing) but the morning-after silence among the debris,
> the sort of *mise en scène*, all litter and breeze, which makes me a sucker
> for holiday resorts out of season.[26]

At heart, Mahon's poetry is about a literary consciousness
profoundly turned in upon itself, the poetry's deepest feeling is for
the state of desire which the widening horizons of literature makes
possible, a desire for desire, for the moment before any activity (with
its attendant possibilities of failure) gets started. From this point of
view, the ideal state is to spend your days dreaming about the days
spent dreaming of a future. The model literary life is a dream of the
literary life. His poems, glowing with visions of the literary future,
cannot come to terms with time and so the end of each poem is a
disappointment, a return to time, which many of the concluding lines
nervously over-advertise ("Will scarcely last beyond today." "Come

in, fifteen, your time is up", "Like clock hands in a bar mirror.")[27]

Sound in Mahon's poetry has a Beckettian affinity with silence. With human vitality draining into those objects on which it acts, or which act on it, the outside world is suggested by a few momentous 'noises off', a milk-bottle being knocked over, "a lorry changing gear at the end of the lane", or even Donleavy's "white pop of a tennis-ball". The poetry's contemplative murmur is given sudden corrective jerks, especially in the habitual contraction from smooth polysyllables to harsh monosyllables. Sounds like these manipulate consciousness by raising fears of intrusion, the frequency with which they occur suggesting that they have long since been ritualised. Ambient, echoing spaces are used to protect consciousness from time. One can find an early example of this pattern in 'An Unborn Child', a poem from his first book where, augmented by the comfort of the broad-shouldered Yeatsian stanza, the embryo subject basks in reassurance, mulling over hints of the world to come:

> I feel them in my bones – bones which embrace
> Nothing, for I am completely egocentric.
> The pandemonium of encumbrances
> Which will absorb me, mind and senses,
> Intricacies of the box and the rat-race –
> I imagine only. Though they linger and,
> Like fingers, stretch until the knuckles crack,
> They cannot dwarf the dimensions of my hand.[28]

The poem seems to look forward to a point where the child will accept the pressure of the world, will take on the responsibilities of knowledge, yet the emotional heart of the poem is clearly in looking back, fondly, at the child's distance from knowledge, experience thinking about experience from the point of view of innocence. An experienced innocent, the unborn child is but a mild disguise, an ephebic apparition, for the student prince. The childish voice, which the title might encourage us to expect, arrives in a state which is altogether over-evolved, reflecting a fascination which Mahon has for all species of warped development, extremes of thwarted promise. What is 'unborn' in this poem will be 'disused' in a later one.

§

Before passing on to a discussion of 'A Disused Shed in Co. Wexford' I want to take a closer look at some of the patterns and techniques at play in Mahon's canon, particularly those which work in favour of inwardness against the pressure of outside influence. These are (a) his use of homogeneous collectives (b) his manipulation of light-effects (c) his use of panoramas and lists and (d) his mixed uses of tone and diction. Returning to my metaphor of the Rosetta Stone, 'A Disused Shed in Co. Wexford' casts light on the rest of his canon by using all of these techniques to their best effect. In this single poem Mahon concentrates a series of patterns which are elsewhere scattered throughout his work:

(a) *The use of homogeneous collectives.* One of Mahon's ways of confronting the outside world, what we might call 'not-Mahon', is his method of describing crowds. These are not, as we might expect, depictions of crowds of people, but crowds of objects mostly small and homogenous: tins, leaves, grapes, anemones, snowflakes, and mushrooms. Their arrival is often signalled by the word 'thousand' (an enumeration which stands in for the innumerable): "A thousand limpets left by the ebb-tide/ Unanimous in their silent inquisition", "A thousand mushrooms crowd to a keyhole".[29] Mahon is not at all interested in the members of such crowds, rather he prefers that ideal-isation of crowds which ironically is one of the things which makes them powerful, especially from the outside – a pure sense of crowd being the keenest way to emphasise, by contrast, a pure thinking solitude.

Suggestive in this context, I think, is the following remark of Giacomo Leopardi, to which Italo Calvino draws attention in his *Six Memos for the Next Millennium*:

> Highly pleasing … is the sight of an innumerable multitude, as of stars, people etc., a multiple motion, uncertain, confused, irregular, disordered, a vague rising and falling, etc., which the mind cannot conceive definitely or distinctly, etc., like that of a crowd, or a swarm of ants, or a rough sea …[30]

Leopardi thinks this pleasurable feeling arises for reasons of variety, uncertainty and not seeing everything. Rather than borrow his expression 'innumerable multitude', I prefer the closely related phrase 'homogeneous collective', because, when thinking about such groupings, I want to put the emphasis, not on the difficulty of count-ing their members, but on their members' lack of individual identity. Although Leopardi is right to associate the contemplation of such groupings with pleasure I think that a wide range of emotional responses is possible. Reading Northern Irish poetry I am often struck by the many references to homogeneous collectives, a prevalence which may owe something to the fact that it is impossible to contemplate the province for long without dwelling on opposed collectives. Such collectives are extensively used, for example, in the work of Louis MacNeice – to illustrate his musings on the One and the Many – in the poetry of Ciarán Carson – as examples of a hostile, unknowable System – and in Mahon's work – combining a teasing otherness which threatens the self with a means of transmitting the self's interiority. Mahon's collectives could not dramatise his uncertainties about the self's boundaries if any of their members had an individual identity, for at every moment they must be held open, blankly, for possible occupation by the speaker's ego.

In Mahon's poem, 'Leaves', for example, we encounter one such homogeneous collective. Reading this poem we certainly experience something of the pleasure which Leopardi mentioned, but it is only a minor part of our overall response:

> The prisoners of infinite choice
> Have built their house
> In a field below the wood
> And are at peace.
>
> It is autumn, and dead leaves
> On their way to the river
> Scratch like birds at the window
> Or tick on the road.
>
> Somewhere there is an afterlife
> Of dead leaves,
> A stadium filled with an infinite
> Rustling and sighing.
>
> Somewhere in the heaven
> Of lost futures
> The lives we might have lived
> Have found their own fulfilment.[31]

In this poem, human beings are a minimal presence, barely established in the first stanza before they make way for their more compelling Dante-esque substitutes, the surging collective of dead leaves. It is worth noting that here again, we find ourselves reading a poem about thought. Following a familiar pattern, the poem excludes

descriptions of labour in order to leave a bigger space for conscious-
ness. It is consistent with the use Mahon makes of his other
homogenous collectives that the leaves' propulsion is not self-gener-
ated, that instead they are *propelled*. Like the state of contemplation
to which they owe their existence, they are chronically passive. The
unknown human beings of the first stanza are defined only by a single
attribute, choice, which makes them seem distant from us, especially
when the key noun attracts a modifier as abstract as 'infinite'. Like
the speaker, these human presences fade into an involved white cloud
of thought. The poem defines our hopes, especially those we will not
fulfil in this life, against a general background of insignificance and
ineffectuality. The conclusion of the poem is positive, because Mahon
has the confidence, at this stage of his career, to laud the possible at
the expense of the actual.

This is one of many poems which dwell on the acoustics of possi-
bility. Waiting for the silence to be broken – and then waiting for it to
resume – enacts the poem's own periodicity, its own manipulations
of sound and silence. The poem propels itself forward with a mixture
of sensual intensity and evocative abstractions, an intensity which is
matched by the delicacy of the sound-effects. The combination of
unvoiced fricatives with thin vowel sounds, for example, closely
evokes the faint friction of leaves. The abstract quality of the poem is
supported by the non-specific diction, which has a marked utopian
expansiveness: "infinite" (used twice), "afterlife", "heaven",
"futures", "fulfilment". These airy terms remind us that Mahon's
poetry is fond of disembodied states, an extreme example being
'Matthew V. 29-30' where the speaker reduces himself, "To a rubble
of organs, //A wreckage of bones". Consistent with such an objective,
Mahon's homogeneous collectives tend to remind us of groups of
limbless human beings – that is to say if one thinks of a human as a
mushroom, a leaf, or an anemone, then in that imaginative transfor-
mation, we think of a body shorn of appendages, like a skittle ready
to be toppled. The voiced fricative of "lives" gives way to the unvoiced
fricative of "fulfilment" and this movement from the voiced to the
unvoiced is a kind of celebration of the incorporeal, a sly triumph for
thought. While the author of the poem is effectively disembodied, his
consciousness has been magnified, the endless play of its possibilities
have been housed securely in the sound-filled stadium that is the
poem itself.

Another poem which combines the presence of homogenous
collectives with the possibilities of silence is 'The Snow Party'. Again

Mahon makes good use of the ambiguity of the homogenous collective. What does it stand for? Does it stand for anything? Should we see the snowflakes as no more than a ghostly version of those "thousands" which the poem claims are dying elsewhere? Or do they stand in, more expansively, for humanity in general? These questions cannot be answered definitively, of course – the presence of this glowing collective is suggestive rather than explicit.

In 'The Snow Party' Mahon again transfers his presence to a ghostly surrogate, this time to the Japanese poet, Basho, who is, minimally introduced in the first line (shades of the "prisoners of infinite choice") and then promptly disappears. The poem's key term is silence which, as we have seen in 'Leaves', Mahon closely associates with the operations of consciousness. The poem opposes the fatal hustle and bustle of the outside world with the silent contemplation of exotic locations – Nagoya, Kyoto, Irago. As in 'Lives', Mahon is not interested in the human disasters mentioned towards the end of the poem, but he is interested in the poetic effect of their brisk dismissal:

> Elsewhere they are burning
> Witches and heretics
> In the boiling squares,
>
> Thousands have died since dawn
> In the service
> Of barbarous kings –
>
> But there is silence
> In the houses of Nagoya
> And the hills of Ise.[32]

The brief burst of plosives which he associates with the executions ("burning", "boiling", "barbarous") is effectively erased by an eerie silence, a silence which the poem evokes with a thin-vowelled sibilance ("city", "sea", "silence", "Ise"). Given that Mahon generally evokes his collectives in a spirit of anti-humanism it is no surprise to see that 'The Snow Party' ends with "houses" and "hills" rather than people. The concluding scene of over-refined civilisation is coloured with a suggestion of holocaust.

(b) Mahon's mixed uses of tone and diction. As we might expect from a poet with a divided sensibility, Mahon's poetry is tonally various and

accommodates frequent changes of diction. Like the dilations and contractions which are depicted in 'Lives', his tone tends to fluctuate between extremes. Consistent with their student sensibility, Mahon's poems tend to fret about their own worldly competence and so, by way of compensation, they often adopt a briskly superior tone, even as they disparage worldliness. Whereas poems like his elegy for Louis MacNeice offer a positive vision of what poetry can do ("Rinsing the choked mud, keeping the colours new.")[33] other poems, and particularly those which consider the value of his own work, emphasise its trivial nature. 'Heraclitus On Rivers', in which Auden's suspicion that "poetry makes nothing happen" is a ghostly presence, is a good example:

> Your best poem, you know the one I mean,
> The very language in which the poem
> Was written, and the idea of language,
> All these things will pass away in time.[34]

While this poem disparages human effort in general, it is written with such an air of assumed authority that one is inclined to wonder how the speaker can affect such certainty. Also one wonders why the negation of human endeavour is so extreme, unless the speaker has some stake in the unqualified nature of his statement? Rather as a student will assume an air of worldliness to pre-empt the challenge of the fully adult world, the tone which is used here is at once beguiling and unpersuasive. We are not being told anything which we do not already know – rather it is the fact of our being told and the possible motives behind the telling which work upon us. Another example of Mahon's dramatic-sounding negations can be found in 'After Nerval':

> Your great mistake is to disregard the satire
> Bandied among the mute phenomena.
> Be strong if you must, your brusque hegemony
> Means fuck-all to the somnolent sun-flower
> Or the extinct volcano[35]

In a typically paradoxical manner, the poem criticises the "brusque hegemony" of the powerful in a tone of voice which is itself brusquely hegemonic. It is again hard to discern the speaker's stake in what is being said or what the reader is supposed to make of it. What seems to be the message of the poem is drastically undermined by the chosen means of transmission. Here and elsewhere, the poem impresses as a performance. Its dismissiveness is enjoyable and energetic, but it is most usefully read as the performance of a divided self. Hence the diction of the poem divides between the grandiose and the throwaway, between the sonorously poetic "somnolent sunflower" and the anti-poetic "fuck-all". Generally speaking, the mixtures of tone and diction represent personal uncertainty about the poet's preferred state of inwardness. That is to say, when his diction is elevated and his tone is grandiose then the poem feels secure about its status in relation to the world. When the diction is colloquial and his tone is morose then that security has been lost.

(c) Mahon's use of panorama. In portraying his inner world as rich, Mahon generally contrasts it with an impoverished outer world. One of the primary techniques he uses to subordinate the external world to the inner one is that of panorama. By the term 'panorama' I have in mind Mahon's sweeping visual treatments of time and space, a function which, I think, is traceable to some of the more grandiose moments in Auden's poetry, like "The Summer holds...":

> The summer holds: upon its glittering lake
> Lie Europe and the islands; many rivers
> Wrinkling its surface like a ploughman's palm.
> Under the bellies of the grazing horses
> On the far sides of posts and bridges
> The vigorous shadows dwindle; nothing wavers.
> Calm at this moment the Dutch sea so shallow
> That sunk St. Paul's would ever show its golden cross
> And still the deep water that divides us still from Norway.[36]

This Chorus comes from a play which was one of many that Auden wrote for the Group Theatre, a company which had an explicitly public purpose. The sweep of the language aims for a healing accessibility, and is intended to provide a vision in which the audience has a stake. The reference to 'Europe' is as much political as it is geographical, intending to offer a ghostly vision of unity between nations – this is a poem unambiguously involved with history. In Mahon's work, by contrast, such panoramas may be accessible but they are not intended to be healing. They intentionally evoke feelings of distance and emptiness, which, in the verse-letters and later poetry, sits oddly with the speaker's casualness of manner.

The light that left you streaks the walls
of Georgian houses, pubs, cathedrals,
coasters moored below Butt Bridge
and old men at the water's edge
where Anna Livia, breathing free,
weeps silently into the sea,
her small sorrows mingling with
the wandering waters of the earth;[37]

This is the penultimate stanza of 'Beyond Howth Head'. Like the panorama from Auden's Chorus, it creates a dramatic sense of space. The reader has an impression of viewing a number of widely separated realities all at once, gradually seeing further and further, and in that tumbling vision experiences an involuntary thrill. Mahon allows his tone to drift towards a thin-sounding grandiosity, which is particularly evident in the last several lines. One of the features of such panoramas is that their conclusion often feels like the conclusion of the poem as a whole. Because 'Beyond Howth Head' contains several such panoramas the poem seems to 'end' several times, each occasion requiring a slightly awkward 'restart'. This pattern of conclusion and restart is used to better effect at the beginning of 'A Disused Shed' where – as I shall argue – it makes more emotional sense.

In Whitman's poetry, where panorama is a recurrent device, the accumulative drive of his long lines seems to issue from his unforced enthusiasm for the world around him. So involved are his poems with the affairs of others that their capacity for attention is naturally turned outwards. Mahon's accumulative ethos functions differently. Instead of signalling an involvement with the affairs of others, his panoramas are more like reminders of what to avoid. Such long perspectives, as disclosed by the panoramic trope, and the related device of the list, tend to universalise whatever they include and enable the poet to range from one moment in space or history to another at high speed. When Mahon uses them in his verse-letters and elsewhere it is as a means of putting himself beyond the illusions of society, to face the simple reality of the elements:

morning scatters down the strand
relics of last night's gale force wind;
far out, the Atlantic faintly breaks[38]

These lines are of the sort, which Dillon Johnston had in mind, when he wrote, "... Mahon establishes a "theoptic" view in which human endeavour dwindles before the vastness of history and of the heavens."[39] With this wide-screen, elemental picture, he prepares us for the philosophical generalisations, which are to come.

(d) *Manipulation of light-effects.* Hugh Haughton has remarked on Mahon's "fascination with precise calibrations of light".[40] Tellingly Mahon is fond of quoting a phrase of Nabokov's (from *The Real Life of Sebastian Knight*) which celebrates the mystic individuality of things in "the halo around the frying pan". As a clue to the nature of Mahon's poetics, this phrase may not be very helpful – it can be taken in more than one way. Whereas a tough-minded application of the phrase may show us a frying pan as we have never seen it before (because we have never been looking), a tender-minded application will dwell more lovingly on the halo, roughly equivalent to the thinly disguised sentimentality which in Mahon's poetry anthropomorphises inanimate objects. In 'Courtyards in Delft', an example of each type occurs within only four lines:

> I lived there as a boy and know the coal
> Glittering in its shed, late-afternoon
> Lambency informing the deal table,
> The ceiling cradled in a radiant spoon.[41]

The images in this passage are linked by the presence of a mysterious light, even extending to the dark multitude of coal, and, as in other poems, the light is compressed into a small space. Mahon's use of light may be thought of as an infusion of the poet's spirit into a selected portion of the outside world, a Zeus-like descent which transmits his imagination and power. This trope is often combined with the presence of homogeneous collectives which become animated by the touch of the poet's inwardness. The play of light which we witness in 'Courtyards in Delft' is understood as the vision of an imaginatively gifted child, which animates that which would otherwise be banal. It is no coincidence that the speaker in 'The Last of the Fire Kings' contemplates escaping through fields where "fireflies glow" and that some of Mahon's more successful poems, 'Leaves', 'The Snow Party' and, of course, 'A Disused Shed in Co. Wexford', meditate in extended fashion on such images.

In 'A Disused Shed in Co. Wexford', this kind of godlike imaginative power is transferred to the human realm – a clever reversal – because the "flash-bulb firing squad" which appears near the end is even more anonymous than the mushrooms. Mahon's use of light is finally a means of distributing his inwardness to surrogates. Instead of situating it in the lives of artists that he admires, he distributes it to favoured objects. Still, we should be clear that this is not a hymn to alterity – the halo around the frying-pan is himself.

§

It is time to turn our discussion towards 'A Disused Shed in Co. Wexford'. Here I want to explain the poem's special status by identifying it as the end-point of Mahon's work, the point beyond which further travel was unnecessary. I also want to offer an elaborate new reading of this poem and, by extension, of his career in general. The poem, I will argue, is not about history. It is about consciousness. What gives the poem its complexity are the conflicting attitudes towards consciousness which it keeps in play. On the one hand, the poem is a celebration of thought, of the ability of the imagination to weave new visions, of the ability of inwardness to distribute itself, absorbing, commanding, conquering what would seem to exist at a distance from it – and in these moments of self-praise, it has an unmistakeable buoyancy. On the other hand, the poem contains the speaker's doubts about consciousness – is it sufficient? Is it wise, in nurturing consciousness, to leave the world behind? Are the chosen vehicles of consciousness – words, poems – too much contaminated by the influence of others? I believe that the poem succeeds because it holds these competing considerations in beautiful tension.

The various means by which Mahon distributes his inwardness are all present at once in this poem. The poem begins, for instance, with a characteristic panorama, a total vision, which as rapidly shrinks through a gothic keyhole into a miniature Gormenghast. The Nabokovian halo of attention drifts uneasily into the Wexford shed to rest on the ultimate homogeneous collective, a group of mute inglorious mushrooms that have festered unseen for fifty years. Light-effects, too, are plentiful. Indeed, the poem uses these in highly contrasting ways, dramatically framing the lives of the mushrooms for which the glow from the keyhole is at once a source of hope as well as a possible means of annihilation. In keeping with the poem's subtle ambiguities of attitude both its tone (by turns, wistful, grandiose, oracular, witty, exhausted, ironic, buoyant, nostalgic, and finally anxious) and its diction (encompassing triffids, Treblinka, moonmen, and Indian compounds), are wildly unstable:

Even now there are places where a thought might grow –
Peruvian mines, worked out and abandoned
To a slow clock of condensation,
An echo trapped forever, and a flutter of
Wildflowers in the lift-shaft,
Indian compounds where the wind dances
And a door bangs with diminished confidence,
Lime crevices behind rippling rainbarrels,
Dog corners for shit burials;
And in a disused shed in Co. Wexford,

Deep in the grounds of a burnt-out hotel,
Among the bathtubs and the washbasins
A thousand mushrooms crowd to a keyhole.
This is the one star in their firmament
Or frames a star within a star.
What should they do there but desire?
So many days beyond the rhododendrons
With the world waltzing in its bowl of cloud,
They have learnt patience and silence
Listening to the crows querulous in the high wood.

They have been waiting for us in a foetor of
Vegetable sweat since civil war days,
Since the gravel-crunching, interminable departure
of the expropriated mycologist.
He never came back, and light since then
Is a keyhole rusting gently after rain.
Spiders have spun, flies dusted to mildew,
And once a day, perhaps, they have heard something –
A trickle of masonry, a shout from the blue
Or a lorry changing gear at the end of the lane.

There have been deaths, the pale flesh flaking
Into the earth that nourished it;
And nightmares, born of these and the grim
Dominion of stale air and rank moisture.
Those nearest the door grow strong –
Elbow room! Elbow room!
The rest, dim in a twilight of crumbling
Utensils and broken pitchers, groaning
For their deliverance, have been so long
Expectant that there is left only the posture.

A half century, without visitors, in the dark –
Poor preparation for the cracking lock
And creak of hinges. Magi, moonmen,
Powdery prisoners of the old regime,
Web-throated, stalked like triffids, racked by drouth
And insomnia, only the ghost of a scream
At the flashbulb firing squad we wake them with
Shows there is life yet in their feverish forms.
Grown beyond nature now, soft food for worms,
They lift frail heads in gravity and good faith.

They are begging us, you see, in their wordless way,
To do something, to speak on their behalf
Or at least not to close the door again.
Lost people of Treblinka and Pompeii!
Save us, save us, they seem to say,
Let the god not abandon us
Who have come so far in darkness and in pain.
We too had our lives to live.
You with your light meter and relaxed itinerary,
Let not our naive labours have been in vain![42]

The reading which I offer of Mahon's poem opposes much of
the current criticism and it certainly does not agree with the readings
offered by Paulin and Haughton, over-reliant as I think they are on
the chameleon category of history. Before going any further, then, it
seems important to consider these readings – is this, after all, a histor-
ical poem? It depends, of course, on how the word 'historical' is used.
It is notable that when Haughton and Paulin discuss 'A Disused Shed'
both refer to the time in 1973 when they first read it, and both think
of the poem as closely bound to the tragic period of Northern Irish
history in which it was composed. In the sense which they imply,
'historical' would come to mean something like 'directly engaged with
current events', or perhaps less narrowly, 'directly engaged with those
historical phenomena which lie behind current events.' In his study
of the poet, Hugh Haughton flatly states that 'A Disused Shed in Co.
Wexford' is "about contemporary violence", although he then has to
admit that, "the poem nowhere mentions contemporary violence".
To get around this apparent obstacle he lays great stress on the
poem's publication date:

   …1972 was the bloodiest year in the conflict, with the imposition of direct
   rule from Westminster, an escalating IRA bombing campaign, the British

Army's Operation Motorman leading to a violent Protestant backlash and the introduction of internment for loyalists. In other words, the horrific violence of the Anglo-Irish war and Civil War was being re-enacted, a brutal reminder that the Treaty of 1921 had left unresolved political differences in Ireland to fester and grow, like the mushrooms in Mahon's poem …[43]

The contention seems to be that since the poem was written during a particularly violent phase of the Northern conflict, the poem must be about that period. This is hardly a convincing line of argument since it would arbitrarily bind all poems to any events that occur in their immediate historical radius. Haughton's point is further weakened by the fact that not only does the poem fail to mention contemporary violence it barely mentions violence at all. True, there are references to a burnt-out hotel and to the apparent kidnapping of a mycologist, but, in the time-line of the poem, these events, which are not even described, occurred fifty years previously. The mushrooms emerge to face a "flash-bulb firing-squad", this is also true, but, in the poem's value-system, this event seems to be at once good and bad – good, in that the mushrooms want to be recognised, bad, in that such recognition may kill them. It is hard to believe that Mahon would be in favour – however ambiguously – of the kinds of firing-squad that were circulating in 1972. Another weakness of Haughton's argument is that the suffering of the mushrooms, central to the poem, is caused by neglect rather than violence. I suppose one could argue, with some strain, that *neglect* was one of the major causes of the Troubles but if the speaker thinks that neglect is a cause of violence why is that violence scarcely evident in the poem?

Here, one of the difficulties of this kind of interpretation arises. Haughton draws a doubtful analogy between the festering mushrooms and festering 'political differences', which merely demonstrates that as soon as one tries to make any kind of equation between the mushrooms and political or historical groupings the reading becomes incoherent. The analogy is implausible because the poem's vivid anthropomorphism likens mushrooms to human beings, not to the political differences which human beings generate. His reading is also implausible because the various descriptions of the mushrooms could hardly stand for a recognisable pattern of political allegiances. What are the politics of Magi, moonmen, and triffids? The major political difference which has bedevilled Northern Ireland, has been – need we say it? – sectarian in nature, but the poem nowhere even hints at the presence of sectarianism. The mushrooms function as one community, not two rival communities in conflict. Haughton's reading is an example, I believe, of the impulse to read poetry in an excessively decent and civic-minded way. It reflects a desire to associate an admired poet with socially desirable attitudes even at the price of significant omissions and distortions. One might think of this as a kind of default critical reading in which the pressure to fold poems into urgent public narratives takes unfortunate precedence. His example indicates that any publicly-directed reading of the poem will want to say that the mushrooms stand, at least in part, and decently, for one or other aspect of the Northern Irish conflict. We can see this impulse at work, when Tom Paulin scolded me for not mentioning the poem's political dimension:

> Among other historical subjects, Mahon's poem, which dates from early in the Troubles, gives a voice to the victims of political violence – violence which a substantial section of Ulster Unionism is trying to ensure continues.[44]

Paulin's analogy varies from Haughton's in its details but remains just as unlikely. He wants to equate the mushrooms, amongst other historical subjects, with the *victims* of political violence in Northern Ireland. But why not also equate the mushrooms with the *perpetrators* of political violence? Presumably, that would complicate our reading because it would make us lose 'sympathy' with the mushrooms. But if the mushrooms are victims, where are their persecutors? Given the apparent absence of persecutors, and the absence of a motive for their persecution, does it seem useful to think of mushrooms as the victims of a deliberately inflicted suffering? The answer must be 'no'. Like Haughton, Paulin does not acknowledge that the primary cause of the mushrooms' suffering is neglect, because this does not fit in with his picture of the poem as a commentary on the Troubles.

One simple, but strong, argument against a historical reading of the poem is Mahon's record of avoiding The Troubles in his work. Indeed in a quote used by Haughton, the poet declared:

> It's possible for me to write about the dead of Treblinka and Pompeii: included in that are the dead of Dungiven and Magherafelt. But I've never been able to write directly about it.[45]

This disclaimer needs to be qualified a little. 'Afterlives', the first poem in *The Snow Party* does refer explicitly to the Troubles but it does so almost in the manner of an apology. Returning to the province after many years away, the speaker of the poem suggests that he is not adult enough to engage with the turmoil:

Perhaps if I'd stayed behind
And lived it bomb by bomb
I might have grown up at last
And learnt what is meant by home.[46]

Mahon may have intended a dark irony when, in these lines, the speaker refers to his own immaturity. After all, what kind of growth is it to live amongst bombs? This is also a clue to the poet's preoccupation with his own unfinished evolution.

To equate the mushrooms with one community or another – Northern Irish Catholics, Northern Irish Protestants, victims of political violence, victims of disaster, the forgotten of the world (and it says something that mutually contradictory readings of this sort have occurred) – leads the well-meaning interpreter into a tangle. The same problems afflict even those 'historical' readings which are vaguely and carefully phrased like, for example, Seamus Deane's assessment of the mushrooms:

They seek to escape from the brutality of a dark, instinctive and lethal struggle into the light of recognition. Mahon has here inverted his usual procedure. The lost lives are not lived beyond history, but before it. Their fulfilment is in history.[47]

Again the analogy is strained. Deane's reading gives the impression that dark, instinctive, and lethal struggles occur only before history (however that might be defined.) But, as we know only too well, such struggles occur in the world on a continual basis. Like the earlier analogies this one crumbles in the face of the simplest questions. Who or what has caused the mushrooms' suffering? Are the mushrooms to blame for their travails? What group of people does the plural pronoun represent? If 'we' save the mushrooms, how are 'we' in a position to do so and how have 'we' escaped their fate? The mushrooms' plight is pathetic but if any historical community was characterised in the manner suggested by the poem, such a portrayal would rightly be seen as patronising and misleading.

By way of illustrating this point we might note another minor critical dispute which this poem has generated. In an essay which touched lightly on a variety of other Northern Irish writers, and which made passing remarks on 'A Disused Shed', Seamus Heaney associated the mushrooms not with blameless victims but with potentially blameworthy sectarian precursors:

> ...[Mahon] makes the door of the shed open so that an apocalypse of
> sunlight blazes onto an overlooked, unpleasant yet pathetic colony of
> mushrooms. What they cry out, I am bold to interpret, is the querulous
> chorus that Mahon hears from the pre-natal throats of his Belfast ances-
> tors, pleading from the prison of their sectarian days with the free man
> who is their poet-descendant ...[48]

No longer are the mushrooms equated, here, with festering polit-
ical differences, with the victims of violence, or with a pre-historical
community – here they represent Mahon's 'sectarian' ancestors. While
Heaney felt the urge to associate the mushrooms with a definite
historical group, his reading is completely at odds with those of Paulin
and Haughton. Peter McDonald was not impressed by Heaney's
identification, describing it as "inadequate", and claimed that Heaney
was wrong to take for granted, "Mahon's freedom from the situation
the poem embodies."[49] I think this correction is useful. As my own
psychological reading of the poem proposes, Mahon's situation is
indeed intimately bound up with the destiny of the mushrooms. To
be fair to Heaney, I should point out that in an earlier essay he had
warned against drawing easy analogies:

> To reduce the mushrooms' lives and appetites to counters for the frustra-
> tions and desolations of lives in Northern Ireland is, of course, one of
> those political readings which is perfectly applicable, but we recognise
> that this allegorical approach ties the poem too neatly into its place.[50]

This is a more cautious judgement. Taken as a lesson in history,
'A Disused Shed' would simply be grotesque, just as its implicit
equation of Treblinka with Pompeii is maladroit. The various analo-
gies do not stack up, whether we deploy them singly, all together at
once, or as part of some patchwork of resemblances. The poem is not
interested in history. It wants to escape it.

I think my disagreement with the historical interpretations offered
by Paulin and Haughton reflects, to some degree, a generational
difference in interpreting Mahon. It is quite understandable that
someone reading the poem in 1973 would read the poem in the light
of pressing current events. Most of the early writing about Mahon
emphasised how glamorously cosmopolitan the poems were. *Night-
Crossing* and *Lives*, his first collections, with their versions and
translations of Villon, Breton, Rimbaud, and Baudelaire, were seen as

bringing a fresh idiom into Irish poetry. The critic Brian Donnelly, an early fan, recalls how Mahon's face – unsmiling and goateed – on the cover of *Night-Crossing*, was "suggestive of things foreign and exotic". But the thrilling impression of worldliness was misleading. Mahon's modernity was a sought-after effect which did not, as Rorty likes to say, go all the way down. From the admittedly partial perspective of 2008, Mahon's self-mythologisation as a modern cosmopolitan looks like the creation of a studious provincial which was accepted by a generation who wanted to see certain 'modern' values embodied. After *The Hudson Letter* and *The Yellow Book* it is hard to see Mahon as an enthusiast for modernity in any of its forms.

If historical readings of the poem tend to get mired in contradiction, then why should my contrary thesis, that the poem's main concern is consciousness, be accepted? Well, for the good reason that the poem says so – in its very first line: "Even now there are places where a thought might grow". It is strange how often this announcement goes unremarked. Perhaps this is because, in relation to the main 'action' of the poem, it has the air of a preamble – or, perhaps better, a preamble to a preamble. What readers are apt to remember about the poem is, I would suggest, the arresting central image of the mushrooms, and when they reflect on the first stanza what they remember is a kind of bold panoramic prelude. The 'blink-and-you-might-miss-it' quality of the poem's opening line finds a suggestive match in Robert Frost's "She is as in a field a silken tent", where the reader flitting over the pronoun may forget that the poem is about a woman and only secondarily about a tent. It is easy to forget that the first line has announced the subject of 'A Disused Shed', which is thought, or at any rate the conditions in which thought might grow, and that the rest of the poem is a series of examples – most quite sketchy, one very elaborate – illustrating what the first line proposes. It is also convenient to forget the first line if, anxious to provide a default historical reading, one wants to steer away from the inner psychological drama proposed by the opening. As the rueful-sounding "Even now" suggests, the conditions in which inwardness prospers are as likely to be temporal as spatial. The opening phrase is almost Yeatsian in its theatrical belatedness, as though we were encountering yet another *fin-de-siecle* speaker possessed of an outworn heart in a time out-worn. For Mahon, though, this opening represents a backward look, not to an earlier public state, but to an earlier private self.

We might think of the poem as the ambivalent soliloquy of the

Belfast student prince. Like Hamlet's famous meditation on life versus death, the speaker of 'A Disused Shed' is radically undecided about the value of his existence, and his uncertainties are projected, hazily but persistently, on the nervous and vulnerable mushrooms. Although Mahon's speaker wants to believe in his own imaginative virility, he is self-aware enough to consider its possible limitations. According to Seamus Heaney, "['A Disused Shed'] is about the need to live and be known, the need for selfhood, recognition in the eye of God and the eye of the world, and its music is cello and homesick."[51] This is beautifully phrased, but it is only partly persuasive, I think, because it makes the poem sound much more melancholy than the actual reading experience. The poem's popularity is partly due to the fact that large parts of it are so thoroughly entertaining. In the opening and the middle section the speaker is obviously enjoying himself and this enjoyment is transferred to the reader. The lives of the mushrooms are supposed to be wretched, but what the reader feels is much more a function of a speaker who is relishing his own performance – how different this is from a reading of poem like, say, Paul Celan's 'Todesfuge'. Responsible as he is, Heaney makes the poem sound more adult than its slightly reckless references to "Treblinka" and "Pompeii" might lead us to suppose. In the midst of his enthusiastic performance, Mahon's speaker, like his shadowy equivalent in 'Lives', sharply reduces these disasters, subordinates them to the joy of his own phrase-making – any large-scale disaster would do. "Treblinka" and "Pompeii" are on a par with the first stanza's use of "Peruvian" and "Indian". It is precisely because the speaker lacks a root in categories like "Peruvian" and "Indian", or in places like Treblinka and Pompeii, that he feels free to use them. To mention Dungiven or Magherafelt – places in which he has a root, and a corresponding moral stake – would entirely alter the poem. We do better to read 'A Disused Shed' against the desire (often felt by students) to escape those scenes of moral responsibility which might inhibit imaginative freedom.

Auden once said that it is wise for a poem to announce its subject in the first line. The words 'thought' and 'growth' vibrate, in this opening line, with rapt uncertainty. Do thoughts grow? Do we grow as we think? Is thought an enemy of growth? Is the speaker thinking? Is the speaker growing? The colourful anthropomorphism at the heart of the poem (which is of a kind that might appeal to children) is a hint that its personality is not fully adult. Because the mushrooms themselves can hardly be characterised as grown-ups, we are obliged to ponder questions of maturity and immaturity. The embryonic feelings of 'An Unborn Child', are extended into the not-quite-adult state of 'A Disused Shed'. Cadences from the former which have a resonant ruminative hum like, "The pandemonium of encumbrances", are reproduced in the latter's, "Indian compounds where the wind dances". The objects which we find in 'A Disused Shed' and 'An Unborn Child' similarly convey a foetal softness of thought: a curled-up kitten, clouds of goldfish, a bowl of cloud, rhododendrons – like the "little oval soul-animals" of Plath's 'Balloons'. These absorb the power of the poem's stupefying opening line where the beginning of the psychodrama is flatly announced. We might think of the forms of the poem as like thoughts coming into being, prepared to luxuriate forever in their own formation – "What should they do there but desire?"

Poems – to adapt a dictum of Richard Poirier – are about other poems more than they care to say. And also more than critics care to say. A publicly directed reading of 'A Disused Shed' is disinclined to see a poem as some kind of competition with an earlier poem for it suggests that art is a kind of sealed continuum in which creations endlessly feed on each other. I think it is against such a background that we should view the fact that Hugh Haughton, in writing the first major study of Mahon's work, does not mention the two most obvious poetic influences on 'A Disused Shed', namely Seamus Heaney's 'Bye-Child' and Sylvia Plath's 'Mushrooms'. Instead he focuses on a source of influence to which Mahon himself draws attention – the novels of J.G. Farrell. In his own account of the poem's germination, Mahon mixes up the Farrell novels from which he claims inspiration, an instructive mistake which reminds us to be wary of any poet's account of his or her influences. There is no doubt that Farrell's writing is powerfully present in 'A Disused Shed', but it is far from being the only major influence. The poetic influences on the poem especially matter because one of the poem's central preoccupations is the very fact of being influenced. One of the reasons why the poem contemplates out-of-the-way places where a thought might grow is because it associates seclusion with imaginative fecundity. It turns out, however, that the language used to summon this seclusion before the mind's eye is itself compromised and so the poem swerves from one set of influences towards another.

All poems are compromised by having their sources – to some degree – in other poems and this impurity is more or less troubling depending on the temperament of the poet. For a writer as committed to his imaginative sovereignty as Mahon, the drive to be original is keenly felt, and the horror of derivativeness is correspondingly strong.

One way to ease your influences is to overturn them, deflect them, and something like this movement, which in most poems takes place at a micro-level, from moment to moment, occurs with a drastic level of intensity in 'A Disused Shed', at the point where stanza one shifts to stanza two. Mahon's poem opens with a kind of panorama of panoramas, an ecstatic dilation which vibrates with distant poetic voices. Most prominent amongst these is the voice of Auden whose method of dilation the poem appropriates only to terminate. We sense we are in Auden-territory right away with the reference to abandoned mines – indeed the first stanza of the poem occupies territory much like Auden's 'Who stands, the crux left of the watershed' with its "long abandoned levels", its "damaged shaft", and "dismantled washing-floors".[52] Other well-known Audenic panoramas can be distantly discerned, from 'The Fall of Rome' ("In a lonely field the rain/ lashes an abandoned train") to 'In Praise of Limestone', a poem which "the lime-crevices" of 'A Disused Shed' brings to mind, ("... beneath/ a secret system of caves and conduits; hear these springs/That spurt out everywhere with a chuckle".)[53]

As though afraid of becoming "An echo trapped forever" the poem swerves away from this composite dilation with an abrupt contraction of its vision. An opening which had promised an Audenesque continuation is decisively interrupted. The quest for poetic originality is prosecuted, here, by a kind of deliberate blindness, whereby one secondary world is shut down in favour of another. So against the sound of Auden, the poem inside the shed begins to overhear Roethke, Plath, Heaney, Farrell, and Beckett (the interior of the shed would make an excellent set for *Endgame*.) The poem stops being one kind of echo, empties itself out in order to admit other voices. This is not to suggest that the poem is unoriginal but it does suggest that its originality lies less in what it chooses to say than in what it chooses to hear. In many ways a visual triumph, 'A Disused Shed' is even more an auditory celebration, a symphony of overhearing. The extravagant onomatopoeia of its diction reminds us of Bachelard's phrase that "Words are clamour-filled shells."[54] Beyond the echoes it has chosen to amplify, the poem listens for a silence that is not there, the united silence of end and start.

Let us take a look at some of these influences. To mention Heaney's first, this has already been discussed by the critic Heather Clark who has pointed out similarities of diction, theme and setting between Heaney's 'Bye-Child' and 'A Disused Shed', some of which suggest an extremely close relationship between the poems:

Mahon and Heaney even use the same words to describe their prisoners:
the child is a 'little moon man' who gapes with 'wordless proof'; the
mushrooms too are 'moonmen' who beg 'in their wordless way' not to be
abandoned by their liberators.[55]

Apart from Heaney's 'Bye-Child', the most obvious influence on
the poem is Plath's 'Mushrooms' (which was published in *The Colos-
sus.*) Although one might initially be surprised by a linkage of Plath
and Mahon, the two writers have more in common than one might
think. Both are inward visionaries; both are intensely literary; both
(in their poetic personae) seem uninterested in other people; both
have a narrow range; both return to subjects obsessively; both are
quick to appropriate historical disaster for projections of their own
suffering; both readily contemplate de-peopled environments, and
both have a peculiar feeling for childhood which awkwardly mirrors
a sense of incomplete personal development. While Plath's use of the
Holocaust in a poem like 'Lady Lazarus' may be more tendentious
than Mahon's use of Treblinka in 'A Disused Shed', the parallel is
nonetheless suggestive.

It is worth dwelling, too, on some of the similarities between
Plath's 'Mushrooms' and 'A Disused Shed'. Like Mahon's magnum
opus, Plath's characterisation of her mushrooms is distractingly
anthropomorphic. One factor which makes the influence a little less
explicit is the use of pronouns. In Mahon, the mushrooms are a 'they',
while in Plath they are a 'we'. In the course of depicting her
mushrooms as a surging collective, Plath erases their individual
identities. Reminding us of the enforced humility of Mahon's collec-
tive, Plath's mushrooms are said to move "very quietly", and are
"asking//little or nothing" In both poems, the mushrooms expand,
unseen, towards the light, a movement which climaxes at a door.

Both poems make a good deal of silence. 'A Disused Shed', in
particular, is drenched in the acoustic of alertness, a quality which
infuses the poem's duration with tense possibilities. At any moment,
we feel, the quiet might be compromised – the poem's consciousness
appears to be constantly alert for intrusion or variation, an intrusion
which of course decisively occurs. Heaney, in discussing 'A Disused
Shed', speaks of "a voice from beyond", which is, "beamed back out
of a condition of silence and Zen-like stillness...," and although he
does not intend it in this sense, that would make for a good descrip-
tion of the poem's alertness for other poetic voices.[56] Hence while
Plath's mushrooms operate discreetly and quietly, Mahon's have
"learnt patience and silence". While Plath's poems are "Perfectly

voiceless", Mahon's communicate in a wordless way. Whereas Plath's creatures exclaim, "So many of us!/ So many of us!", Mahon's appear to cry "Save us, save us." In neither case does the collective perform a convincing allegorical function. The play with silence, instead, associates the mushrooms more closely with consciousness. The door banging "with diminished confidence", the "slow clock of condensation", and the "lorry changing gear at the end of the lane" are in effect pondered for years by the omniscient ear of 'A Disused Shed'.

Plath's mushrooms declare that they are "Nudgers and shovers/ In spite of ourselves", and that first unusual noun, alerts us to one of Plath's sources, who is also, I think, one of Mahon's. That influence is Theodore Roethke who, in his poem, 'The Minimal', uses the same plural noun, "nudgers", to describe a non-human life-form. Roethke's so-called 'greenhouse poems', scattered through *The Lost Son and Other Poems* (1948), lie at the heart of a tendrilous network of influence which runs back and forth between the canons of Heaney, Plath, and Mahon. Like 'A Disused Shed', the greenhouse poems link a sense of warped development to soft, faintly sinister life-forms which grow in an enclosed darkness, a scenario oft-repeated in *The Colossus*. Some of Roethke's phrases and word-choices are suggestively close to Mahon's. In 'A Disused Shed', the mushrooms' cry of, "Elbow room! Elbow room!", which recalls the threateningly acquisitive Nazi concept of 'Lebensraum', is prefigured by a similar vegetable exclamation in the sequence, 'The Lost Son':

> Scurry of warm over small plants.
> Ordnung! ordnung!
> Papa is coming![57]

It would take us too far away from our topic to consider Roethke's influence in the detail which it deserves. In any case, the poems in *The Lost Son* tend to overlap each other in such a way that it is not a matter of their individual influence so much as their collective effect. Nevertheless, even a cursory glance at poems like 'Root Cellar' ("Nothing would sleep in that cellar, dank as a ditch,/ Bulbs broke out of boxes hunting for chinks in the dark,") or 'Weed Puller' ("Me down in that fetor of weeds") or 'Dolor' ("The unalterable bathos of basin and pitcher" – Mahon's poem contains some notably dolorous wash-basins and pitchers) or 'Big Wind' ("Creaking the cypress window-drams,/ Cracking so much thin glass" – Mahon uses the same verb-combination) should be persuasive enough.[58] Even a line like, "the world waltzing in its bowl of cloud" may owe something to

Roethke's 'My Papa's Waltz'. Roethke psychologises the cultivation of plant-life to such a degree that the associated qualities of softness, wetness, and mustiness cannot be separated from the fragile formation of the speaker's sexuality. This sexual element is obviously present in 'A Disused Shed' – "What should they do there but desire?" – although critics tend to focus more on the poem's general sense of failed promise. For our purposes, it is enough to say that the relative ease with which Mahon can be introduced into this extensive poetic continuum is itself evidence that the poem is more fruitfully approached from the angle of psychology rather than history.

Plath's influence, like Roethke's, also casts suggestive light on the poem's gothic quality, and this is something which can be connected with its theme of growth. Like a much-distorted, pocket history of the human race, 'A Disused Shed' parodies evolutionary processes and vibrates with some of those anxious literary ripples caused by Darwinism in the nineteenth century, especially those which emerged in fin-de-siècle Gothic. One of the ways in which Darwinism undermines the notion that the human being is an integrated whole is its suggestion that we are composites of other creatures. Exploring this topic in her study, *The Gothic Body*, Kelly Hurley deploys a useful concept of abhumanity which she defines as follows:

> The abhuman subject is a not-quite-human-subject, characterized by its morphic variability, continually in danger of becoming not-itself, becoming other.[59]

This abhuman subject is a mainstay of gothic literature where it is generally a source of a fascinated ambivalence. Similarly mixed feelings radiate from 'A Disused Shed', where neither the speaker nor the reader seems sure what to make of the abhuman mushrooms. On the one hand, their distorted shapes are a possible source of disgust. On the other hand, their mutability is a possible source of excitement – after all, the imagination which has transformed the mushrooms may cause further exciting transformations. Hurley's catalogue of abhuman types in gothic literature indicates that Mahon's mushrooms are not a category unto themselves:

> ... one must note ... the variety and sheer exuberance of the spectacle, as the human body collapses and is reshapen across an astonishing range of morphic possibilities: into slug-men, snake-women, ape-men, beast-people, octopus-seal-men, beetle-women, dog-men, fungus-people.[60]

Both Plath and Mahon align the evolution of the body with the evolution of individual poems. Just as the human body may be seen as a patchwork composed of little bits of other species, so poems may also be seen as patchworks, composed of little bits of other poems. The loss of the unitary human subject is paralleled with the loss of the unitary author. Hurley relates this to Darwin's picture of the human being as a patchwork:

> Such a body is not just liable to abhuman becomings, but also reveals itself as always already abhuman, a strange compilation of morphic traits, fractured across multiple species-boundaries. [H.G.] Wells ... would describe the human body as a modified fish-body.[61]

The poem's links with gothic literature extend beyond the concept of abhumanity, especially in its choice of setting. We might note that the title of the poem is focussed on the shed rather than the mushrooms. As Robert Harbison has pointed out, such obscure spaces are regularly psychologised in gothic literature:

> The real justification for calling Gothic a nonprogressive fiction of pure setting is that the fears of intrusion on the self are not exorcised but only manipulated. The Gothic battle is the attempt of self-control to withstand the onslaughts of the irrational, their subject is staving off madness, and they give the contention spatial form.[62]

One can find, for instance, many parallels between Mahon's poem and one of the high watermarks of gothic literature: Poe's 'Fall of the House of Usher'. In each case a kind of obscure and secret process of evolution is brutally aborted. One could link, too, the extreme sensitivity which Mahon's speaker evinces to the slightest stimulus to the hyperaesthesia of Roderick Usher. The poem begins and ends with references to individuals who have something like the status of the "cool scientific teller" – as Robert Harbison describes him – of Poe's story.[63] The mushrooms plight is book-ended by a mycologist, at the beginning, and a set of photo-journalists, at the end. So the poem flirts with the kind of dilated pseudo-objectivity which we get at the beginning of Auden's 'Spain' or at the end of 'The Fall of Rome'. This is the pseudo-scientific voice which Heaney's readings of Mahon tend to get wrong, the impression such a voice gives of efficiency and capability is a mask for chronic neuroses. Mahon's references to publicly-understood disasters can be read, then, as opportunities for consciousness to wrap itself up in the right kind of feelings, rather in the way that Harbison describes the reader being manipulated at the beginning of Poe's tale. As Harbison makes clear, the presence of a rational speaker in Poe's tale does not mean that the story performs a discursive function – Poe's story is less of an argument and more of a blend of ambivalent moods.

> It does not matter what the words exactly are, only that the reader should understand that he is to steep himself, close himself up entirely in a unitary feeling, as later when a long list of Usher's theosophical books is included, the impalpability of the tale is unviolated because they only elaborately suggest the kind of thing we might think of, tell us topics for our brooding.[64]

The fantasy of 'A Disused Shed' takes place in a world apart, a delicious secret, made all the more delicious by dwelling on those faults of the self which have swelled over time to an idiosyncratic fungal bureaucracy. 'Treblinka' and 'Pompeii' are cues to signal our feelings, they give us "topics for our brooding". For the poem to be effective, it doesn't matter that Mahon has juxtaposed, in the words of Fran Brearton, "... natural and 'manmade' disasters ...," a juxtaposition which would matter in any straightforwardly discursive context.[65]

'A Disused Shed' makes significant parallels between different forms of development: human evolution in general, the psychological journey of the self, and the poem's own unfolding. This is one explanation for the poem's fascination with distortion. The phrase, "beyond nature", points to another one of its influences, the exotically shut-in protagonist of Huysmans' *A rebours*, another figure who is in quest of imaginative sovereignty. As Bachelard puts it, "... to achieve grotesqueness, it suffices to abridge an evolution."[66] All forms of evolution in the poem are interrupted and each form feels threatened by the others: the privatised self fears that its proper growth will be thwarted by solitude, human evolution, as parodied by the mushrooms, is presented as coarsely primitive, and the poem's own progress is threatened by the existence of previous poets, by a kind of self-disgust and by time itself.

The poem's various contradictions are concentrated in its least satisfactory stanza, which is the last: What are the naïve labours of which the mushrooms speak? From what we have been shown, we can only conclude the mushrooms have passed their time in an environment which, typical of Mahon's poetry, is labour-free. Perhaps the mushrooms are re-imagining their own activity and romanticising

their coming "so far"? In *The Secret Life of Poems*, Tom Paulin offers
the following suggestion:

> This is the poet as tourist, a role Mahon is repudiating through the final
> demand made by the mushrooms. A poem, too, can be a naïve labour,
> can look home-made, and this highly sophisticated poem draws the naïve
> and primitive into itself at the last minute in order to offset its own sophis-
> tication, its carefully wrought stanzas, half and full rhymes, patterns of
> assonance, elegantly pitched lines.[67]

While this reading conflicts with Paulin's earlier interpretation (it
would associate the victims of sectarian violence with the naïve and
the primitive) it does point to a difficulty with the poem's conclusion.
Again, I think Paulin is making the mistake of separating Mahon's
speaker from the mushrooms. The subtitle from Seferis speaks of the
"weak souls among the asphodels", but those who died at Pompeii
and Treblinka did not do so because they were "weak". What should
we remember the mushrooms for? Is it possible to read their collective
outburst, and the final stanza as a whole, as awkwardly sentimental?
Giorgio Agamben has remarked on the difficulties which many
poems encounter at their conclusion:

> ... it is possible to see the inner necessity of those poetic institutions, like
> the *tornada* or the envoi, that seem solely destined to announce and
> almost declare the end of the poem, as if the end needed those institu-
> tions, as if for poetry the end implied a catastrophe and loss of identity
> so irreparable as to demand the employment of very special metrical and
> semantic means.[68]

The ending of 'A Disused Shed' is best understood as an unsat-
isfactory return to time from the realm of a highly literary
consciousness. It is the self (and poem) which wants to be remem-
bered. It is the self (and poem) which wishes not to be "in vain". As
anxious about origins as it is about outcomes, the poem presents us
with a beginning and an end which are theatrically broken-off. Just
as the 'real' cause of the mushroom's condition is not the departure
of "the expropriated mycologist" so their 'real' fate is not in the hands
of "the flash-bulb firing-squad". These are surrogates for points of
embarkation and arrival which must remain cosmically inaccessible,
even though the poem does its best to access them through its massive
dilations and contractions, through a 'Big Bang' of creation and a 'Big
Crunch' of apocalypse – the twin explosive stars of keyhole and flash-
bulb.

Returning to the chasm where we began, it is possible to reach a conclusion. The difference between Mahon's poetry, early and late, was located above all, in his attitude to privacy. Whereas his early poetry was private and inward, his later poetry was not. At the beginning of his career, the hopes and fears of the Belfast prince of thought had not been proved against experience. It was possible for Private Mahon, then, to trust in the self-sufficiency of poetry and the purity of his inwardness, even while fearing that, in worldly terms, he might be left behind. While he hoped that thought could and would conquer all, that his daydreams were their own reward, he feared that thought would not and could not suffice, that his abstention from conventional forms of activity would be severely punished. Since, in Mahon's early work, his hopes and fears were in balance, the poems, in their ritualistic way, tended to dilate as much as they would contract. In pessimistic moments, self (and poem) would shrink into a state of generalised negativity while, in optimistic moments, self (and poem) would expand until the serpent of consciousness was over all. In Mahon's later poetry, however, his hopes and fears were no longer in balance. Experience had settled the issue: thought was not enough. The dilations and contractions of each poem were accordingly reduced – the speaker was painfully, theatrically aware of his limitations and was no longer prepared to push against them. Although the speaker could look back, with varying degrees of nostalgia, to the hopeful life of a student, his heart was not in it.

Notes
1. John Redmond, 'Perish the Thought', review of *Selected Poems* by Derek Mahon, *London Review of Books*, February 8 2001.
2. Tom Paulin, Letters, *London Review of Books*, 8 March 2001
3. Hugh Haughton 'On Sitting Down to Read "A Disused Shed in Co. Wexford".Once Again.' *The Cambridge Quarterly* 31, no. 2 (June 2002): pp. 183-98, p. 185, p. 198.
4. Mahon has since produced a *New Collected Poems* (2011) which contains a handful of new poems and *Raw Material* (2011), a selection of versions and translations.
5. W.H. Auden, *The Dyer's Hand* (London: Faber, 1963), p. 338.
6. Peter McDonald, 'Incurable Ache', *Poetry Ireland Review*, 56 (Spring 1998), p. 118.
7. Tim Kendall, 'Beauty and the Beast', *Poetry Review*, 86, 1 (Spring 1996), p. 52.
8. Derek Mahon, 'The Hudson Letter', *The Hudson Letter* (Oldcastle: Gallery, 1995), p. 37.

9. Derek Mahon, 'Dusk', *The Yellow Book* (Oldcastle: Gallery, 1997), p. 40.
Derek Mahon, 'At the Chelsea Arts Club', *The Yellow Book*, p. 35.
10. Derek Mahon, 'To Eugene Lambe in Heaven', *The Yellow Book*, p. 24.
11. Derek Mahon, 'shiver in your tenement', *The Yellow Book*, p. 18.
12. Seamus Heaney, 'The Pre-Natal Mountain: Vision and Irony in Recent Irish Poetry' in *The Place of Writing* (Atlanta: Scholar's Press, 1989), pp. 36-53: p. 48.
13. Derek Mahon, 'A Ghostly Rumble Among the Drums' in *Journalism* (Oldcastle: Gallery, 1996), pp. 220-223, p. 223.
14. Hugh Haughton, *The Poetry of Derek Mahon* (Oxford: OUP, 2007), p. 14.
15. Derek Mahon, 'The Sadness Lurks So Deep' in *Journalism* (Oldcastle: Gallery, 1996), pp. 185-188, p. 188.
16. *ibid.*
17. Derek Mahon, 'J.P. Donleavy's Dublin', *Selected Poems* (Middlesex: Penguin, 2000), p. 18.
18. Derek Mahon, 'Girls in Their Seasons, *Night-Crossing* (London: OUP, 1968), p. 2.
19. Paul Muldoon, 'Gathering Mushrooms', *Poems 1968-1998* (New York: Farrar, Straus and Giroux, 2001), p. 106.
20. Derek Mahon, 'Alien Nation', *The Hudson Letter* , p. 62.
21. Haughton, *The Poetry of Derek Mahon*, pp. 228-9.
22. *ibid.*, p. 227.
23. Frank O'Hara, 'A Step Away from Them', *Lunch Poems*, (San Francisco: City Lights, 1964) p. 15.
Frank O'Hara, 'Personal Poem', *Lunch Poems*, (San Francisco: City Lights, 1964), p.32.
24. Derek Mahon, 'Lives', *Lives* (London: OUP, 1972), p. XX
25. Derek Mahon, 'Tihonus' in *Selected Poems* (Oldcastle: Gallery, 1991), pp. 169-70.
26. *ibid.*, pp. 220-223, p. 220.
27. Derek Mahon, 'Legacies', *Night-Crossing*, p. 38.
Derek Mahon, 'September in Great Yarmouth', *The Snow Party* (London: OUP, 1975), p. 29.
Derek Mahon, 'J.P. Donleavy's Dublin', *Night-Crossing*, p. 13.
28 Derek Mahon, 'An Unborn Child', *Night-Crossing*, p. 25.
29. Derek Mahon, 'Rock Music', *Selected Poems* (Middlesex: Penguin, 2000), p. 76.
Derek Mahon, 'A Disused Shed in Co. Wexford', *Selected Poems*, p. 54.
30. Italo Calvino, *Six Memos for the Next Millennium* translated by Patrick Creagh (London: Vintage, 1996), p. 19.
31. Derek Mahon, 'Leaves', *The Snow Party*, p. 3.
32. Derek Mahon, 'The Snow Party', *The Snow Party*, p. 8.
33. Derek Mahon, 'In Carrowdore Churchyard', *Night-Crossing*, p. 3.
34. Derek Mahon, 'Heraclitus on Rivers', *Poems 1962-1978* (Oxford: Oxford University Press, 1979), p.107.
35. Derek Mahon, 'After Nerval', *The Snow Party*, p. 23.

36. W.H. Auden, *English Auden* (London, Faber, 2001), p. 281.
37. Derek Mahon, 'Beyond Howth Head', p. 38.
38. Derek Mahon, 'The Sea in Winter', *Poems 1962-1978*, p. 110.
39. Dillon Johnston, *Irish Poetry after Joyce* (Notre Dame: University of Notre Dame Press, 1985), p. 241.
40. Haughton, *The Poetry of Derek Mahon*, p. 117.
41. Derek Mahon, 'Courtyards in Delft', *The Hunt by Night*, p. 9.
42. Derek Mahon, 'A Disused Shed in Co. Wexford', *The Snow Party*, pp. 36-38.
43. Hugh Haughton, *The Poetry of Derek Mahon*, p. 115.
44. Tom Paulin, *London Review of Books*, 8 March 2001
45. Eamon Grennan, 'Derek Mahon: The Art of Poetry', *Paris Review*, Spring 2000, p. 165.
46. Derek Mahon, 'Afterlives', *The Snow Party*, p. 2.
47. Seamus Deane, 'Derek Mahon: Freedom from History': p. 163.
48. Seamus Heaney, 'The Pre-Natal Mountain: Vision and Irony in Recent Irish Poetry' in *The Place of Writing* (Emory: Scholar's Press, 1989), pp. 36-53, p. 49.
49. Peter McDonald, *Serious Poetry: Form and Authority from Yeats to Hill* (Oxford: OUP, 2002), p. 157.
50 Seamus Heaney, 'Place and Displacement: Recent Poetry from Northern Ireland' in *Finders Keepers* (London: Faber, 2002), pp 112-133: p 120.
51. Seamus Heaney, 'Place and Displacement': p. 120.
52. W.H. Auden, 'Who stands, the crux left of the watershed', *Selected Poems* ed. Edward Mendelson (New York: Vintage, 1979), p. 1.
53. W.H. Auden, 'The Fall of Rome', *ibid.*, p. 183.
   W.H. Auden, 'In Praise of Limestone', *ibid.*, p. 184.
54. Gaston Bachelard, *The Poetics of Space*, p. 179.
55. Heather Clark, *The Ulster Renaissance: Poetry in Belfast, 1962-1972*, (Oxford: OUP, 2006). p. 171.
56. Seamus Heaney, 'Place and Displacement', pp 112-133: p. 120.
57. Theodore Roethke, 'The Lost Son', *The Collected Poems of Theodore Roethke* (London: Faber, 1968), p. 57.
58. Theodore Roethke, 'Root Cellar', *ibid.*, p. 38.
   Theodore Roethke, 'Weed Puller', *ibid.*, p. 39.
   Theodore Roethke, 'Dolor', *ibid.*, p. 46.
   Theodore Roethke, 'Big Wind', *ibid.*, p. 41
59. Kelly Hurley, *The Gothic Body: sexuality, materialism, and degeneration at the fin de siècle* (Cambridge: CUP, 1996), pp. 3-4.
60. *ibid.*, p. 4.
61. *ibid.*, p. 92.
62. Robert Harbison, *Eccentric Spaces* (New York: Avon, 1977), p. 85.
63. *ibid.*, p. 90.
64. *ibid.*, p. 91.
65. Fran Brearton, *The Great War in Irish Poetry* (Oxford: OUP, 2000), p. 209.
66. Gaston Bachelard, *The Poetics of Space*, 1st ed 1958, translated by Maria Jolas 1964 (Boston: Beacon Press, 1994), pp. 108-109.

67. Tom Paulin, *The Secret Life of Poems* (London: Faber, 2008), p. 217.
68. Giorgio Agamben, *The End of the Poem: Studies in Poetics*, 1996, translated by Daniel Heller-Roazen (Stanford: Stanford University Press, 1999), p. 112.

GLYN MAXWELL: THE SPECTRAL ADOLESCENT

These days, at least where poetry is concerned, we hear less about the deadly rivalry between Britain and America. Back in the 1960s, one heard of little else. Anthologies of the period regularly – and tendentiously – defined American and British poetries against each other. Those were the febrile days when Al Alvarez scolded British poets for their "gentility", while David Wright dismissed American poetry as "more an industry than an art".[1] If we assume that mutual hostility has not, in the meantime, merely been replaced by mutual ignorance, is there a reason why the America v Britain contest appears to have receded? One can think of a few: the spectacular, dominating rise of poets from the North of Ireland, the lasting influence of translated poetry from Eastern Europe, and, above all, the collapse of 'Britishness' into a rebarbative regionalism which has made it hard to identify a 'Britain' against which to pitch America.

Yet, putting those factors to one side, has much really changed? Is it not the case that American poetry, vaguely led by John Ashbery and Jorie Graham, is as campus-oriented and experimental as ever, and that *English* poetry – exceptions like the Cambridge School apart – is every bit as suburban and traditional? Opening our contemporary anthologies do we not find that, on the whole, prominent English poets pursue a very recognizable and conservative poetic model: a mixture of Auden and Larkin with some up-to-date shadings of Heaney and Muldoon? Answering both questions affirmatively, I dwell, in this chapter, on 'the parochial eye': a major ingredient in the traditionalism of English poetry, and one that marks it off starkly from its American cousin. By 'the parochial eye' I mean a poetic stance which has three principal characteristics: (a) a stance which dwells to an unusual degree on local, visible surfaces, on that which appears to be near at hand; (b) a stance which imagines for itself a neigh-bourly audience, an audience which is a natural extension of the local and visible; and (c) a stance which is distrustful of experiment, inter-nationalism, and higher education. Although the adjective 'parochial' is sometimes intended to be pejorative, in what follows I want the term to be descriptive rather than negative, acknowledging that the style which it describes has allowed many successful poems to be written.

Some of those successes appear in landmark post-war collections like Larkin's *The Whitsun Weddings* and Douglas Dunn's *Terry Street* – with emboldening models of this sort, the parochial eye has become a dominant phenomenon in British poetry. To measure its effect one need look no further than the high-profile career of Tony Harrison, who quickly traded the cosmopolitan stance of his first collection, *The Loiners*, for the defiant localism of mid-career books like *The School of Eloquence* and *Continuous*. The opening lines of his long poem, 'V', are typical of the style with which he is now associated:

> Next millennium you'll have to search quite hard
> to find my slab behind the family dead,
> butcher, publican and baker, now me, bard
> adding poetry to their beer, beef and bread.[2]

Echoing a children's rhyme in the third line, the poem immediately acquires an air of time-worn good sense. Using a 'bread and butter' technical scheme (alternate full rhymes with five-beat lines), this poem, and others like it, invokes a traditionally organized community in which people are defined by well-understood roles. Set in a graveyard, the poem organizes itself around the two-dimensional pressure of the headstones, a literal reading which tends towards a flattening and foreshortening of public space. Meanwhile, the voice is carried forward by the unpretentious plosive bluffness implied by beer, beef, and bread. A similar public flattening, though one which is less comforting, can be discerned in Paul Farley's 'Establishing Shot':

> It might as well come here as anywhere.
> Pick any card: street-lamps, tall leylandii,
> rotated ryegrass in available light.
> A long, slow take. Half-closing day. No one
> playing out. A goal-mouth chalked on brick
> is a frame within a frame just for a moment
> before the artless pan resumes: bollards
> and gutter-grass; ...[3]

The shot is not so much establishing as established, a view so dismally familiar the voice sounds tired even thinking about it. It is a view of the played-out English suburb/estate/inner city, which the poem, elaborating its movie metaphor, drolly contrasts with the fireworks of the camera. Here the parochial eye is imprisoned by a state of mind which merges with the surfaces which it cannot see beyond. Harrison's studied bluffness and Farley's graceful self-aware-ness are but two ways among many – other, influential versions of 'the parochial eye' can be encountered in the work of Sean O'Brien, Craig Raine, Christopher Reid, and Simon Armitage (to name but a few). In this chapter, I will be looking at a well-developed example of the phenomenon as represented by the poetry of Glyn Maxwell.

Born in 1962 of Welsh parents, Maxwell is closely associated with the most successful promotional event of 1990s British poetry, the grouping known as the 'New Generation'. One of the most startlingly energetic of the younger English poets, he is already the author of eight collections of poetry, several verse-plays, and a novel. Maxwell's eye was on the parish from the start. "Divide the town into eleven parts," one of his early poems declared, "throw ten of them away, and look at this". In the remaining nine percent of suburb, the dismissive (yet charming) speaker prepared to strike another of his sweeping blows against blandness, adolescent misery, and Just Being Young in England. Appearing in the title-poem of his first book, *Tale of the Mayor's Son*, these lines, with their strange, mathematical figure (eleven parts?) exemplified how enumeration would become a favoured vehicle for the speaker's alienation. The scene displayed would be repeated – compulsively, and in any number of surreal variations – in poem after poem: the victory of a chippy Solitude over an always pathological Togetherness:

> They skated on the ice at the ice-rink,
>   Elizabeth and a black-trilbied boy
> who kept his hat on. I'd have hated that
>
> had I seen it. I hate people who
>   make such alert decisions to impress.
> I'd have him on his arse. Oh good, he is.[4]

The town was Welwyn Garden City, part of the Greater London commuter belt, and the poems were propelled through this somewhat anonymous backdrop by a powerful, adolescent *schadenfreude*. In a puzzling, but arresting, manner the book made consistent use of names, groups and numbers. Whereas the sources of the narrator's resentment were multitudinous – the resentments – it might be imagined – of anyone young in suburban England – the objects of his resentment were actual multitudes. Instead of the kind of inhuman

homogenous collectives which, as we have seen, haunt Derek
Mahon's writing, Maxwell's poems were swamped by crowds of
homogenous cartoon-like people. Still, the impulse, in both cases, was
the same: a reduction of the visible (especially evidence of other
consciousnesses) in order to magnify the speaker. *Tale of the Mayor's
Son* was a parade of mobs, teams, gangs – familiar and unfamiliar –
that all stood up to be discounted ("pleasers", "non-enemies",
"highnesses", "kidney-donors", "Northern correspondents"). Just as
the book's more humdrum assemblies acquired charm by being
counted ("twelve drivers", "sixteen guests", "seventy-five teabags",
"seven hundred cabs"), so those curmudgeonly home-county types
who could not be dismissed merely by naming ("Mr. Gem", "Dr.
Pools", "Major Crammer") multiplied on the narrative petri-dish into
more easily-dismissed families ("the five Cliftons", "furious old
Coles", "the unlucky Greens").

    As these various groups occupied the theatrical middle distance,
the speaker usually looked out of, or in to, those scrappy redoubts so
beloved of a rebel adolescence (the book's first poem was set on a
playground, the last on a ball-pitch). Tracing the surfaces of a too-
familiar world, the parochial eye which gazed out of these poems
usually aligned the spectator with the spectral, a link most intensely
felt (as we will see) in his fifth book, *Time's Fool*. In contrast to
Emerson's famous transparent eyeball, the parochial eye of Maxwell's
poetry was unable to see beyond the boundaries of its parish and this
atrophy gave rise to all manner of gothic distortions. As much a
function of his anger as of his energy, the speaker's agitated manipu-
lations of his environment were often linked with a desire for
vengeance. This was a society the narrator knew well and, knowing
well, kept carefully at arm's length. His revenge, to borrow Heaney's
vocabulary, was to be tribal and intimate:

> ... But never mind how they laugh,
> the moody soldiers and the snappy teens:
>
> yours is the last if not the longer
> when this one comes, when this one means it
> at the top of the stairs, and your short breath
>
> blows all their laughter to what it is,
> a loud sadness.[5]

    The groups which roamed his early verse were amplifications of

a trait, surreal multiplications of an attitude. While the self-contra-
dicting speaker could be described as 'multitudes' – in the sense that
we associate with Walt Whitman – the groups themselves were essen-
tially simple organisms formed from the same cell ("… in dismal
Cliff-Town, the hundred men/ huddle and wipe again, and stir the
beer"), and the public world was reduced to a kind of pantomime
Greek Chorus straight out of *The Ascent of F6*:

> We billion cheered.
>> Some threat sank in the news and disappeared.
> It did because
>> Currencies danced and we forgot what it was.[6]

Typical of the book, these lines disarm the reader. While the plural
pronoun is attached to an improbably large number, the tone is so
boyishly enthusiastic that there is no space to challenge the speaker.
The alternation of short and long lines creates a double pace in which
childish hesitation is followed by childish verbiage.

Maxwell is a rapid writer, and his early poems seemed dramati-
cally off-the-cuff, deliberately improvised – one sentence, or clause,
often a reaction (contradiction, modification, or extension) emphat-
ically made to the preceding one. Taken on a succession of rides, his
readers were meant to enjoy being knocked about, to feel improved
by chaos, even as the relentless roving of the parochial eye
approached the condition of a village-tent performance:

> It reeled across the North, to the extent
> That even Northerners said 'This is North!'
> And what would you have said, to see a sky
>
> Threatening the children with great change?
> Extraordinary clouds! Spectaculars![7]

As this illustrates, there was no emotional registering of distance
beyond immediate neighbourhood – the North of England became a
cardboard stormcloud with "The North" painted across it in very
large letters.

Throughout *Tale of the Mayor's Son*, dull conventional precisions
of time, space and name were isolated from their context and multi-
plied (or divided) until they became starkly unconventional. The
strange play with names and numbers was mirrored by a fascination
with oddly specified, or non-existent, times such as "all o'clock", "the

negative-seventh day of Xmas", and – this, the subject of a whole poem –'Five-to-four (3.55 p.m.)'. Time, like everything else outside the speaker, was converted to space, then drastically warped and shrunk to suit the outlines of the local. The fascination with time was often revealed by multiple changes of tense:

> But what we didn't know, they were.
> What we don't believe, they are.
> There they are.
> Out floating out and still alive.
> We will breathe and cock and drive
> But not, now, far.[8]

Like a miniature version of Auden's 'Spain', this poem darts rapidly between past, present, and future. Exhibiting a kind of perpetual grammatical restlessness, such poems seemed to prepare every part of speech to turn into its opposite, its plural, its past tense. Objects and events would appear and disappear in such a haphazard manner that the reader could not forget the poem's fictionality and this made them seem even more self-consciously performative.

As he has admitted, the major influence on Maxwell's early work was the vatic Audenesque style of the 1930s. Dramatically protruding from the surface of *Tale of the Mayor's Son*, this ur-language was a fragmentary appropriation, an adaption of one particular phase of Auden's writing. Like Larkin, Maxwell had a special affection for the 'English Auden' of the mid-1930s, particularly the phase between *The Orators* and *Another Time*. Maxwell has been happy to confirm this in interview:

> I was trying to make an Auden sound but without having Auden's opinions or knowledge or understanding or intellectual breadth–just the facility of expression.[9]

Indeed, many of the groups prowling *Tale of the Mayor's Son* – "captains", "second sons", "crooked neighbours" – looked like they had dropped in from an Auden poem without bothering to change. The pattern of influence, however, was not a simple one. Maxwell, we might say, divided Auden into eleven parts and threw ten away. What he kept was the surface level: the sense of disease, the prevalence of gangs, the hostile presence of Them, the kind of mixture which drives classic Auden poems like 'Consider':

The game is up for you and for the others,
Who, thinking, pace in slippers on the lawns
Of College Quad or Cathedral Close,
Who are born nurses, who live in shorts
Sleeping with people and playing fives.
Seekers after happiness, all who follow
The convolutions of your simple wish,
It is later than you think; ...[10]

What Maxwell absorbed from passages of this sort was the dismissive, half-humorous assurance and the surreal sense of sweep. What he did not, or could not, absorb, was the deeper level of organizing myth. Enumerating the sources of Auden's secondary England, Randall Jarrell once provided a lengthy list which ran from Marx, Freud, and Groddeck, to mysticism, fairytales, and parables. Most of the elements which he listed have a negligible bearing on Maxwell's poetry (this is especially true of the intellectual sources), but there is one category which is revealingly influential. This is the category which Jarrell described as "boyish sources of value" and on which he elaborated as follows:

> ... flying, polar exploration, mountain climbing, fighting, the thrilling side of science, public-school life, big-scale practical jokes, "the spies' career" ...[11]

It might be said that such boyish sources of value often seem like the only sources in early Maxwell. In 'Farm Close', for example, we find a speaker who appears to be much younger than the author. Set, typically enough, on a sports field, the poem emphasizes the narrowness of the speaker's vision with a faux-naif repetition of the word 'small':

> The small field by my house is the small field
> I mean: the old green field of incidents,
> small teams, comments, and the planned insult.[12]

Heavily advertising its own informality, and challenging the reader to react to its immature voice, the poem is itself a kind of small green field. Like its three-dimensional predecessors it is a site of contests, a place where the author, now armed with sophisticated literary weapons, may finally triumph over the antagonists of his youth. The speaker adopts a voice which is Young, certainly, but of uncertain age. While he can sound, at times, like he is six or seven

years old ("my book/ with the Straw Witch on page 9, the fright-
ener!"), elsewhere he speaks as though he is in his late teens or early
twenties. Auden's fingerprints are on virtually every phrase from the
use of conflicting double modifiers in the final stanza ("small, deter-
mined planet", "mad, beloved Time-traveller") to the psychologised
generalizations which reach their climax in "the planned insult".

This poem reminds us that Maxwell, in the manner of many of the
poets of the 1930s, used the definite article in order to close the gap
with the reader. Referring conspiratorially to a shared body of knowl-
edge, he applied a battery of effects to presentation of super-typical
scenes and situations, a pattern which was quite in line with faux acces-
sibility of much British poetry in the 1990s. Whereas poets of the 1930s
actually wanted to close the distance between the poet and the
audience, Maxwell simply pretended that the distance was not there.

Whereas Auden's poetry took a bird's-eye, panoramic view of
England-in-Europe – including its history, technology and geology –
Maxwell's was a view of England-in-Welwyn, a view of the parish.
Beyond a few centre-left decencies, *Tale of the Mayor's Son* said
nothing large-scale about England because, the poems implied, there
was largely nothing to say. Not that it seemed to matter. The success
of the book (published in 1990) was that it so *enjoyably* caught a
mood, after three Thatcher victories, of public hopelessness. In
contrast to the gloom of the Seventies, Maxwell's *non serviam* for the
Nineties was fun – a prolonged, theatrical recoil from the plural, with
the emphasis firmly on 'theatrical'. Like some other notable postwar
collections, *Tale of the Mayor's Son* was all presentational vigor and
locally observed character (it is worth pointing out that Maxwell has
staged a number of his verse-plays in the very local setting of his
parents' back garden.) Large-scale ideas not already domesticated
were absent. Public life consisted, for good or ill, of Major Crammer
being spotted on the village green.

This did not prevent explicitly public interpretations of his work.
Ian Gregson, for example, has chosen to give a political slant to
Maxwell's postmodernism, notably when writing about the early
mock-epic, 'Tale of a Chocolate Egg':

> [The] mingling of languages [in 'Tale of a Chocolate Egg'] deliberately
> poses problems of reader response which suggest the difficulty of adopt-
> ing simple moral or political attitudes towards postmodernist culture,
> which suggest that reader and author are inevitably in an ambiguous
> position which wishes to condemn what is merely materialistic but finds
> itself nonetheless implicated in and complicit with it.[13]

"Consumerism" and "reification of women," Gregson goes on to suggest, are some of the features of contemporary life which Maxwell might wish to condemn. This strikes me as quite a clear example of a critic enlisting a poet to his own outlook. Gregson adopts a perspective where abstractions in harmony with a postmodernism of which he approves – 'diversity', 'dialogism', and polyphony' – serve as ghostly stand-ins for 'correct' political attitudes. By way of illustrating the difficulty with this, here is how the advertisement of the egg is described near the beginning of the poem:

> The advertising was quite marvellous.
> I even saw a lad discard his Mars
>
> in open-mouthing awe at the vast ad.
> It was enormous, a whole building's wall!
> The walls of a whole block! The chocolate egg
>
> alone in bed, its slogan, as I said,
> itself. Look, like this: O. But obviously
> magnified a million more times.[14]

As the strenuous exclamations attest the focus throughout the poem is on the narrator's self-advertising performance. Far from being a hindrance to the speaker, the omnipresent, over-the-top advertising provides a space in which he thrives. The poem offers not a hint of disapproval. In Gregson's eyes, Maxwell's lack of explicit positions – political or ethical – cannot remain, merely, a lack. But I do not find such political positions to be even an implicit presence. In the same way that Hugh Haughton drew Derek Mahon into the kind of relationship to the public sphere of which he (Haughton) approved, so Gregson orientates Maxwell towards the public sphere in ways unsupported by the poetry itself.

Although Maxwell's work was more strenuously concerned with youth than Derek Mahon's, he is, like the Irish poet, troubled by a sense of thwarted promise. Like Mahon (and, indeed, like Auden,) he has made negative public remarks about his own early writing. In an interview with Robert Potts, for example, he expressed dissatisfaction with certain patterns in his first three volumes and, at the same time, spoke of the corrective ambitions behind his subsequent collections:

> Time will wipe away most of it and leave some of it. There was a lot of
> ostentation and display, a lot of verbal relish and sometimes too little

inside. From *The Breakage* [Maxwell's fourth book] onwards, I think I've just felt the world to be graver and quieter, and nothing has preoccupied me more than time itself. That's what a poet who has lived only in good times will have to come to in the end.[15]

Reluctant to develop out of easy verbal habits, Maxwell's evolution was slow. If youthful charm was the indispensable veneer of his early work, masking numerous gaps and cracks, it was also an obstacle to growth. Whatever the circumstances, Maxwell's speakers seemed to be spry and puckish, constantly bending and twisting the reader's attention. The abundant energy of the poetry was ultimately expended on evasion rather than revelation, extending the speaker's adolescence through the unsatisfactory means of role-play. Stephen Burt, in his study of adolescence in twentieth century poetry, reflects, in helpful fashion, on how this desire to hold true to the values of a particular age-group, (he traces it back to Rimbaud), is increasingly relevant to our own literature and society:

> The notion of youth as goal seems paradoxical in Rimbaud, which is one reason he surrounds it with sorts of self-contradiction and paradox. The same notion becomes almost a cultural commonplace in certain parts of 1990s America, with its Generation X and Yers, indie rockers, perpetual students and "kidults" …[16]

Not only do these remarks seem pertinent to Maxwell's "kidult" speakers, they illuminate the wider embrace of immaturity in the Britain of the 1990s. Equally, the forms of self-contradiction and paradox which Burt associates with Rimbaud find their matches in Maxwell's work.

Struggling to accommodate the grown-up world, Maxwell's poems sharply recoiled from labour. Many of his "kidult" characters seem to be at a permanent loose end. Take, for example, the aptly titled 'Sulk':

> What we are at is pining for our lost
>   Future. How we are doing that is simple:
> Slouching beside our low glass tables dressed
>   In shimmering precious suit from nape to ankle.[17]

A reluctance to describe work was strongly felt in his longer poems, where it created problems of exposition. How did Maxwell's unlikely protagonists spend their time? In order to deflect attention from this gap, the poems would refer to occupations of a particular type, those which might populate a boy's adventure story: kings, queens, detectives, soldiers, explorers. There was, too, a noticeable, perhaps compensating, fascination with sporting activity. In the course of describing Auden's early style, Burt throws a sideways light on the varieties of thwarted development which we also find in Maxwell's poetry:

> Auden's early poems describe not a generalized immaturity but a partic-
> ular kind of adolescence, enabled and mediated by all-male boarding
> schools ....Auden's homosocial, and sometimes homosexual, groups and
> teams find nothing worth developing into or toward, and they refuse the
> clearer rules of adulthood for the obscurities of in-groups and codes.[18]

It is noticeable that some of Maxwell's more successful early poems were those where he set such mannerism aside – at least for a while. Two poems in *Rest for the Wicked*, 'Younger Than That Now' and 'The Night Is Young', were consistent with the "graver and quieter" attitudes to which the later Maxwell aspired. Both poems are concerned with aging, with the past surveyed from the perspective of a reduced present.

In 'The Night Is Young', we encounter a typical Maxwellian stand-off, in which two groups of men are depicted in a bar. Across this murky parochial space, one man from each side recognizes the other, and they meet, briefly, in the middle:

> I was with some friends when I noticed with some strangers
> One of the Gang. And we rose like we'd won awards,
> Reluctant and delighted, to a position
> Halfway between our tables, and began,
> Began with a tale of now and ourselves, but soon
> Were hurrying back in the years like children
> Yelled out of the light of their inexplicable game,
> Into the brooding houses to be held.[19]

The I-persona is clearly meant to be Maxwell himself. Compared with much in *Tale of the Mayor's Son*, the pacing is slower and clearer, and the action is framed with the same anecdotal clarity which characterizes many of Larkin's representative narratives (Larkin's style represents a kind of default mode for most New Generation poets.)

Reflecting on the hectic role-play which some of the early poems uncritically embodied, the eye of the poem stabilizes, and the public world is revealed in its banal homogeneity. The poem appears to suggest that personality is situational – what ultimately determines our behaviour is the gravity of whatever social body we happen to be orbiting. The two men enter a space where their respective acting routines mirror each other and these routines, in turn, acquire a vertiginous life. And, if being 'One of the Gang' is little more than a role-playing game, can the same reductive thing be said about other parts of life, like home and family? The poem ends sourly:

> I returned to my circle,
> Shaking him off as doubtless he shook me off,
> Answering who he was with an oh someone,
> Settling to the night, uncomfortable, gruff,
> And feeling about as young as the night is young,
> And wanting it all, like one who has had enough.
> You don't forgive what's left of what you loved.[20]

By echoing the concluding phrase of Larkin's 'An Arundel Tomb' ("What will survive of us is love"), Maxwell's conclusion aims for an unusual liturgical sonority which, like the poem's slower pace, seems to register the effort of self-recognition. It may be that the construction of this poem was surer because its preoccupations – the end of youth, group feeling, the public world as stage – were ones with which Maxwell, as a playwright and actor, felt at home.

Theatricality was even more directly at issue in the thematically-related, 'Younger than that Now', a poem which presented Maxwell loitering backstage, reflecting on his life in the theatre:

> Open the door one crack and you are backstage.
> The closest of the bright unanswering faces
> you love and know, but away down the crowded passage
> They get much gloomier longer to recognise.[21]

In general, those poems by Maxwell that do not crush banalities are crushed by them. Here, as the speaker gradually comes to a halt amongst the props and costumes, he seems to realize that not only is his work dependent on cliché (the props), it is also vulnerable to it. As the urge to knock over straw targets declines, the straw-targets acquire a kind of resurrected menace.

While the Dylanesque title is optimistic in spirit, Maxwell's intention appears to be darker. This valedictory account of life in the theatre has an uncertain, unhappy mood. The space which Maxwell describes is representatively theatrical, filled with types and figures, the kinds of type which one could expect to see in any dramatic season. Although Maxwell seems to be saying goodbye to the stage we are not told where he is going and the poem seems to hint that there is nowhere else to go. By the end of the poem he has made his way to an obscure area "at the end of the theatre" and finds himself sitting on a paint-spattered chair. Against the poet's habitual buoyancy, the journey which the 'you-persona' undertakes is strikingly negative, passing from "a frozen chorus", "vast and icy rooms", and "dresses coldly hung", to a broken image of himself in glass:

> Pass by yourself in brown and broken glass,
> By planks and crates at the foot of a storage tower,
> By what seems rubbish to you but will be of use,
> And then the rubbish ....[22]

The kind of modesty demonstrated by these two successful examples of the parochial eye in action was, however, overshadowed by Maxwell's developing attachment to epic procedures, a development which tended to lay bare his contradictions. The longer his poems got, the more they seemed to feel their own pointlessness, and their protagonists, in the absence of an obvious goal, compensated with greater narrative extravagance. One way of explaining Maxwell's attachment to peculiar times of day is the difficulty his fictional creations have in spending their time. In this context, Seamus Deane's association of boredom with apocalypse is suggestive:

> Boredom has to pay close attention to chronology in order to define its own condition – entrapped by the passage of time it elaborates an escape from that by envisaging the passing away of time. The bored have to find a way of passing the time; in doing so, they arrive at the position where time passes them by.[23]

Deane is writing here about Irish literature but the analysis is apt for Maxwell's work, particularly his poetic epics where creation and destruction seem to arise from impatience with ordinary reality. Maxwell's God, in 'Out of the Rain', provides a notably camp example. Inflicting a cartoonish deluge on a ramshackle contemporary world, he seems motivated by having nothing better to do:

> More obviousness then. Sheet lightning.
> God's face in it, bored, on His chin.
>
> One of us shouting, 'Knock it off!' to Him.
> And suddenly it stopping, at our shins.[24]

In 'Out of the Rain', Maxwell's embryonic epic, the I-persona experiences life in an about-to-be-flooded world as a kind of exaggerated Sports Day, where communal life is sustained, to a preposterous degree, by winning games. Even as such revels unfold, the narrator informs us, ominously, that a shadowy adult is elsewhere building an Ark. Like most examples of labour in Maxwell's work this activity is not described in detail, and the product is (characteristically) dismissed as an "embarrassing huge boat". When the Flood eventually arrives, the narrator wonders exactly how this Noah-figure managed to gather the various animals on to his Ark. His failure to find an answer is symptomatic:

> The animals. Big question, yes, of course:
> How did the son-of-a-prophesying-bitch
>
> find them all? – what's the word – the logistics.
> Answer: haven't a clue.[25]

As these lines illustrate, Maxwell's narrative informality is, on one level, an invitation to imagine a more comprehensive, or polished, style of narration, rather as a pantomime actor might make a virtue of fluffing his presentation. 'Not knowing about the logistics' is an aesthetic decision rather than an accident.

Foreshadowing the extravagance of *Time's Fool*, 'Out of the Rain' plays off public apocalypse against extremes of private eccentricity. The deluge in which the speaker's make-believe town is submerged, feels disobliging rather than destructive – and comes without any sense of human cost:

> I swam, and thought of the dead. I thought 'They're dead.'
> (I was known as a thinker at school, I'll have you know.)
>
> I thought of the things I'd seen, and thought 'I didn't
> see those things'. (I was known as a liar, too.)

As usual, the psychological interest of the poem is generated by the speaker's distracting narrative style. Ian Gregson uses the above lines to illustrate the poem's lack of depth:

> The emphasis [in 'Out of the Rain'] is not on moral or political misdemeanours but upon a kind of inadvertence and shallowness, an inability to concentrate on things of genuine significance which is reflected in the silliness of the first person narrator ....[26]

Another 'silly' narrator lay at the heart of Maxwell's fifth book, *Time's Fool*, a long poem running to almost 400 pages. This peculiarly spectral vision of adolescence, was on a much larger scale than anything Maxwell had attempted before. The book can be read as an attempt to swerve away from his earlier style, although, ultimately, in its search for gravity it tried too hard. Amongst the stylistic consequences of Maxwell's early refusal of the adult world was the difficulty of creating a sustaining adult myth along the lines of, say, Yeats's Gyres, or Eliot's Fisher King. Since luxurious youthful boredom and grand teenage refusals do not suit a man of thirty-seven (Maxwell's age when writing *Time's Fool* – he described this, revealingly, as "the last year of youth"), in *Time's Fool* he finally attempted something in the grand manner, a prolonged goodbye to his earlier style.

Whereas in the early work the contemptible pluralities of modern life had little or no meaning, in *Time's Fool*, they had all too many meanings. Whereas the early poems were narrative jumbles of no particular identity, *Time's Fool* was awash with generic identities – at once, thriller, ghost-story, travelogue, autobiography, and science-fiction. Likewise, its hero was an 'identity-magnet', at once adolescent, commuter, murderer, ghost, victim, poet, and messiah. But did all this adding amount to increase or dilution?

Unusual numbers did not disappear from Maxwell's work, quite the reverse. Edmund Lea, the narrator of *Time's Fool*, is cursed to remain forever seventeen – the spectral adolescent par excellence. "Hell had made a number out of me", he says, and that number is seven.[27] Seven times for seven years he rides a train of seven cars which stops at his home station, Hartisle, seven times – here, the parish is as gothic as it is inescapable. Lea triggers his curse by 'killing' the poem's villain, Cole, at a most Maxwellian time: 3.21 a.m. (7 = 21 divided by three). A small child who sees the incident calls Lea '007'. Lea repeatedly arrives in Hartisle at 4.19 p.m. (259 minutes after noon another number divisible by seven) on Christmas Eve (seven days before the year ends) in '70, '77 ... and so on seven times.

The main inspiration for the poem's schema is Wagner's opera 'The Flying Dutchman', a source which *Time's Fool* makes no attempt to conceal. Indeed it provides one of the poem's epigraphs. Early on, Lea relates his plight to a poet named "Glen" (Maxwell's alter ego) who conveniently points out the analogy. When Glen gives Lea the nickname "The Flying Scotsman", (the name of a famous steam locomotive – there was a "Flying Dutchman" too) he reminds us that transposing the legend from ship to train is an idea which has occurred to others. Among literary works, for example, there is 'Dutchman', Amiri Baraka's polemical play set on a subway. Using the legend as a rough symbolic backdrop, Baraka's play inverts Wagner's image of redemption through a woman's love by allowing its black hero to be murdered by a domineering white woman. Like *Time's Fool* the play contains a number of anonymous and ghostly passengers who, in their passivity, seem to be accessories to something awful. Maxwell's adaption of the myth is, however, much more elaborate and explicit.

Amongst the poem's many flaws the principal one is exposition. Whereas Gothic tales often rely on an outwardly objective 'frame', a solid sober narrator, like Coleridge's Wedding-Guest, who helps the reader to accept the tale's extravagance, *Time's Fool* is supposed to be a 'firsthand' account completed by Lea on his final return to Hartisle, a premise which leads to problems. For example, we have difficulty believing, as we are asked to believe, that Lea is writing the poem as events occur. He begins writing in 1985 in order to explore the cause of his curse fifteen years earlier. Not only is this poem-within-the-poem a sort of *aide-memoire* (through writing it he recalls events which he has – quite implausibly – forgotten), he intends it to be a confession, which, on his next return to Hartisle, may release him from his curse. Ludicrously in 1991, he is still making copies of the poem even as he pulls into the station (truly a man who works to a deadline):

> … my thousand poems
> I'll throw from here, paving beloved ground
> with these exact confessions of my crime.
>
> You who have read so far, this is your town
> I inch towards: you do not know my face.[28]

Leaving aside the odd decision to confess his crime in the form of a verse-novel – and to copy it out a thousand times by hand – the author does not seems to care if anyone could be expected to pick up a discarded poem and read "so far". The conceit that the poet is 'writing this as he speaks' or that 'you' the reader are in the room with him – a sudden shortening of fictive distance – are off-the-shelf postmodernist techniques from Maxwell's shorter poems that seem misplaced in a longer work.

... Now every night
I sit in the same food buffet with the same
macabre servant present and I write,

I make the thousand copies of this poem
I'm going to need in – I can calculate –
four hundred and five days, for when I come

to Hartisle once again at Christmas, late
Christmas Eve of 1991.
All these copies can survive the night

Because I've backed them up. I took a carbon![29]

Confusingly then, the copies are copies of copies. The reader must decide whether the tonal shift from "macabre servant" to banal "carbon" is intentionally comic or merely clumsy – Lea's final exclamatory burst seems peculiarly playful for someone suffering the psychic equivalent of solitary confinement. Nor does Lea in fact need these copies, but the poem, in order to account for its own existence, needs him to be writing it.

Why does Lea's writing take poetic form? To account for this the plot must twist again. Apparently, those supernatural powers which have Lea in their grip are, aesthetically speaking, arch-conservatives. When Lea tries committing anything to paper it simply fades away – unless it rhymes! That said, no explanation is provided for his adoption of *terza rima* and, as Lea does not seem to be even moderately well-read, we must presume that his *hommage* to Dante is unconscious. In interview, Maxwell partly explained the adoption of terza rima as a way of managing a poem of such length:

> Terza rima seemed to be the strongest form to take a poem of this length, because it had to be stanzaic. Terza rima approximates to thought, or the place where two elements–thought and light–connect. The first line of a terza rima is already an echo – it's an echo of the middle line from the stanza before – so it's a thought that's being processed, using rhyme as a metaphor for thought. So the second line is a new rhyme, the new light striking you, "What about this?" The last line is the last echo of the previous thought, so you get what I call the fourth line, the white space, which allows you to continue the process. .... For me it.s an eternal form; like DNA, it can absolutely reproduce itself.[30]

Like this explanation, when the writing is not implausible, it is

often awkward. Take, for example, the dialogue. Maxwell's early
poems often feature little caricatures of contemporary speech which
enliven the texture ("Me fuckin' sweet'art's buggered off, sweet'art!/
'ere – 'ave a fiver, that'll do it. Oi/watch it matey! ..."). *In Time's Fool*
there are vast stretches of such 'nowspeak'. These are often wildly
inappropriate. For example, during a key scene, the evildoer Cole,
when confronted by Lea, stands on the edge of a deadly drop,
perversely hoping to be pushed. To that end, he announces that he
has slept with Lea's girlfriend, and asks a question:

> ... 'What makes you think I'd want to jump?'
> I stared at Cole and answered, 'Where you are
> is what. I thought you'd be –' 'You thought I'd stop
>
> at Thingummy's? You thought I'd be with her?
> I do not stop, I never stop, I reach
> this place and I take anyone. It's where
>
> I come to when I'm thirsty. It's the ditch
> I drink in.' 'That's my town, that is,' I tried
> to lighten things. ...'

One would think that Lea, at this moment, would have more on
his mind than the good name of his town (and that preposterous
"Thingummy's"!), just as the narrator's wish to lighten the mood is
psychologically implausible. As usual, the characters, especially the
interchangeable minor ones, never sound convincing as characters.
They sound, instead, like short Maxwell poems.

None of this would matter if the ride were enjoyable – consistency
is not an important virtue in Maxwell's poems. The sheer length of
the poem, however, ensures that the reader, like Lea, is soon searching
for an escape hatch. While Lea's rail journeys, washed-out and shut-
in, eventually make the reader feel like they are stuck on a branch
ley-line, the numerous cantos are the verse equivalent of leylandii:
dark, monotonous and fast-growing. The narrator, meanwhile, lapses
into grim horrorisms which would defeat even Vincent Price and the
best dry-ice machine:

> ... I was lodged in Hell,
> my Hell. Yours may be stuffed until it shrieks;
> mine, love-avoiding, gapes like any skull.31

As Auden ends his train's-eye view of Britain, 'Night Mail', with "the postman's knock", Larkin ends his, 'The Whitsun Weddings', with London's "postal districts packed like squares of wheat". Each poem suggests that their visions are transmissible, capable of being shared. In both cases, the train, as an icon of the Industrial Revolution, marks an uneasy interface between the local and the national. Whilst harbouring an uneasy community of strangers it also represents the technological erosion of community. Loosely following this pattern, *Time's Fool* ends with the spectacle of Lea, now released from the train, as an isolated old man, who is passing his time by occasionally writing letters. After 49 years of travel, however, his message seems, even to him, barely worth transmission:

> .... I write these things,
> I add them to the old account I had
>
> By heart the night I came, so many things,
> I try hard not to shape it, it's just there,
> The life I went through. As to what it means,
>
> I leave to whom I leave it to.[32]

Leaving us to shape the text, however, does not help, because the poem's gothic heart is empty. The Flying Dutchman is cursed thanks to the sin of pride, the Ancient Mariner kills the albatross, but Lea, as it turns out, has done no obvious harm. Cole, whom we think he has killed, was never alive in the first place – an undead, rather, who reappears towards the poem's close. Learning neither the source nor the significance of Lea's curse, it is hard for us to care about it.

Maxwell's versions of apocalypse in 'Out of the Rain' and 'Time's Fool' disturbed time but persistently declined into boredom. When Seamus Deane argues for a close connection between boredom and apocalypse in the literature which flowed from the Celtic Revival, the period backdrop of disappointed expectations is important. In that case, a utopian, vitalistic conception of the national spirit was constantly thwarted by a grimly humdrum Irish reality. In Maxwell's parochial eye, by contrast, there was only the humdrum. There was no national spirit against which to play it off. When Maxwell took on the Audenesque machinery of a national myth he could only deploy it on an individual basis, not on a collective one. Maxwell's narrator in *Time's Fool* wanders in a literary structure whose function is elsewhere, an Audenesque landscape which, ironically, made abandoned function an essential trope of its public criticism – one way of reading *Time's Fool* is as a failed attempt to escape the second-ary world of another.

If Maxwell's early work represented vigor without a project, and *Time's Fool* was a project without vigor, then his later work in *The Nerve* and *The Sugar Mile* was more obviously transitional. After *Time's Fool* drew a line under the 'English Maxwell', such books intro-duced, tentatively, the 'American Maxwell'. The results were mixed. In these collections there was hardly a poem without a very good line and hardly a poem without a bad one. New philosophical notes were uncertainly sounded. *The Nerve*, for example, opened with a somber rumination in the manner of Stevens, 'The Sea Comes in Like Nothing but the Sea', and closed with another, 'The Snow Village'. In these the poet discoursed, with unexpected solemnity, on abstrac-tions like knowledge and nothingness. The parochial eye started to acquire a belated American openness.

Like many a poet from Northern Ireland – especially Paul Muldoon – Maxwell took to citing Frost as an influence, and to suggesting that Americans do not know the New England poet as well as they might. Maxwell tended to sound, however, more like Muldoon first and Frost second, as in the short 'Colorado Morning':

> Looping around the more or less dead straight
> lines where skiers were,
>
> some shy, nocturnal creature's one and only
> shot at its signature.

In four lines we encounter a succession of Muldoon effects: the typically airy colloquialisms "more or less" and "one and only"; the playfully extravagant rhyme of "skies were" and "signature", the looped syntax, plus a loud echo of 'Quoof', one of the Northern Irish-man's best-known poems ("… some other shy beast/ that has yet to enter the language".)

While the spectral adolescent was no longer central to Maxwell's work, and the poems often flourished a grown-up, married 'we', strik-ingly he retained the urge to domesticate his surroundings with a faux childishness. In 'The Weather Guy', for example, he adopted a sort of Stevie Smith voice, "Hurricane This is playing wolf/ to New York city's clever pig …." There were seriously-intentioned poems which rendered American society through the kind of lurid types which English audiences especially enjoy, for instance, an eccentric country music singer and a tragically eccentric backwoods hunter. The result of all this was an American book in an English style, an uneasy mixture of new material and old manners. 'Playground Song', for instance, seemed like a ghostly transfer of the parochial eye:

And tiny things too late to do
  have gone so far they can't be seen
except at dusk by me and you
  and though I hide till Hallowe'en

you never come, …

In *The Sugar Mile* Maxwell was still happy to play games with the time of day. 'Harry Pray In His Coat', for example, begins with the line "Something like five o'clock."[33] Given that the book glanced at an event (9/11) that has been remembered by a date this seems appropriate. In the following excerpt, a monologist draws attention to the year in which New York was attacked:

Wouldn't have thought I'd ever write the year
2000 … 2001! doesn't look right.
Looks more like the year

aliens land, with all those zeroes there
like faces, and this 1 … it looks like what?
Beginning all over. Right,

when what's to begin again?[34]

Making extensive use of dramatic monologue, *The Sugar Mile* attempted to filter contemporary events – and particularly the relationship between Britain and America – through the filter of a pub conversation. In this, the book may have been nodding towards *The Age of Anxiety*. Bearing a family resemblance, the voices in the poems were often hard to differentiate, although what counted for more was their ability to tell stories.

One comes away Maxwell's canon feeling that here is a poet of such energy and talent that he might do anything – or nothing. The mixed effects of his later work are sharply captured in 'Farm Animals Are Childhood'. This poem begins by considering the difference between English cows and those in Massachusetts. The poet, out on his bike, spots some children throwing stones at cattle. Prompted to think about the nature of childhood, the speaker throws out a series of verbal equations: "Watching children isn't childhood", "Believing's

childhood", "Caring isn't quite". None of these is especially striking
– the poem seems to be drifting to an undistinguished close. Then,
quite suddenly, it gathers itself around the motif of a stone's throw
(recalling the parochial distance of the early poems) and fires a
magnificent parting shot:

Childhood is a well a mile from home,
in which things go on falling till they're here.[35]

Notes:

1. A. Alvarez ed. *The New Poetry* revised ed. (Middlesex: Penguin, 1966) pp. 28-
9
    David Wright 'Introduction' to *The Mid-Century: English Poetry 1940-1960*
(Middlesex: Penguin, 1965), p. 17.
2. Tony Harrison, *V,* p. 7.
3. Paul Farley, 'Establishing Shot', *The Ice Age* (London: Picador)
4. Glyn Maxwell, 'Tale of the Mayor's Son', *Tale of the Mayor's Son* (Newcastle,
Bloodaxe Books, 1990), p. 11.
5. Glyn Maxwell, 'A White Car', *Tale of the Mayor's Son,* p. 85.
6. Glyn Maxwell, 'We Billion Cheered', *The Boys at Twilight: Poems 1990-1995*
(Tarset, Bloodaxe, 2000), p. 66
7. Glyn Maxwell, 'Flood Before and After', *Tale of the Mayor's Son,* p. 22.
8. Glyn Maxwell, 'Song of Our Man', *Rest for the Wicked* (Newcastle, Bloodaxe,
1995), p. 46.
9. John DeStefano, "Breath and Daylight" [an interview with Glyn Maxwell]
Atlantic Unbound June 14 2001 http://www.theatlantic.com/unbound/poetry/
maxwell.htm (accessed Feb 22 2009)
10. W.H. Auden, *Selected Poems,* ed. Edward Mendelson, 1979 (New York:
Vintage, 1989), p. 15.
11. Randall Jarrell, 'Changes of Attitude and Rhetoric in Auden's Poetry' in *The
Third Book of Criticism* (London: Faber, 1975), pp. 115-150: p. 116.
12. Glyn Maxwell, 'Farm Close', *Tale of the Mayor's Son,* p. 112.
13. Ian Gregson, *Contemporary Poetry and Postmodernism: Dialogue and Estrange-
ment* (London: Macmillan, 1996), p. 120
14. Glyn Maxwell, 'Tale of a Chocolate Egg', *Tale of the Mayor's Son,* p. 96.
15. Robert Potts, 'Glyn Maxwell', *The Daily Telegraph* August 24 2005
16. Stephen Burt, *The Forms of Youth: Twentieth-Century Poetry and Adolescence*
(New York: Columbia University Press, 2007), p. 14.
17. Glyn Maxwell, 'Sulk', *Rest for the Wicked,* p. 81.
18. Stephen Burt, *The Forms of Youth: Twentieth-Century Poetry and Adolescence*
(New York: Columbia University Press, 2007), p. 45.
19. Glyn Maxwell, 'The Night is Young', *Boys at Twilight,* p. 133.

20. Glyn Maxwell, 'The Night Is Young', *Rest for the Wicked*, p. 35.

21. Glyn Maxwell, 'Younger Than That Now', *Boys at Twilight*, p. 126.

22. *ibid.*

23. Seamus Deane, 'Boredom and Apocalypse: A National Paradigm' in *Strange Country: Modernity and Nationhood in Irish Writing Since 1970* (Oxford: OUP, 1997), pp. 145-197, p. 169.

24. Glyn Maxwell, 'Out of the Rain', *The Boys at Twilight: Poems 1990-1995*, p. 91.

25. Glyn Maxwell, 'Out of the Rain', *Out of the Rain*, p. 44.

26. Ian Gregson, *op.cit.*, p. 121.

27. Glyn Maxwell, *Time's Fool*, p. 227.

28. *ibid.*, p. 176.

29. *ibid.*, p. 157.

30. John DeStefano, 'Breath and Daylight: a conversation with the poet and playwright, Glyn Maxwell' http://www.theatlantic.com/unbound/poetry/maxwell.htm (accessed 2/3/09)

31. Glyn Maxwell, *Time's Fool*, Houghton Mifflin, 2000 (London: Picador, 2001),p. 174.

32. *ibid.*, p. 394.

33. Glyn Maxwell, 'Harry Pray In His Coat', *The Sugar Mile* (London: Picador, 2005), p. 16.

34. Glyn Maxwell, 'Joey Folding *The New York Times*', *The Sugar Mile*, p.40.

35. Glyn Maxwell, 'Farm Animals are Childhood', *The Nerve*, p. 17.

ROBERT MINHINNICK AND ECO-POETRY

Near the end of, *The Song of the Earth*, his influential book of eco-criticism, Jonathan Bate asks, "What are poets for in our brave new millennium? Could it be to remind the next few generations that it is we who have the power to determine whether the earth will sing or be silent?"[1] It would be good to know what poets are for – even better if we could be sure they were designed for a purpose, particularly the kind of noble purpose which Bate has in mind. The idea of an eco-poetics, so strenuously promoted by *The Song of the Earth*, holds out the prospect that poetry, so long marginal to our cynical consumer society, might find something dramatically worthwhile to do. It is the general thrust of this book, however, that such seductive public goals tell us more about critical priorities than they do about poetic ones. When confronted by rhetorical appeals to a singing planet, we need to remind ourselves that the only songs which issue from the Earth are those we pretend to hear. As Richard Rorty once wrote, "The world cannot speak. Only we do."[2]

I put forward these thoughts as a way of framing the subject of this chapter: the poetry of Robert Minhinnick. A Welsh poet who writes in English, Minhinnick does not feature in Bate's book, although given the shape of his career, he might easily have been included. As a private citizen, Minhinnick could hardly have greener credentials. He is, amongst other things, an active environmental campaigner, the co-founder of the Welsh version of Friends of the Earth and of the charity, Sustainable Wales. The environment is also prominent in the texture of his poetry. From Pen-y-fai, the small village in south Wales where he grew up, to nearby Porthcawl, the coastal resort where he currently resides, Minhinnick's literary outback takes in the crumbling post-industrial side of Wales. The second poem in his first book, *A Thread in the Maze*, refers, with characteristic spikiness, to a, "coast poisoned/ By people, crossboned with shipwreck."[3] As a young man, he worked in a number of spectacularly dilapidated parts of south Cardiff and these experiences later bore fruit in such poems as 'A Profile in Iron'. One of these early jobs was at a scrap-yard. It is worth observing how, during an interview I

conducted with him many years later, his memories of that youthful
phase seem bathed in a narrative of environmental corruption:

> Getting to the scrapyard meant you had to drive through the steelworks
> and that was like driving through hell, with flames bursting out of the
> ground. The people working at the scrapyard were pretty hard-bitten.
> Those who sold scrap cars for metal for example, were known as 'tatters'
> – in Cardiff parlance, 'gypsies'. So, at an early age, you were exposed to
> people who were rough, strange, extraordinary.... The area was very
> polluted. You don't hear much about Cardiff beaches – I'm not sure what
> they're like now – but at that time they were absolutely covered in scrap
> metal.[4]

Another aspect of Minhinnick's writing which might have been
expected to appeal to Bate is that the Welshman is decidedly *engagé*.
Minhinnick has been happy to operate as a public intellectual – for
example, as editor of *Poetry Wales*, weaving an enhanced political
awareness into the discourse of the magazine. Though a notable
cosmopolitan, he has been confronted with a literary discourse which
is self-consciously national – even, provincial – in character. Writing
about Anglo-Welsh magazines, Roland Mathias once observed that
a literary editor in Wales always occupies a delicate position:

> The smallness of Wales brings great benefits, or can: it also brings terror
> to the choicemaker compelled to fraternise with those who want his
> blood. The editor realises then, if he did not before, not merely that his
> part is a lonely one but that he cannot hope to be given his deserts, much
> less to be popular ...[5]

Although he sometimes appears dissatisfied with the "smallness
of Wales", Minhinnick seems at home with controversy. Favouring
the kind of pugnacity associated with critics like Geoffrey Grigson,
he frequently scolds the Welsh writing fraternity to take more risks,
to be more broadminded. In attempting to project *Poetry Wales* on an
international basis, he spent a good deal of time overseas, a happy
counterbalance to the local jealousies of home. While one might have
expected that the considerable workload of editing a poetry magazine
would have interfered with his vocation, this risk did not materialise.
On the contrary, the role proved to be a liberation.

If we were to review Minhinnick's CV in the abstract, then, he
might seem to be the very model of the modern eco-poet for which
The Song of the Earth yearns. But while it is tempting to read the
Welshman's work as part of an unambiguously public project, to see

his poems flowing through some dappled green continuum, it would also be a mistake. Despite his undoubted status as an ardent environmentalist and public intellectual, Minhinnick's *poetry* has increasingly drifted away from the public sphere. I will argue that the very qualities which have come to the fore in Minhinnick's writing make it difficult to describe him as an eco-poet.

§

Minhinnick's career evinces a clear split between his early work – dutiful, solemn, formally anxious – and his later poetry – radical, outrageous, formally extravagant. As the poet has grown older, his poems have got younger. The most radical of his books – *King Driftwood* – is also his most recent collection of new work, although it was the preceding work, *After the Hurricane*, which proved to be truly pivotal. The latter had a kaleidoscopic range and depth unmatched by anything in his career. As we will see, this breakthrough was partly prompted by his experience of translation and by his editorship of *Poetry Wales*.

Although Minhinnick's poetry has undergone a radical evolution, many of the thematic motifs of his recent work – the skin, the stranger, the journey, varieties of damage, aspects of translation – are also motifs of his early work. *A Thread in the Maze*, his first book, contained an introduction by Cary Archard which, as well as stressing Minhinnick's Welshness, presciently noted that he, "dislikes the contemporary trend toward skeleton poetry." By this Archard meant the habit of imaginative self-impoverishment, the kind of self-limiting writerly processes which one might associate with the Movement poets or even with writers like R.S. Thomas.[6] What Archard put his finger on, however, was an aspiration rather than an accomplishment. Viewed from this distance, the poems in *A Thread in the Maze* do not have much flesh on their bones.

Some of the conventional flavour of the book is captured by a poem like 'Oxford'. An early example of the encounter theme, it is typical in its dependence on an over-tasteful diction:

> Two strangers revealing themselves
> In the winter evening's vitriolic gloom,
> Discovering each other, sharing that sacrament
> Of the conjunction of lives that comes once.[7]

Quite apart from the sentimental metaphor of a "sacrament", and the limp association of a winter evening with "gloom", the whole poem is sunk in a tone of manufactured wistfulness (exactly the kind of tone which often plagues poetry readings.) It lacks the idiosyncratic fizz which sets off his later work. One redeeming feature, though, is the use of the modifier, "vitriolic". From his time working at the scrapyard to his later globe-trotting, Minhinnick's awareness of landscape has a consistent mineral focus. 'Vitriol' is one of his favourite words – the only word in the passage which he really owns.

This geological motif reminds us that one of his major influences is Seamus Heaney, a literary presence which is easy to spot in an early poem like 'The Midden':

> In a drench
> Of heat, I am a rooky archaeologist
> Fingering dry midden earth
> History's black
>
> Sediment
> Lies under my nails. Fine irony.[8]

Various Heaneyesque touches are evident here: the pervasive digging metaphor, the use of a subterranean diction, and the adoption of a structure which has the look of a linguistic cross-section. Additionally the poem depends upon a somewhat wooden use on the first person pronoun, a kind of solemn self-announcement in the manner of Heaney's line, "I am the tall kingdom over your shoulder".[9] There are other problems too. One notes how the armour-plated noun 'History' is wheeled out anxiously, as though to bestow a kind of rhetorical grandeur, while the concluding expression, "Fine irony", invites the reader to notice – how ironic – the fineness of its irony. Burdened with an excessively clotted diction, the poem's central justification mimics the layering of which the poem speaks, rather in the manner of Heaney's so-called 'artesian' stanzas.

'The Midden' also reminds us of Minhinnick's ongoing obsession with marked skin. Throughout the early books the theme of scarring suggests the inescapability of the environment, a motif bound up with the poet's celebration of danger. As much as the environment may be damaged, in Minhinnick's poetry, it is also capable of causing damage. That which can be marked can also be punctured. In the following encounter with wildflowers, for example, Minhinnick seems to recall the exploratory bite of Heaney's 'Death of a Naturalist':

The anthers were like arrowheads
I pricked against my skin, daring

Their pale dust to enter me. I played
A game, a child's experiment with fear,
Discovering in the beautiful
The pain of betrayal.[10]

While the poem relies on the resonance of its slightly unusual choice of verbs ("pricked", "daring", "enter", "discovering") its tone, which is sober and controlled, records the experience in a documentary manner. Early poems like this rely heavily on earnest personal testimony, as though fulfilling some kind of unspecified obligation to be confessional. Aiming for decorum, they lack the colourful roughness which Minhinnick enjoyed in the Cardiff scrapyard, the same quality which distinguishes his later poems.

Set against the background of his compliant early work, the mood of *After the Hurricane* is bracingly imperative ("Put your foot on the rail", "Think of a pilot light", "Step carefully")[11] Rather than being aimed at the reader, these commands, which are heard at regular intervals, have the sound of inner urgings, encouragements to the self. The book relies on an unsettled relationship between writer and reader, putting both on their interpretive mettle. Readers are neither coldly excluded nor warmly embraced. A good example of such interpretive tension arises in the poem, 'Regulars'. Set in the unpromising heart of a dive bar, an environment which puts the newcomer on guard, it invites the reader to occupy a position close to, or perhaps identical with its speaker, as he scans the room:

Men with 43 per cent and rising
Johnnie Walker Black Label complexions;
Men drowning in stonedust
And men with lunar phrenology;
Men with wall-chained Staffordshire
Mastiffs in riveted collars
And brass-studded leather belly-belts;
Solitary men in corners about whom
Plays the violet light of a thunderstorm;[12]

In the infernal glow of this poem where some of the customers "are wearing dead men's clothes", Minhinnick strikes a note – typical of his later work – of gregarious scepticism. While he could never be described as an anti-social poet, he seems happier to encounter individuals rather than crowds, and happy, too, that these individuals should, like himself, be individualists. Hence the poetry is generously sprinkled with 'characters' who intercept the speaker on a one-to-one basis. As much a way of life as a compositional strategy, this is also a model for how each Minhinnick poem intercepts its readers.

Raymond Garlick once remarked that, "[among] the best things in twentieth century Anglo-Welsh poetry are the memorable portraits of Welsh men and women," and he went on to identify R.S. Thomas's portrait of Iago Prytherch as a prime example.[13] Minhinnick is deeply influenced by Thomas's theatrically negative take on Welsh life, and his poetry is a good illustration of Garlick's point. Each encounter with a stranger is portrayed as a kind of sacred adventure, a privileged disruption. Present in his work from the beginning, this motif gradually assumes greater depth and complexity – 'La Otra Orilla' from *King Driftwood* is a well-developed later example. For Minhinnick a genuine relationship with the reader – with anyone – can only take place when the usual expectations have been set aside. For the encounter to be real it must be 'naked' – no safety net.

Although he is markedly suspicious of the 'herd mentality', Minhinnick is nonetheless drawn to the drama of collectives. In 'Regulars' the kind of admirable permanency achieved by the group of working-class men has been attained at the high price of ossification. Dannie Abse may have had this kind of poem in mind when he wrote,

> it is evident that many poets in Wales, rightly or wrongly, believe themselves to be members of a defeated nation. That awareness leads them, in the signature of their poems, to side with the losers of history and of life's procession – the underdogs, the outsiders, the downtrodden.[14]

The comments could fairly be applied to many of the poems in *After the Hurricane*. Although standing to one side, the everyman 'you-persona' in 'Regulars' remains loosely attached to his particular "losers of history". The speaker addresses the reader in the second person but rather than inviting companionship, this mode of address creates a shifting triangular relationship, with interpretive power passing uncertainly from speaker to reader to group. The title of the poem identifies a defining habit, but the men are, in an important sense, irregular, every bit as "rough, strange, and extraordinary" as Minhinnick's early work-companions. Excluding women completely, the poem reports back from a lost, male world which has something of the "secret, bestial peace" of Larkin's 'The Card Players', as well as the fraternal warrior ambience of David Jones's 'The Hunt'. The regulars are indelibly stained – we shall see that this is a major theme – a condition which appears to be associated with their gender. By the time the landlord slides a glass in front of 'you', the reader, is faced with a decision, and the choice to be made is compressed into to the phrase, "the beads around the glass are a muck sweat." This is the unhealthy price if you want to join the tribe .

Although 'Regulars' is a good introduction to the edginess of *After the Hurricane*, it is far from being the most ambitious or spectacular poem there. Minhinnick has been an occasional maker of documentary films, a pursuit which has coloured the technique and subject-matter of his poems, and this influence can be perceived in 'The Ziggurat', for instance, a poem which has some of the pressure of a short story. Based on a period when Minhinnick was shooting a documentary in Iraq, it dwells closely on the speaker's relationship with the film's cameraman, who is known only as 'Nazaar'. The relationship between the two men is set against the incidental demands of labour, especially – and this is something the Welshman probably takes from Seamus Heaney – the use of tools. During the shooting, Minhinnick's role was to protect the camera tripod and accordingly the poem is keen to mention the presence of technical instruments – a velcroed sleeve, a Sony cartridge. Although the political purpose of the documentary in question is not made explicit by the poem, we gather that the film was intended to cast an environmental glance at conditions in contemporary Iraq.

A holist by conviction, Minhinnick, in his early poems staked out an environment which works on, and through, us. Because labour and labourers have always been central to his subject-matter, his poetics makes a virtue out of evidence of wear. Even in their idle moments the characters which populate his writing are defined by the tasks which they are not undertaking. Or, indeed, the tools they are not using. In 'On the Llyn Fawr Hoard in the National Museum of Wales', for example, the speaker contemplates an ancient collection of artefacts which has been rescued from a lake. While the physical appearance of the objects is duly appreciated, the speaker indicates that what really interests him is how they once were used – sentiments which seem happily pragmatistic:

> History is not this gear of bronze,
> Its patina teal-green;
> Rather, it is how it was used,
> The association of metal and mind.[15]

Musing on man's place in the world, the American eco-poet, Gary Snyder, has written that it would be desirable to see, "far less population, and much more wilderness."[16] Minhinnick, by contrast, does not dismiss humanity as an unhappy virus. In his work, human beings cannot be peeled clean from the environment, nor vice versa. Damage to one is damage to the other. At the centre of this reciprocal process is the body, particularly the outer layer of skin which, in Minhinnick's poems, usually bears some kind of visible mark – a wound, a stain, a tattoo. Rather than worshipping the body as a temple, his poetry depicts it as a thoroughfare, impure, worked over – a compromised condition which is at once threatening and seductive. In one of his early poems called 'The Party', for example, the slaughter of a pig is the prelude to a typically ambiguous baptism:

> A joke, or ritual, alarming to some:
> The youngest child placed inside the split carcase,
> And lifted out laughing from the wound's long slot.[17]

Alarming, yes, but note: only to *some*. This queer staining ceremony would seem to suggest that, being born into impurity, we should accept that no child is innocent. To have mixed feelings about the stained body – what, in another context, might be termed 'original sin' – is a predicament typical of his work. While such early treatments of this theme are relatively gentle, the mixed feelings are nevertheless a constant. Minhinnick's attitude to the transformations that human beings have wrought in the environment – from shopping-malls to nuclear reactors – is never simply pro or con. At times the poems thrill to the roar of extravagant change, at other times, they recoil.

Such ambivalence runs through 'The Ziggurat', balanced as it is between mid-life adventure and apocalyptic report. The reader is not allowed to forget the foreign-ness either of 'Nazaar' or of the landscape. At various points, the friend's name is repeated, and there are pointed references to 'Babel', 'Basra', and 'Badiet esh Sham'. Although the relationship between the speaker and the cameraman follows a conversation which flows one way from the former to the latter, there is, as in 'Regulars', a prevailing uncertainty about who is speaking and to whom. While delivering his narrative the speaker seems to address Nazaar rather than the reader, and gives a running commentary on their experiences: "We stand at the crater's edge", "We are Babylonian ghosts/ And follow the road uphill".[18] Since this type of address has a necessary redundancy, (Nazaar presumably knows where he is standing) the reader is placed in the somewhat tense position of purposeful overhearing.

The fact that Nazaar remains silent throughout the poem is exploited by the speaker as a mark of cultural distance. As well as suggesting that the purposes and perspectives of the two men are not identical, the silence also has political and existential dimensions. Nazaar, significantly, has negative habits and the poem follows their contour. The reader is made aware of what the cameraman does not see or hear (or chooses not to see or hear), and, even more significantly, what he refuses to say:

> Yet Nazaar
> There is a word
>   You never use
> No matter how I prompt
> Or make any other answer impossible.[19]

The word is 'Saddam'. It transpires that the ziggurat of the title is one of the sites which the camera-crew is forbidden to film, because it belongs to the dictator. As the poem moves back and forward through time, the speaker's reflections on their trip reach a kind of climax, when he urges Nazaar at last to whisper the dictator's name. By the end of the poem, their friendship finally gives way to the more intimate relationship between Nazaar and his family:

> Take the sweets from him, Nazaar.
>   Give them to your quiet sons.
> Take the medicines he offers to your daughter
> Palsied in her cot:
>   And for your wife
> Who waits in your room by the marketplace
> And who swells once more, golden as figmilk,
> Take all the dollars and the dinars and the royal Jordanian pounds
> And buy her a bracelet
>   Of watermelon seeds.[20]

Concluding with a litany of imperatives Minhinnick demonstrates the confidence of his contrariness. The sudden labial sweetness of this passage owes a lot to the contrast between the simple watermelon seeds and the large-scale evidence of environmental damage which the poem has already portrayed. As Nazaar joins his family, the speaker reverts to his default solitude, still open for further adventures.

Of the many formal departures in *After the Hurricane*, one of the most significant is that of length. 'The Zigurrat', is typical in this respect extending over several pages. While such authorial expansion has various benefits – making space for repetition, revision, and recapitulation – it is also a sign of an underlying personal attitude. In the interview which I conducted at his home in Porthcawl, Minhinnick said that he was aware of the expanding size of his poems, and explained that there was a conscious formal contrariness in their refusal to end:

> as I've grown older the poems have got longer. I think they now want to tell a story, but tell that story obliquely. Also you want to go into new territory. After a lot of reading, you learn what is not being written. If you're an editor, of course, you're inundated with what *is* being written. So I ask myself, what's wrong with extending a poem, what's wrong with going from 35 lines to 85 lines to 325 lines? Of course you're not supposed to do that. Nobody is interested in long poems *at all*, they're like *death*, but you think I'm just going to keep going and see what happens.[21]

This identification of the long poem with contrariness may seem unusual but the link has also been made by Paul Muldoon in his critical book, *The End of the Poem*. There the Irishman offers a possible definition of the long poem as, "a poem that resists coming to a close, or drawing its own conclusion."[22] To resist coming to a close suggests an external pressure to conclude, for instance, from the expectation that a well-made poem be little longer than a sonnet.

Apart from the value of formal independence the poems in *After the Hurricane* use their extra space to incorporate technical variations. Many adopt a loose conversational refrain, which enriches and unsettles the longer descriptive passages. In 'Lac la Ronge', for example, the refrain in question opens the poem:

> I dream
> Of a lake that is endless
>   Of a lake
> That is a white mind. [23]

While this seems to promise an abstract philosophical meditation, in the manner of Wallace Stevens, the poem swiftly grounds itself in the details of the Saskatchewan landscape. Completing the stylistic swerve, the speaker draws a series of witty portraits of the locals, who are driving snow-cats and Chevrolets. Minhinnick, in his travel writing, rarely identifies with wealthy people, and in this poem he seems to sympathise with the desperate self-entertainment of the locals, versions – it might be said – of Abse's "losers of history". As it moves forward, the poem shifts register and genre – by turns veering into autobiography, travel narrative, and gothic description. Each new pass over the territory is like a different poem:

> Beneath the lake is a basement room
> With the furnace turned down low
> And a family around a dead TV.
>   Above their heads is a single star
> That transfixes them:
>   Venus,
>   like the eye
> Of a wolverine.[24]

While the tone of this passage suggests a kind of appalled excitement, the reader is once again challenged – is this portrait a factual account? Or should we interpret these lines which refer to a wolverine (a symbol of the Canadian wilderness) as a kind of surrealist critique? At this point, the endless lake of the opening returns, its effect now modified by seeming to have drifted in from another species of writing.

Public debate about the environment, as conducted in the media, television, and online, is often urgent in tone, imperative in mood and dense with facts: "Reduce your carbon footprint!" "Recycle more household waste!" "Save the panda!" Minhinnick's non-fictional *prose* does not stray far from this style. In *Green Agenda*, for example, he often strikes an uncomplicated note of fact-based advocacy:

> The sewage of seventy-five percent of the Welsh population ends up in our seas, twenty percent of the total pumped raw from some of the 230 outfalls between Chepstow and the Dee Estuary .... British Steel at Margam and Llanwern, one of the most significant polluters, is allowed to disgorge almost 1,800 tonnes of oil and grease and 87 tonnes of cyanide each year into the Severn Estuary, which because of discharges from Avonmouth, Barry and other industrial centres, is also a U.K. hotspot for cadmium, a highly toxic heavy metal.[25]

Although his poems are tinged by this discourse, they do not sound nearly as heavy and mechanical. His poetry may contain lists, commands, and facts, but it lacks doctrinal certainty and refrains from political statement. Despite their bursts of imperatives, poems

like 'The Zigurrat' and 'Lac la Ronge' are shot through with an inter-
rogative spirit. Partly this reflects a simple wish not to preach to the
reader. In his interview with Sam Adams, Minhinnick is explicit on
this point:

> I don't think the poet has a moral role though a moral message might be
> perceived by the reader. Of course I have a moral standpoint on many
> aspects of life, but I wouldn't wish it to intrude too obviously in my
> poems, because I simply don't see myself as some kind of moral arbiter.[26]

Blurred intentions and hazy identities are also evident in 'The
Bombing of Baghdad as Seen from an Electrical Goods Shop'. Here
the character of Nazaar re-appears and the meeting between the two
friends is framed by a dining ritual. The bond of labour is once again
evident:

> Eating was serious work.
> I watched you arrange as an evening ritual
> The hummus rough with lemonrind
> And bread dusted with Jordanian thyme.
>
> Every supper, you said, might be the last.
> So maybe that's the way to live
> The way that we should read our books [27]

The poem structures itself around a shift in time, moving from
the Baghdad past to the Welsh present. The speaker, we gradually
realise, is remembering the dinner with his friend from a distance, an
act of retrieval which is also a way of thinking about the war and
worrying about what it might mean for Nazaar. As he watches the
conflict play out in a shop-window, the speaker has the second-hand
experience of any western consumer. The obliquity of this perspective
is unsettling – the televisions are arranged for the technical excellence
of their display, not to harmonise with what they are displaying. The
conflict, here, is visited on casual bystanders, although in this case the
collateral damage it causes is to the soul. The oblique reference to
The Last Supper highlights the democratic nature of eating – every-
one must do it, even Christ. The poem reminds us how easily we
could be in the position of Nazaar, dining with the darkness.

§

Compared with his careful early poems, Minhinnick's later work seems hugely altered. What happened? Any major swerve in a poet's career is likely to have diverse causes – biological, psychological, sociological. In Minhinnick's case we can point to at least three principal factors: the habit of travel, the practice of translation, and the contingencies of editing *Poetry Wales*. Minhinnick himself has admitted a similar range of factors:

> I think what I learned from the editorship, and to some extent from translation, was a sense of freedom, a feeling that you might as well go for it. As editor, you encounter a lot of poetry that hasn't gone for it ....Also, I became really interested in sound because I had to translate – or failed to translate – *cynghanedd*. That's a system of strict metres, where you have to make widely separated sounds match up in a complicated and untranslatable way. This kind of poetry made me aware that a lot of poets in America and Britain neglect the sound of their poems.[28]

Archard's introduction to *A Thread in the Maze* reminds us of the poet's Welshness and any analysis of the highs and lows of Minhinnick's career has to take into account his attitude to various national questions. Probably the most important of these is linguistic. Although he has been described as an 'Anglo-Welsh poet' – a term with which he has shown impatience – Minhinnick is a fluent speaker of his native language. His translations of Welsh-language poetry, were prominently published in *The Adulterer's Tongue*, a landmark book for his own career. As he is well aware, linguistic allegiances have cultural consequences. For one thing, to write in Welsh is to express a view of the nation's future, to hope that the language remains at its core. For another thing, a close concern with the language's well-being brings one face to face with issues of conservation and extinction. In interview, Minhinnick has spoken of how these issues are closely entangled:

> Compared to the English language version, the Welsh language establishment is more complicated because of the danger of the language becoming extinct. The language issue makes all Welsh writing political. To write your name in Welsh is a political act.[29]

While such problems of cultural priority have also arisen in Scotland and Ireland, there is, in the Welsh case, a difference of intensity because of the relatively large size of the native-speaking community. As a result, the Welsh writer is perennially faced with the question as to how their literary habits do, or do not, contribute to the survival of the language, a question most sharply turned on those who choose English as their medium.

Part of the difficulty of seeing Minhinnick as an 'eco-poet', is that his poetry is attracted to vulnerability and danger. His writing likes to put itself in harm's way, or in the way of that which is likely to be harmed. It can be hard to admire the song of the Earth when listening to the hum of the deep-water reactor. What goes for the physical environment also goes for the cultural situation. In some of his writing the Welsh language stands in for everything in the world which is likely to be swept away by cultural or technological 'progress'. Although it would be an exaggeration to say that Minhinnick enjoys the cliff's-edge status of both the Welsh language and the Welsh writer, he is clearly uncomfortable with comfort. His introduction to *The Adulterer's Tongue* links Welsh-language poetry to a kind of enlivening peril. Explaining that his method of translation was relatively liberal, even hazardous, he compared it to, "… driving at night without headlights." The description was not meant to be pejorative.[30] For Minhinnick the process of translation was only worthwhile if it could be made risky:

> Certainly, I would never claim to be a 'faithful' translator. I'm not inter-
> ested in the mimetic, and, to this writer, faithfulness has a dogged, indeed
> doggish, quality. My English version of the Welsh poems here are not
> conceived as copies or echoes of the originals. If I was translating them
> next year they might look very different.[31]

Neither aiming for an embalming faithfulness, nor converting Welsh poems into some form of Minhinnick-ese, his translations in *The Adulterer's Tongue* alerted the poet to new possibilities for his own poems. One of the translated writers to whom he seemed to be especially drawn was his friend, Iwan Llwyd. In Minhinnick's later work, where the poems often aim for a loose music of repetition, something of the spirit of Llwyd's 'Far Rockaway' may be discerned:

> Though it's far way will you follow me down
> to Far Rockaway, Far Rockaway,
> its name sings golden as guitarstrings
> or a street choir becoming an ocean,
> or lovers who have turned in here
> off the night's turnpike, whispering over black coffee,
> gasoline and fine rain on their clothes
> two moonwatchers touching fingertips,
> counting back the backroads' roadkill,
> certain there's been no one like them before.[32]

By offering a romantic vision of vagrancy while, at the same time, undermining it, these lines speak to Minhinnick's later style. Throughout this poem about a Welshman in NewYork one senses how much the word 'far' appeals to its translator. In this translation and in others, the reader feels the pull of a journey undertaken, and the promise of a journey which is there to take. This is one reason why the last line of this first stanza has a special resonance. The voice is certain not only that there have been other lovers like those it describes but similar poems about similar lovers, a motif of sameness which mirrors the relationship between the original Welsh poem and its translation. This is one way that Minhinnick's work (like Llwyd's) invites agonistic reading, an activity which, through a constant process of self-interruption and self-interrogation, it often carries out itself.

Randall Jarrell once compared the late cosmopolitan style of W.H. Auden to, "an air plant in a window box of the cloud city of the exiled *Wandervögel*."[33] Although Minhinnick is by any standards a *Wandervögel* the effect, in his poems, is not of rootlessness, but, paradoxically, of excessive connection. In the sequence, 'A Welshman's Flora', for instance, the speaker claims to have, "put down more roots/Than InterCabletel or Microsoft."[34] And this is indeed the ethic of *After the Hurricane*: attachments multiply as the poems aim to bear the impress of as many environments as possible. Such proliferation is partly reflected in a number of poetic sequences which are built around lists. There are many examples: in 'A Welshman's Flora' each section of the poem gives voice to a different flower, in 'Elementary Songs' each gives voice to a different element, and in 'The Porthcawl Preludes' each gives voice to a different maritime object. Such forms have their contrariness built in, enabling Minhinnick to manipulate a complex set of contrasting or competing attitudes. Meanwhile everything from coelocanths to bathyspheres is given a fictional personality, blurring human characteristics with the natural world. At the same time the poems are cheekily topical – 'Nettle' speaks about the contemporary Welsh politician, Ron Davies, 'Lithium' refers to the rock star, Kurt Cobain, and 'Lawrencium' makes mention of "the AcceleratorTunnel/ At Berkeley". In contrast to the competing forms of rock and soil to which Auden's 'In Praise of Limestone' gave voice, Minhinnick's elements speak in an off-the-cuff, charmingly throwaway style. Here, for example, is the section entitled 'Sodium':

There's not a boy-racer on Wyndham Street
To touch me. You hear that engine revving in the night?

Think of the glow as the petrol tank explodes
At 3 a.m. on the forestry track.[35]

Like Llwyd's 'Far Rockaway' this combines the thrill of romantic exploration with a clear-eyed practical sardony. Although the daring of male adolescents may end in disaster, the poem does not disown their energy – it is obviously thrilled by the illuminated fastness of the forestry track. While the surrounding trees are threatened by the rampaging machine, the push of the rhetoric bathes in the glow of destruction, as a child in a science-class might admire the flaring of sodium.

Contrariness is also evident in Minhinnick's travel-writing, where one of his abiding fascinations is with American culture. Despite adopting left-of-centre political positions he has complicated feelings about the United States, as has been noted by M. Wynn Thomas:

> For Minhinnick, America's is a culture unravelling as it restlessly, cease-lessly travels. Part of him delights in travelling and unravelling along with it, letting his imagination run riot, even in the violent meaning of that phrase; allowing the United States to reform him of his rectitude, to recall Gwyneth Lewis's expression. But another part of him holds its Welsh ground, keeping its distance, eyeing American warily, viewing it as a warning of how bad things might get.[36]

This accurately draws attention to the way Minhinnick is inclined to embrace that which threatens him, experiencing America from the perspective of someone who is only passing through. In *To Babel and Back*, he describes some of the country's more blatant vulgarities with tolerance, even affection. It is especially noteworthy how he takes issue with Bill Bryson's *The Lost Continent*, a jaundiced and impatient account of Middle America. While accepting the tart validity of some of Bryson's criticisms, Minhinnick takes the book to task for playing up to easy prejudices and attempts to even the score:

> The US has destroyed its history and environment. It delights in the disneyfication of its own psyche. But the US teems with mysteries. Despite the wagon-trains, Hollywood and rock 'n' roll, it remains unexplored.[37]

What he especially seems to value about America – or at any rate his own idea of it – is the opportunity which it offers to test the self. Appearing as a dramatic character in a large number of his own poems, the Minhinnick-character is usually portrayed as active and adventurous, ready to embark on any number of foreign journeys, to expose himself to all manner of hazard including radioactivity. In this sense, he fully agrees with the Beat proposal that the self become a laboratory of the future – the poems seem to say, *Forgive us for not trespassing*. But the actions of the Minhinnick-character do not form part of any kind of recognisable program, do not support an obvious environmental world-picture. As he travels here and there, his signifi-cant encounters arise as often by accident as by design, The Minhinnick-character is often portrayed as puzzled, compromised, admitting his own ignorance – he is certainly not a green messiah. Running through many of these poems are some of the same anxieties which surface in Elizabeth Bishop's poetry, most famously in 'Questions of Travel':

> What childishness is it that while there's a breath of life
> in our bodies, we are determined to rush
> to see the sun the other way around?[38]

If one reason to travel is to question, another reason is to be questioned. By roaming over the map of style, Minhinnick has a chance to leave others behind. One of the poems in *After the Hurri-cane*, 'From the Rock Pool', for example, deploys an obviously provocative personification of the sea. This comes into focus in the second section of the poem where the speaker has wandered into the departures section of an airport:

> Last week at the airport I met the sea in Terminal 1.
> She was drinking Finnish coffee and reading the Dead Sea Scrolls.
> On one ankle was a tattoo of Australia
> while Greenland was inked in blue over her breast.
> This is fate, I said. Do you come here often?
> And I stared into the icebergs in her eyes.
> Fate, she said, has nothing to do with it.
> And if the Welsh could swim
>   they'd be Irish.[39]

Quirkily provisional, shabbily anecdotal, the tone of this passage is characteristic of much of his later style: it contains flashes of mockery, a vein of cheekiness, whilst radiating a high level of poetic self-confi-dence. In such poetic encounters with individuals, real or imaginary, the speaker often seems passive, as though awaiting instructions. The scenario is not that far removed from Mersey Beat surrealism, or the kind of ironic vignettes of contemporary consumption which we associate with Paul Muldoon. By reminding us that the national distinction made between 'Welsh' and 'Irish' is principally a matter of an aquatic boundary, the sea, here, is an ambiguous embodiment of global culture. Those civilisations which it allows to form are the civilisations by which it is shaped. At the same time as the sea erodes our coastlines, its skin – note the tattoo – is marked by us. Hence it is waiting, as we are, for departures, literary and otherwise.

§

King Driftwood, the follow-up to *After the Hurricane* pushes the experimental style of its predecessor even further. In this collection, his most recent, the habit of travel is even more entrenched and the poetry's air of difference is immediately obvious in its diction, especially the use of place-names. The world that we encounter in *King Driftwood*, is like that of any foreign country which is new to us: a challenge from moment to moment, often on the most basic level. What is the local drink called? What verbal formulae is it courteous to use? What are the names of the local rulers? The poet so enjoys such linguistic and experiential challenges, that he passes them on to his readers. Flexible and topical, it is hard to imagine what kind of material it would think worthy of exclusion. Everything makes it in: from Radiohead and Nebuchednezzar to Ecuadorian botanists and Tesco cash-back. The vocabulary, too, is aggressively varied. As well as simpler words we find "promethium", "jalabiya", "Megablitz", "vermiculations", "fulgurite", and "tributyl chloride".

As in *After the Hurricane*, the reader often finds the author playing the role of a travelling-companion. A visit to Argentina, which is recorded in 'La Otra Orilla', gives us the flavour (this section of the poem has hint of Heaney's 'Oysters' about it):

> Learning the language
> was like eating its seafood
> – chipirones, pulpitos –
> when Gotan, my friend, took me to the café
> and every word was squidgy as a mussel
> under its blue door.[40]

Generally, the reader occupies a position in relation to Minhinnick as his speaker occupies here in relation to 'Gotan'. We feel like we are in the presence of a benevolent, knowledgeable, and occasionally provocative, guide, who knows how to enjoy himself with others.

In *King Driftwood* the poems are ever more animated by an ethos
of accumulation. Characters are often shown eating and drinking,
and we experience each poem, to a considerable degree, as a feat of
consumption – just how much stimulation can the speaker swallow
without bursting? The poems make good on their author's observa-
tion that if "[a] poem is going to die, better that it die of a surfeit –
better to over-eat than starve,"[41] This helps to explain why it is a long
book. The poems are generally composed in strophes – long verse-
paragraphs of varying length – which another poet might have
worked into separate poems. Unfolding in a space where lyric turns
into epic, the ruling principle of *King Driftwood* is the risk of going
too far. Being reluctant to end the poems give the impression that on
some Parnassian plane to which the writer has occasional access, they
survive and grow longer. In one of the sections of 'On Listening to
Glenn Gould Play Bach's Goldberg Variations', Minhinnick identifies
with the speed of the pianist:

> we must go faster
> if we want
>   to leave ourselves
> behind.[42]

Favouring energy over organisation, most of the poems read
quickly, as though they were afraid of staying in one place for too
long – each is a kind of mini-Big Bang. This sense of drama is under-
lined by an attachment to the present moment. One of the key words
in the book is "now", which is often used to introduce a dramatic
scene, or at the point where a monologue shifts from past tense to
present. From a long list of possible examples we find, "Now, my
mother is hissing", "Now what's that sound?" "Now the sea drinks
with me ..." "Now here comes the gravedigger". Similar formulae
occur elsewhere: "Listen:/ Surely that's her:" "Here the rose/ returns."
"Look here./ It's Mrs Dawes-Llewellyn," Just as the identity of any
speaker in any given poem is provisional the same can be said of the
poetic time-frames.

If Minhinnick's poems increasingly give a voice to rocks and trees,
that is not to persuade us that rocks and trees have their own language
but to make us more aware of our linguistic limits. An extravagant
example of this motif may be found in 'The Hourglass'. The poem is
framed as a journey, beginning mundanely in Britain, then gradually
moving outward to encompass more exotic locations. As with many
poems in the book the reader encounters a thin layer of realism which

is then overlaid with a stream of deliberately provocative metaphors. The speaker is an aging geography teacher who, after falling asleep in class, experiences a dream-vision. During this surreal episode the teacher is given his own geography lesson by an unlikely travelling companion, the personification of sand. This hazy entity is described in various unlikely ways: "a haemophiliac boy/ with highlights in his hair", a library, a gospel, and "a sorcerer full of secrets." Running through this dream-vision is a broad streak of comedy – the teacher engages with sand in unlikely repartee – at one point, telling it to stop complaining and take some Ritalin.

Minhinnick's loose personification of environmental phenomena draw comic attention to their own inadequacy – for the desire that sand would speak back to us says more about our wish for centrality and significance that it does about sand. As the speaker journeys with sand to locations where the effects of erosion and desertification are obvious he comes to realise that "there's no oblivion." This realisation is central to *King Driftwood*: apocalypse is not a void but a transformation. Since, in the eye of eternity, all is due to be transformed, metaphor, or if you prefer the poetic imagination, is just another name for what happens – and what is likely to go on happening. Ashes to ashes and dust to dust. This awareness is neatly underlined when the personified sand points out that it was its own movements which led to the discovery of those papyri on which the Iliad was written. In this sense, sand gave birth to literature.

In 'An Isotope, Dreaming' we find a good example of Minhinnick testing his environment by exposing us to extreme cases. The identity of the poem's speaker is unstable but at least some of the time it is an isotope which has "waited in my cave/ for a billion years".[43] As the poem evolves from section to section, it transmits increasingly startling images. When faced with the beguiling question, "What's the half life of the half life?" it answers with oblique, but charged, parallelisms:

> It's in my mouth, I said. It's on my skin.
> It's in the earth under my nails and the fillings in my teeth.
> It's in the water I drank and the mesquite I chewed.
> And from now it's in my words and they will never let it out
> because words are the green bones we bend to make a child.[44]

The last line is richly suggestive, an example of Minhinnick's late style at its best. While it offers a subversive song-like hint of 'Fern Hill' in its surreal, fairytale use of 'green', it also conveys the same sense of verbal imprisonment which emanates from Thomas's conclusion ("Time held me green and dying/ though I sang in my chains like the sea.") Other sections of Minhinnick's poem have a discursive clarity, but the above lines provoke urgent questions of interpretation: In what sense are words supposed to be "green bones"? In what sense do words make a child? As an unexpected modifier for 'bone', is "Green" supposed to make us think of innocence and newness? The last line is somewhat contextualised by the poem's concern for children who have been damaged by radioactivity. As the example of 'The Party' confirms, childhood is not a protected or privileged state, rather it is as compromised as anything else.

'An Isotope, Dreaming' is organised around three journeys to sites which have been damaged by radioactivity, and on each of these journeys the speaker, who sometimes becomes Minhinnick himself, has an encounter in which the effects of radioactivity are crystallised. Much of the imagery is disturbing, as the occasionally diabolical speaker seems to enjoy the subordination of spiritual values to material ones. We are told, for instance, that, "The soul perishes/ but matter can never be destroyed."[45] Framing these journeys are portraits of the speaker at home in Wales, as he waits for an apocalyptic-sounding redemption. A useful point of comparison might be with Ted Hughes's 'Pibroch':

... A pebble is imprisoned
Like nothing in the universe.
Created for black sleep. Or growing
Conscious of the sun's red spot occasionally,
Then dreaming it is the foetus of God.[46]

In Hughes's poetry rapid changes of scale are commonly combined with personification of the natural (and supernatural) environment, a method which can seem hubristic and grandiose. The reader might wonder how the speaker is able to make such confident announcements about the nature of God and the Universe. Minhinnick avoids such pitfalls in a number of ways. Down-to-earth and drawn to the everyday, his poetry's self-deflating charm arises from an awareness that it is in competition with other discourses, giving no reason to think it will defeat its competitors. While the poems imply a listener who is being challenged by what is being said, the first person being challenged is Minhinnick himself.

§

How useful, then, is the concept of 'eco-poetry' in Minhinnick's case? In a recently published lecture where he expands on, and refines, some of the themes rehearsed in *The Song of the Earth*, Bate distinguishes between two kinds of eco-poetry, one traditional, one postmodern. The former he traces back, "to Romantic ideas, most obviously to Samuel Taylor Coleridge on the imagination as the organic unifying principle." To the latter, more recently developed type of eco-poetry, he applies the labels of 'postmodern' and 'ironic', as well describing it as more, "scientifically informed and politically engaged." He proceeds to characterise, "contemporary eco-poetry as being nicely poised with a foot in each of these important camps."[47] This forked definition of eco-poetry is relatively permissive and casually phrased – it would be surprising if Minhinnick's work evaded it altogether. While I think it would be fair to say that Minhinnick's poetry is in touch with both ends of Bate's definition, the definition itself seems too limited to apply completely to the Welshman's work.

It might be more illuminating to return to Bate's original question: is it the purpose of poetry to help us hear the song of the Earth? By entertaining such a notion, by implying that it is the poet's role to fine-tune the metaphysical static, Bate stands against Richard Rorty's picture of the poet as a trafficker in contingencies, as one ever reweaving the terms of their private perfection. For, as Rorty reminds us, there is nothing beyond humanity which humanity should feel compelled to worship:

> ... as long as we think that "the world" names something we ought to respect as well as cope with, something personlike in that it has a preferred description of itself, we shall insist that any philosophical account of truth save the "intuition" that the truth is "out there".[48]

Nevertheless, the public narrative of environmentalism looms powerfully over contemporary literature, and many poets and critics are happy to bask in its emerald glow. A comparison between Minhinnick and another of the poets in this book, John Burnside, is revealing. The Scottish poet would no doubt be gratified with a description of his work as eco-poetry, indeed he encourages just such a reading in his essay, 'A Science of Belonging: Poetry as Ecology'. There he not only refers approvingly to Bate's notion of a song of the earth, he is happy to confirm that his role as a poet is to hear that song.[49] By way of illustrating his point, he includes one of his own poems, 'By

Kautokeino', which he tells us, had a specifically environmental purpose:

> What I wanted to emphasize here [in the poem] was the sound of the Arctic north, and the deliberate, conscious work of attuning one's art to the song of the earth. To do this, it seems, the contemporary poet in a consumer culture needs to step outside that culture, to step away from the narrowly human realm – as delimited by consumerist mores – and connect with something larger and wider, with the more-than-human.[50]

Amongst other things this is a very explicit example of a poet aligning his work with a publicly-oriented critical narrative. Burnside is anxious to confer significance on his own work, furnishing the reader with an interpretive road-map so that they will arrive at the 'correct result'. But this manoeuvre, however noble its intentions might be, is confused and self-defeating. Just as it is unconvincing to speak of a "narrowly human realm", it is unwise to talk about getting in touch with "something larger", with the "more-than-human." As pragmatists never tire of saying, we are already in the world and the only values and preferences which we can satisfy are our own. The idea of the "more-than-human" itself aims to satisfy purely human, and mainly sentimental, ends. It is a point which the Polish poet, Szymborska, makes sharply in her 'View with a Grain of Sand':

> We call it a grain of sand,
> but it calls itself neither grain nor sand.
> It does just fine, without a name,
> whether general, particular,
> permanent, passing,
> incorrect, or apt.
>
> Our glance, our touch means nothing to it.
> It doesn't feel itself seen and touched.
> And that it fell on the windowsill
> is only our experience, not its.
> For it, it is not different from falling on anything else
> with no assurance that it has finished falling
> or that it is falling still.[51]

When oil-slicks wash ashore and when chemical plants explode, it goes without saying that such disasters matter, but that is only because they interfere with our own dreams and purposes, not because they are breaking an imaginary law of nature. There is always a state of things, but there is never a *natural* state of things.

Revealingly when Burnside goes on to elaborate what the eco-poetic role might be, it proves to be a struggle. He is driven to lay an unlikely emphasis on the simple act of walking. We should be encouraged, he tells us, to get in touch with the elements, to "smell the wind" and to "taste the starlight".[52] Of course, this is commonsense advice for healthy living – a spot of fresh air – but the desire to merge with a grandiose public narrative tempts into some ringing overstatements:

> ... walking is the basic discipline of science of belonging, for this is a science based almost entirely upon field work. On foot, we are able to imagine an accord between poetry and ecology, a full-scale and rounded knowledge of what Gary Snyder calls the 'Earth House Hold'.[53]

It seems to me that this elevates the harmless habit of pottering about into a kind of cosmic virtue. As with much writing of this type, what sounds like some kind of systematic argument is, on closer inspection, merely an accumulation of "hooray words" (belonging, accord, full-scale, rounded). It is towards incoherence of this sort that the song of the earth leads.

And this is one path which Minhinnick, as a poet, avoids. The kind of public sphere which Auden characterised by "the flat ephemeral pamphlet and the boring meeting" holds no attractions for his poetry. Whereas the private sphere is an arena for ever more daring personal transformations, Minhinnick generally characterises the public sphere as damaged or dysfunctional and holds it at a distance. Rather than being a vatic interventionist on behalf of the environment, Minhinnick *as a poet* might best be read according to Rorty's picture of the liberal ironist. Rorty describes such an individual as follows:

> ... [one who realises] that anything can be made to look good or bad by being redescribed, and their renunciation or the attempt to formulate criteria of choice between final vocabularies puts them in the position which Sartre called "meta-stable": never quite able to take themselves seriously because always aware that the terms in which they describe themselves are subject to change, always aware of the contingency and fragility of their final vocabularies, and thus of their selves. [54]

While reading Minhinnick's poetry does not give one a burning sense that there is something to be done for the planet, neither does it give the sense that we are in a hopeless state – there will always be an environment and it will always transform. Closer in spirit to the unillusioned mood of both *After the Hurricane* and *King Driftwood* are the following remarks of Jerry Fodor:

> We are forever wanting to know what things are for, and we don't like having to take Nothing for an answer .... Still I think that sometimes out of the corner of an eye, "at a moment which is not action or inaction," we can glimpse the true scientific fission: austere, tragic, alienated and very beautiful. A world that isn't for anything; a world that is just there.[55]

What I suspect distinguishes Minhinnick is that he would accept that the world isn't for anything. *King Driftwood* reminds us that there is no melodramatic oblivion, there is only transformation, or in other words, metaphor. For all his environmental activism, what we overhear in Minhinnick's poetry is not "the song of the earth" but a song of myself. Like a geological formation, his poems serve no purpose, no ultimate good – they are "just there." At the end of 'An Isotope, Dreaming', the author, who has concluded his many visitations, is visited in turn by a devilish version of himself:

And here on the peninsula I ask
where is the half moon and who is the half man
and what is the half life of the half life of the half life?

You are very welcome.
I hope you guess my name.

Notes

1. Jonathan Bate, *The Song of the Earth* (London: Picador, 2001), p. 282.
2. Richard Rorty, *Contingency, Irony and Solidarity*, p. 6.
3. Robert Minhinnick, 'Salvage', *A Thread in the Maze*, (Swansea: Christopher Davies, 1978), p. 13.
4. John Redmond, 'Interview with Robert Minhinnick' *Gallous* 1 Autumn 2008, 25-40: p, 25.
5. Roland Mathias, "The Lonely Editor: A Glance at Anglo-Welsh Magazines" in *A Ride through the Wood: Essays on Anglo-Welsh Literature* (Bridgend: Poetry Wales Press, 1985), pp. 289-307, p. 290.
6. Cary Archard 'Introduction' in Robert Minhinnick, *A Thread in the Maze* [no page number]
7. Robert Minhinnick, 'Oxford', *A Thread in the Maze*, p. 49.
8. Robert Minhinnick, 'The Midden', *Native Ground* (Swansea: Christopher

Davies, 1979), p. 12.

9. Seamus Heaney, 'Act of Union', *Opened Ground* (London: Faber, 1998), p. 127.

10. Robert Minhinnick, 'Bittersweet', *Native Ground*, p. 35.

11. Robert Minhinnick, 'Regulars', *After the Hurricane* (Manchester: Carcanet, 2002), p. 16
    Robert Minhinnick, 'Elementary Songs', *ibid.*, p. 17.
    Robert Minhinnick, 'The Orchards at Cwm y Gaer', *ibid*, p. 14.

12. Robert Minhinnick, 'Regulars', *ibid.*, p. 16

13. Raymond Garlick, *An Introduction to Anglo-Welsh Literature* (Cardiff: University of Wales Press, 1972), p. 63.

14. Dannie Abse, 'Introduction' to Abse ed. *Twentieth Century Anglo-Welsh Poetry* (Bridgend: Seren, 1997), p. 13.

15. Robert Minhinnick, 'On the Llyn Fawr Hoard in the National Museum of Wales', *The Dinosaur Park* (Bridgend: Poetry Wales Press, 1985), p. 10.

16. Gary Snyder, "Buddhism and Possibilities of Planetary Culture" in *The Gary Snyder Reader: prose, poetry, and translation, 1952-1998* (New York: Counterpoint, 1999), pp. 41-43, p. 43.

17. Robert Minhinnick, 'The Party', *Life Sentences* (Bridgend: Poetry Wales Press, 1983), p. 26.

18 Robert Minhinnick, 'The Ziggurat', *After the Hurricane*, p. 106, p. 109.

19. *ibid.*, p. 109

20. *ibid.*, p. 106, p. 110.

21. John Redmond, 'Interview with Robert Minhinnick' *Gallous* 1 Autumn 2008, 25-40: p, 31.

22. Paul Muldoon, *The End of the Poem* (London: Faber, 2006), p. 299.

23. Robert Minhinnick, 'Lac la Ronge', *After the Hurricane*, p. 36.

24. *ibid.*, p. 38.

25. Robert Minhinnick, 'Introduction', *Green Agenda: Essays on the Environment of Wales* (Bridgend: Seren, 1994), pp. 7-22, p. 14.

26. Quoted in Sam Adams, "Interview with Robert Minhinnick" <http://www.carcanet.co.uk/cgi-bin/scribe?showdoc=14;doctype=interview>

27. Robert Minhinnick, 'The Bombing of Baghdad as Seen from an Electrical Goods Shop', *After the Hurricane*, p. 12.

28. Interview with John Redmond, *Gallous* 1 Autumn 2008, p. 34.

29. John Redmond, *ibid*, p. 38.

30. Robert Minhinnick, 'Introduction', *The Adulterer's Tongue*, (Manchester: Carcanet, 2003), p. xii

31. *ibid.*

32. Iwan Llwyd, 'Far Rockaway; trans. Robert Minhinnick, *ibid.*, p. 62.

33. Randall Jarrell, *The Third Book of Criticism*, (London: Faber, 1975) p. 155.

34. Robert Minhinnick, 'A Welshman's Flora', *After the Hurricane*, p. 85.

35. Robert Minhinnick, 'Elementary Songs', *ibid.*, p. 17.

36. M. Wynn Thomas, *Corresponding Cultures: The Two Literatures of Wales* (Cardiff: University of Wales Press, 1999), p. 245.

37. Robert Minhinnick, *To Babel and Back* (Bridgend: Seren, 2005), p. 32.

38. Elizabeth Bishop, 'Questions of Travel', *Complete Poems* (Chatto & Windus, 1983), p. 93.

39. Robert Minhinnick, 'From the Rockpool', *After the Hurricane*, p. 111.

40. Robert Minhinnick, 'La Otra Orilla', *King Driftwood* (Manchester: Carcanet, 2008), p. 48.

41. John Redmond, op.cit. o. 38.

42. Robert Minhinnick, 'On Listening to Glenn Gould Play Bach's Goldberg Variations', *King Driftwood*, p. 35.

43. Robert Minhinnick, 'An Isotope, Dreaming', *ibid.*, p. 10.

44. *ibid.*, p. 11.

45. *ibid.*, p. 9.

46. Ted Hughes, 'Pibroch', *Collected Poems*, ed. Paul Keegan (London: Faber, 2003), p. 179.

47. Jonathan Bate, 'The Green Line in Contemporary Poetry: The Michael Donaghy Lecture 2006' *British and Irish Contemporary Poetry* 1 (1) Spring 2008, pp. 1-18, p. 3, p. 9, p. 9.

48. Richard Rorty, *Contingency, Irony, and Solidarity*, p. 21.

49. John Burnside, "A Science of Belonging: Poetry as Ecology" in Robert Crawford ed. *Contemporary Poetry and Contemporary Science* (Oxford: OUP, 2006), pp. 91-106, p. 97.

50. *ibid.*, pp. 91-106,

51. Wislawa Szymborska, 'View with a Grain of Sand', *View With a Grain of Sand: Selected Poems* (London: Faber, 1996), p. 135.

52. John Burnside, *op. cit*, pp. 91-106, p. 105.

53. *ibid.*, pp. 91-106, pp. 105-6.

54. Richard Rorty, *op. cit*, pp. 73-4.

55. Jerry Fodor, *In Critical Condition* (Cambridge, Mass.: MIT Press, 1998), p. 16.

The Influence of Sylvia Plath
on Seamus Heaney

In making a case for the influence of Sylvia Plath on Seamus Heaney, I start, in this chapter with the misunderstood inwardness of the Irishman's poetry, because I believe it is this quality which draws him towards her writing. Then, in filling out the detail of their poetic convergence, I pay special attention to the influence of *The Colossus* and *Ariel* on *Wintering Out* and *North*. The argument has two underlying assumptions: firstly, that Heaney is an inward poet who is generally misunderstood as the reverse and, secondly, that personal repression, which he sees as a private bad, is often interpreted, in the special circumstances of the Northern Irish conflict, as a public good. As I see it, Heaney discovered in Plath's work a psychological cocktail which appealed deeply to his own personality, a mental world in which the self's inwardness is (violently) compromised and misunderstood by others. Towards the end of the chapter I offer some reasons why critics tend to underestimate, or overlook, this literary relationship. Plath's influence on Heaney is, I argue, hard to detect because his poetic personality is, in Bloomean style, enabled and threatened by her role as a strong precursor.

To explain what I mean by describing Heaney as an 'inward poet' let me glance at a parable. It is one which the poet himself selected to occupy a prominent position, the beginning of 'Mossbawn', the first essay in his *Selected Prose*:

> I do not know what age I was when I got lost in the pea-drills in a field behind the house, but it is a half-dream to me, and I've heard about it so often that I may even be imagining it. Yet, by now, I have imagined it so long and so often that I know what it was like: a green web, a caul of veined light, a tangle of rods and pods, stalks and tendrils, full of assuaging earth and leaf smell, a sunlit lair. I'm sitting as if just wakened from a winter sleep and gradually becoming aware of voices, coming closer, calling my name, and for no reason at all I have begun to weep.[1]

Heaney lets the story speak for itself. The desire for absolute

solitude is a powerful one in artists and, here, the adult writer registers
the child's fantasy of becoming a self-sufficient universe. It is the kind
of deserted world which, in the words of the critic Robert Harbison,
is "the most egoistic piece of imagining possible, the world left behind
for the self alone …"[2] I want to mark this parable out as an emblem
of Heaney's inwardness, which is reflected and amplified by poems
like 'Oracle', 'Bye-Child', and 'Exposure'. Heaney has spoken of his
inwardness as bound up with various psychological defences, implying
that his early, isolated child-self remains at the heart of his personality.
But its existence is not something which he finds easy to put across:

> When I recollect myself as a young child, I have a sense of being close to
> …[an] unsatisfied, desiring, lonely, inner core. It – or he – hasn't disap-
> peared but nowadays he dwells farther in, behind all kinds of socialized
> defences, barriers he learned to put up in order to keep the inwardness
> intact but which ultimately had the effect of immuring it.[3]

In his essay on Plath in *The Government of the Tongue*, Heaney
illustrates his thoughts on her work with a parable revealingly similar
to the one in 'Mossbawn', an example, drawn from Wordsworth's
Prelude, of a boy in the wilderness practising owl-hoots in the dark. It
is significant for his own poetry, as well as for Plath's, that Heaney
uses, in Harbison's language, such an 'egoistic' example. If we were
to think of a similar instance, in Plath's work, of childhood withdrawal
we might choose a story related by Ronald Hayman:

> Without quite claiming to have attempted suicide when she [Plath] was
> two, she told a story about learning to crawl. After being put down on the
> beach, she made for the coming wave, and Aurelia [Plath's mother] picked
> her up by her heels just as she had penetrated the 'wall of green'.[4]

Lurid as this childhood parable may be, it is suggestive, nonethe-
less, of how, Plath's desire for separation is more absolute than
Heaney's and, ultimately, is associated with a violent end. As a poetic
model, Plath takes the Irishman a long way but, in the end, her inward-
ness is not enough. This is the final judgment reached in his essay:

> There is nothing *poetically* flawed about Plath's work. What may finally
> limit it is its dominant theme of self-discovery and self-definition,…. I do
> not suggest that the self is not the proper arena of poetry. But I believe
> that the greatest works occur when a certain self-forgetfulness is
> attained…[5]

To overcome inwardness, to achieve "self-forgetfulness", is not easy and Heaney, as a writer, does not always succeed at being more 'social'. Often his attempts in this area seem awkward and unhappy and are tied to questions about violent conflict.

Take as an example, 'Weighing In'. Although not one of Heaney's best poems, it usefully illustrates some of the poet's symptomatic problems when it comes to discussions of violence. Typically, Heaney combines a general reflection on the value of violent resistance with his own particular concerns about shyness and timidity. Here is the third section of the poem:

> To refuse the other cheek. To cast the stone.
> Not to do some time, not to break with
> The obedient one you hurt yourself into
>
> Is to fail the hurt, the self, the ingrown rule.
> Prophesy who struck thee! When soldiers mocked
> Blindfolded Jesus and he didn't strike back
>
> They were neither shamed nor edified, although
> Something was made manifest – the power
> Of power not exercised, of hope inferred
>
> By the powerless forever. Still, for Jesus' sake,
> Do me a favour, would you, just this once?
> Prophesy, give scandal, cast the stone.[6]

The argument here is painfully murky. Among his many strengths, Heaney has never been able to include systematic analysis and, accordingly, his more discursive poetry can get lost in contradictions. But there is more to these lines than conceptual haze. This excerpt illustrates how Heaney's language tends towards impenetrability when he touches on his own repression. It is not an accident that his argument is hard to follow. The pacific example of Jesus, which the speaker seems to admire, and for which he even finds persuasive reasons, is one he advances only to withdraw. At the same time as the speaker is 'weighing in', he appears to be 'wriggling out'. The pattern is repeated throughout his canon. Heaney performs his own lack of performance, treats energetically his own lack of energy.

A further irony is that Heaney, who is by any standards a masterful poet, finds it difficult to be explicit about his desire for that 'mastery'. He is rightly perceived as a mild and generous personality, but this perception has interfered with the way we read his (often

competitive) relations to other poets – and this includes Heaney's own
account of what poets have influenced him. As the extract from
'Weighing In' reveals, Heaney, finds it almost impossible to represent,
in explicit terms, his own aggression – especially his own passive-
aggressive behaviour – whether in matters personal or political, or
with respect to various literary rivalries.

The strongest model of influence we have available to us is the
relatively antagonistic one provided by Harold Bloom in *The Anxiety
of Influence, A Map of Misreading* and elsewhere. At first it seems
strangely difficult to fit Heaney into this model. It is hard to see him
as engaged in a struggle to overcome those literary precursors who
meant the most to him: Frost, Kavanagh, Hopkins, Hughes,
Wordsworth, and, I want to suggest, Plath. The very language of
struggle and overcoming seems out of place in relation to Heaney's
poetic personality – or, perhaps one might say, is displaced *by*
Heaney's poetic personality. One wonders how much this is a
function of his evident graciousness and how much it is a repression,
conscious or otherwise, of more combative qualities. In my view it is
exactly when Heaney is writing about the self-assertive qualities of
his biggest influences that he most misreads them.

Just as Heaney takes the 'struggle' out of his relationship with his
precursors, so practically all of Heaney's meditations on violent
conflict follow a trope of proximity without participation. The situa-
tion is further complicated by the familiar Romantic fissure between
poet as representative man and poet as exceptional seer. Heaney
prefers to conceal his feelings of originality, his awareness that he is
an individual of exceptional quality, for the sake of representativeness,
the impression of being an ordinary man with ordinary appetites, and
this favouring of representativeness (community) over exceptional-
ism (originality) is, in the long run, a distortion.

One thinks here of the final section of 'Station Island' where
Heaney, on his pilgrimage, encounters the shade of Joyce. The novel-
ist advises the poet to pursue artistic independence:

> 'You lose more of yourself than you redeem
> doing the decent thing. Keep at a tangent.
> When they make the circle wide, it's time to swim
>
> out on your own and fill the element
> with signatures of your own frequency,
> echo-soundings, searches, probes, allurements,

elver-gleams in the dark of the whole sea.'[7]

What is strange about this advice is that, even if it is good, it is obvious. Stephen Dedalus, for instance, would scarcely have needed to hear it. And is it not odd that Heaney should use Joyce to channel such wisdom as late as his *sixth* collection of poems? The need for such counsel suggests an exceptional level of repression on the pupil's part, one which is not fully explained by Heaney's desire, in the demanding context of the Troubles, to govern his tongue.

Before his encounter with Joyce's shade, in the less-remarked-on section 9 of *Station Island*, Heaney, in penitent mood, dreams of a trumpet he once found:

> …. Still there for the taking!
> The old valve trumpet with its valves and stops
> I found once in loft thatch, a mystery
> I shied from then for I thought such trove beyond me.
>
> 'I hate how quick I was to know my place.
> I hate where I was born, hate everything
> That made me biddable and unforthcoming.'

The posture of guilty self-reproof is familiarly Catholic (appropriate for the penitential pilgrimage of Lough Derg) and it is one which is frequently adopted in Heaney's work. It constitutes a kind of dramatic and active turning on the self for the very reason that the self has shied away from drama and action. The poet reproves himself for a *way* of having acted, or not acted, a *style* of inertia rather than scolding himself for having adopted one political position or another.

In his early collections – in poems like 'The Forge', 'The Outlaw', 'Thatcher', and 'Requiem for the Croppies' we find Heaney, who was at that point strongly under the influence of Ted Hughes, admiring certain types of stereotyped masculine behaviour. Admiration, in such poems, was almost always for the decisive behaviour of others rather than for any decisive behaviour of the self. So to describe these early poems as a 'project of mastery' or a 'quest for power' might seem misplaced. And yet were these poems not part of such a project, such a quest? Is it not because Heaney has so successfully presented himself as shying away from decisive behaviour – as pathologically modest – that we are disinclined to use critical language which, were it applied to a poet like Yeats, would be unremarkable?

Such rueful passivity separates Heaney from another 'masculine' poet, D.H. Lawrence, a parallel which is raised in 'Clearances', an elegiac sonnet sequence for Heaney's mother. There he contemplates the kind of feminised masculinity which is encouraged by a close identification of a male with his mother:

> In the first flush of the Easter holidays
> The ceremonies during Holy Week.
> Were highpoints of our *Sons and Lovers* phase.
> The midnight fire. The paschal candlestick.
> Elbow to elbow, glad to be kneeling next
> To each other ....[8]

It is worth thinking about the extent to which a disposition to mother-love, which in Lawrence is seen as a defect to be overcome, is presented, in Heaney's poetry, as an ambiguous virtue. Indeed, from the beginning, Heaney allows personal repression to seem like a communal virtue. Holding back is social – a position which concurs with Auden's 'The Truest Poetry is Most Feigning' which concludes by associating, "love, or truth in any serious sense", with, "a reticence".[9] To refrain from doing something may be good for the community, but is it good for the self? Examples of Heaney refraining from action – not saying, biting his lip, or, as he would put it, 'governing his tongue' – are multiple, occurring in poems as different as 'Casualty' and 'Clearances'. On one level, such personal repression may seem desirable, especially as the one negative model of unrepression, or unconstraint, was paramilitarism.

Because there is a pressure to read any personal disposition in a Heaney poem as political, we are in danger, I think, of misreading his own attitudes towards personal repression. When Lawrence attacks the repression (sexual, social, even existential) of English society, or his own repression in *Sons and Lovers*, he does not represent the condition as having any redeeming features. There are not two sides to the question. The same lack of ambiguity – with respect to repression – characterises the poems of Hughes, the one poet in the Blakean genealogy of English poets to whom Heaney is especially close.

From Hughes, and, to a lesser extent, from Lawrence, Heaney learns, or learns the value of saying, that human beings have more in common with animals than they like to admit. He does not, however, draw the same lesson as his forebears. To recommend the instinctive quality of beasts, to admire their at-homeness with respect to their natural environment, is one thing in poems like Lawrence's 'Kangaroo' and Hughes's 'Hawk Roosting' but it would be an altogether more provocative thing in a Heaney poem. The kinds of images which lead Lawrence and Hughes into postures open to the criticism of crypto- or proto-fascism, would have led Heaney into very compromised poetic territory (imagine the outcry if the author of 'Hawk Roosting' had been Heaney.) Perhaps it would be unfair to apply to Randall Jarrell's remark about Marianne Moore to Heaney, to say that he "only sends postcards to the nicer animals", but it is noticeable how, as a poet of conflict, he avoids celebrating animal violence in his work. In 'Badgers', for example, Heaney identifies the creatures with paramilitaries on the run and the portrait is not meant to be flattering. When, at the end of the poem, Heaney half-identifies with a badger we are made conscious of the creature's repressed posture ("The unquestionable houseboy's shoulders/ that could have been my own.")

In this context, the poet who is most troubling for Heaney is the inescapable Yeats. In his essay, 'Yeats as an Example?', for instance, Heaney (again) adopts the position of looking on and admiring the conspicuous activity of another:

> Unlike Wallace Stevens … that other great apologist of the imagination, Yeats bore the implications of his romanticism into action: he propagandized, speechified, fund-raised, administered, and politicked in the world of telegrams and anger, …[10]

Here is another example:

> I admire the way that Yeats took on the world on his own terms, defined the areas where he would negotiate and where he would not; the way he never accepted the term's of another's argument but propounded his own.[11]

But Heaney is also troubled, in this essay, by Yeats's "priapic" posture and tries to steer us away from 'masculine', wilful versions of the master, such as we find, say, in 'Sailing to Byzantium', to the more 'maternal' and forgiving model such as we find, say, in 'Cuchulainn Comforted'. In other words, Heaney attempts to 'Heaneyise' Yeats – or, in Bloomean language, to misread him – and thereby make him less disturbing. He does something revealingly similar in his essay on Hughes, where he again steers us away from spectacularly violent poems, such as those generally found in *Crow*, to focus on that same book's peculiarly quiet coda, 'Littleblood'.[12] This seems to me a good example of a Bloomean literary defence-mechanism. Heaney is in a struggle with Yeats and with Hughes but, in passive-aggressive

fashion, he contrives to give the impression that only Yeats and
Hughes are doing the struggling.

Because Heaney's poetry has difficulty in travelling the relation-
ship between 'me' and 'not-me', especially when it comes to issues of
political violence, he finds the example of Plath helpful. Heaney helps
himself to confront the issue of violent conflict by creating, in *Winter-
ing Out* and *North*, what Auden would call a secondary world – a
world of the imagination which stands in critical relation to the actual
world. Auden, of course, did much the same in his poetry of the
1930s, strikingly using some of the same material we find in *North*: a
psychologised landscape bathed in the revenge mood of the Sagas,
an atmosphere of crisis associated with images of sickness, 'northern-
ness' understood as a metaphysical quality, and a preoccupation with
messianism (it is this early Auden which Heaney, on the whole
prefers, as he makes clear in *The Government of the Tongue*.) But,
important as this connection might be, my aim is not to trace Auden's
influence on Heaney's renderings of conflict. Rather I want to suggest
that Heaney represses another, more significant, influence throughout
North. Up to this point, I have not attempted to persuade the reader
of Sylvia Plath's influence. In this next part of the essay, therefore, I
am going to offer some detailed examples of that influence in action.

*

Alice Entwistle remarks, "[t]here is much work to be done on the way
in which later generations of male poets ... draw on Plath's
example."[13] I agree. Plath, like Heaney, has been read, extensively if
not exclusively, in the light of some highly charged critical agendas.
Determined readings often cause blindness and, in the case of these
two poets, there is a provocative symmetry to what has been
overlooked. Just as we are reluctant to read Plath as an influence on
male poets, we are equally slow to acknowledge the influence of
female poets on Heaney.

Arguably Heaney's best, and certainly some of his best-known,
poems are featured in his fourth collection, *North* (1975). It is
precisely in this collection where I think Plath's influence is at its
sharpest, and so I am going to examine poems from that book in the
light of poems from *The Colossus* and *Ariel*. Beyond being drawn to
Plath's inwardness – and responding to an array of congenial local
details in her style – I argue that what Heaney finds most animating
in her work are her representations of the self's inwardness as

violently compromised by others. The reader might be forgiven for asking, 'if the influence of Plath on Heaney is significant why has this not been obvious before?' I think this is a good question with a complicated answer. Partly, the answer is bound up with Heaney's somewhat feline relationships to those poets who have influenced him.

The main poetic connection between Plath and Heaney which has received some commentary (and which is mentioned by both Neil Corcoran and Helen Vendler) is the similarity of 'Lady Lazarus' and 'Bog Queen'. The connection is particularly noticeable at the end of each poem. As Nathalie F. Anderson comments, "… the last stanza [of 'Bog Queen'] recalls Sylvia Plath's 'Lady Lazarus' in its suggestion of vengeful potency unchained".[14] Critics have been apt to identify this particular link because, unlike the other Bog poems, the retrieved body in 'Bog Queen' is also the poem's speaker. By contrast with the speakers in *Ariel* and *The Colossus* who often appear to be dead or dying, the speakers in *North* are usually observing the death or demise of someone else. In 'Bog Queen', however, the pattern of proximity without participation (the role of onlooker), which is so frequently adopted in Heaney's work, is momentarily suspended and the link between the two poets edges into the spotlight.

Less remarked is the link between 'Bog Queen' and 'The Grauballe Man'. This is because Heaney's I-persona reverts to his usual stance as a spectator and the body is represented in the third-person rather than in the first-person. The change of viewpoint obscures some otherwise startling similarities. Compare:

> … my skin
> Bright as a Nazi lampshade,
> My right foot
>
> A paperweight.
> My face a featureless, fine
> Jew linen.[15]

... with the following famous lines,

> the grain of his wrists
> is like bog oak,
> the ball of his heel
>
> like a basalt egg.
> His instep has shrunk

cold as a swamp's foot
or a wet swamp root.[16]

In each case, the piled-up comparisons, by virtue of their unexpectedness, deliberately draw attention to themselves. Line-length and pacing suggest a closeness of style which would be entirely obvious if the pronouns matched up. This is not the only poem in *Ariel* which 'The Grauballe Man' echoes. Consider the first three lines:

As if he had been poured
in tar, he lies
on a pillow of turf

The third line closely replicates "your pillow a little turf" of 'Elm'.[17] More subtly, the opening echoes the opening of 'Ariel' ("Pour of tor and distances.")[18] And, later in the poem, the unusual verb "perfected" used by Heaney is surely an echo of 'Edge'("The woman is perfected").[19]

All of this would be incidental if these two poems, and others like them, did not share a wide range of features, including narcotized description, a fascination with body-parts, widespread use of metonymy, rapid changes of scale, the consistent blurring of personal boundaries, and a preoccupation with violence. Like Plath, Heaney is fascinated by touch, a fascination which can easily shade into repulsion. Plath often presents body-parts in an alienated, disassociated manner, and likes to convey disgust by imagining a sinister-looking object being handled – one thinks here of her usually disturbing images of babies, presenting a form which, under normal circumstances, we would be happy to touch in a repellent guise. We might consider this in relation to 'The Grauballe Man' where the subject's hair is described as "a mat unlikely/ as a foetus's."[20] Plath uses a similar simile in 'Poem for a Birthday': "Drunk as a foetus/ I suck at the paps of darkness"[21] which in turn is echoed by Heaney's phrase "pap for the dispossessed".[22]

Even the metaphor of digging which is the one most closely associated with Heaney is widely anticipated in Plath's work, especially by the poems in *The Colossus*. Take the following example from 'The Burnt Out Spa':

I pick and pry like a doctor or
Archaeologist among

Iron entrails, enamel bowls,
The coils and pipes that made him run.[23]

Both poets contemplate dismemberment and bodily rupture in a
tone which is sometimes tender, occasionally rhapsodic and repeat-
edly sexualised. We might think differently about Heaney's focus on
female victims if we were to focus more on Plath's influence.
Consider, for example, how these lines from 'Punishment' ("Little
adulteress,/ before they punished you")[24] echo lines from 'Cut'
("Little pilgrim,/ The Indian's axed your scalp").[25]

Other patterns of influence abound. Both *North* and *The Colossus*
(with Auden in mind) construct an early poem around a Breughel
painting. Both *North* and *The Colossus*, amidst an array of poems about
corpses, include one about a dead mole. Both poets (reflecting the
influence of Roethke's greenhouse poems) use 'root' as a key word
and metaphor – compare Plath's line "In the bowel of the root" ('Poem
for a Birthday')[26] with Heaney's passage "This is the vowel of earth/
dreaming its root/ in flowers and snow"('Kinship').[27] Rather than
multiply individual echoes, however, I want to drive home my point
by looking at two extended – perhaps surprising – examples. These
are the links between 'Exposure' and 'Funeral Rites' (outside the Bog
poems, examples of Heaney's best work in *North*) and two poems by
Plath, respectively, 'Nick and the Candlestick' and 'Berck-Plage'.

Let me first take the pairing of 'Exposure' and 'Nick and the
Candlestick'. What I want to suggest, here and elsewhere, is a deep
coincidence of mood which extends beyond the odd verbal echo,
what amounts to a crossing of secondary worlds. In 'Exposure',
Heaney contemplates his poetic vocation in a pastoral setting. The
poem is one of keenly-felt solitude, with the same quality of pastoral
apartness, which we find in Wordsworth's parable of the owl-mimic-
king boy. In 'Nick and the Candlestick', Plath contemplates the play
of candle-light over her baby. On the face of it, there is no overt
relationship between the poems. However, as soon as we move to the
level of mood, imagery, composition, tone, phrasing, lighting, a series
of parallels are thrown up, and these parallels bring to mind other
poems in both books.

The most obvious motif the poems share is one of dripping. Each
takes place in a cold, wet, dark, isolated space, where the encroach-
ment of drops and a continual dripping sound are a reminder of the
outside world. The drops in 'Exposure' are an ambiguous reminder
of the public realm:

Rain comes down through the alders,
Its low conducive voices
Mutter about let-downs and erosions
And yet each drop recalls

The diamond absolutes.[28]

   We might bear in mind here a remark Heaney makes about 'Elm'
in his essay on Plath: "The elm utters an elmy consciousness, it
communicates in tree-speak: 'This is the rain now, this big hush'."[29]
The drops which fall in 'Nick and the Candlestick' are described by
Plath as "tears//The earthen womb/Exudes"[30] – a reminder that in
both *Ariel* and *North* the secondary worlds constantly present us with
images either of being buried alive or (with corpses emerging from
the ground) of being born dead. Both poems begin with description
in the interests of illustrating a negative mood and both arrest this
process, dramatically, with a similar-sounding question. Heaney's
speaker asks "How did I end up like this?" and Plath's speaker asks
"O love, how did you get here?" Again the main difference between
the examples lies in the pronouns. Both poems make unprompted
self-declarations while, in effect, talking to themselves: "I am a
miner" (Plath) and "I am neither internee nor informer/ an inner
émigré" (Heaney) – a crossing which is underscored by the assonan-
tal and consonantal echoes. Persistently provoked by the dripping
atmosphere, both poems range the poet against unspecified and
unseen enemies, in Plath "A vice of knives", in Heaney "… the anvil
brains of some who hate me". In each case the enemies are associ-
ated with a threatening sharpness which is suggested by droplets
coming to a point. Heaney's phrase "anvil brains" extrudes uncom-
fortably from the texture of 'Exposure' – an instance of him
sounding more like Plath than Plath. 'Brains' is a key repeated word
in *North* and this particular phrase recalls another sinister image in
Ariel, "the terrible brains/Of Krupp" in 'Getting There'.[31] Both 'Nick
and the Candlestick' and 'Exposure' suggest light with their titles and
both oppose the dispiriting darkness with a somewhat feeble local
light-source. Both oppose the darkness with a similar colour-range
too: the candle-light, in Plath, associated with yellow, rose, ruby and
red, and the comet, in Heaney, described in terms of "haws and rose-
hips". In each case, a relationship, again reinforced by the dripping
motif, is traced between the local landscape and the universal
skyscape with references to falling stars: "Let the stars/ Plummet to
their dark address," (Plath) and "… I sometimes see a falling star./

If I could come on meteorite!" (Heaney) Both poems have messianic undertones. Heaney's first line, "It is December in Wicklow." invites us to read his comet ("the once-in-a-lifetime portent") as the star of Bethlehem, a complicating commentary on his own (perhaps unwelcome) role as a cultural leader, while Plath explicitly links her baby with Christ in her poem's last line, "You are the baby in the barn."

Both poems bathe consciousness in a protective womblike state which, however, cannot stop the outside from dripping in. The absence of other adults, and therefore of rival consciousnesses, shows the temptation for both poets of a radical inwardness. When that inwardness is threatened, the associated fear and anxiety gives rise (in both cases) to fantasies of violent aggression as well as the desire to escape adult responsibility.

Let me now turn to my second extended example, the influence of Plath's 'Berck-Plage' on Heaney's 'Funeral Rites'. In both *Ariel* and *North*, poems which happen to contain other (living) adults tend to be more discursive, and fragmented, veering from lyric to narrative. Reflecting this generic blur, both 'Berck-Plage' and 'Funeral Rites' are written in sections. Both poems deal centrally with funerals and the sectioning, in each case, seems to allow the speaker, who is, at times, a character peripherally involved in the action, to approach the subject from different angles.

In his essay on ceremonial patterns in Heaney's poetry, Maurice Harmon mentions 'Funeral Rites' as a poem in which the speaker aims to heal the pain of the Northern Irish conflict, where "the ugliness of death is alleviated by agreeable ritual."[32] I think that this reading of 'Funeral Rites' is too optimistic and that the entire poem takes on a different cast when seen in the light of Plath's influence. Before setting out my disagreements with Harmon, it is worth pointing out a few verbal correspondences between 'Berck-Plage' and 'Funeral Rites'. "The long coffin of soap-coloured oak"[33] mentioned in the former is echoed by the "Dear soapstone masks" of the dead in the latter.[34] In both poems cars are described in terms of purring and the "neighbourly faces" around the corpse in 'Berck-Plage' anticipate Heaney's paradoxical phrase "neighbourly murder" in 'Funeral Rites'.

But the parallels between the poems lie more in the gothic – and sometimes surreal – presentation of action. Both poems present a funeral in a dreamlike, disassociated manner, so that the living are made to resemble the dead. Both poems move out from the speaker's apprehensions of death to imagine the reactions of others, including domestic scenes where they are not present. Plath imagines the dead man laid out: "How far he is now. His actions/ Around him like living-groom furniture, like a decor." Heaney has a similar zombie-like focus on interiors: "Somnambulant women,/ left behind, move/ through emptied kitchens". In order to read 'Funeral Rites' in a positive light, Harmon wants to think of the procession, which Edna Longley has described as "a mass trance", as a benevolent, ecumenical event.[35] Such a reading does not convince me. After all, the procession is compared to a serpent (which picks up on the "many-snaked" sea in 'Berck-Plage') and its participants are portrayed like extras in a bad horror movie.

It would seem that the main point of difference between the two poems is the matter of how they end, but this is only the case if you choose to read the conclusion of 'Funeral Rites', where Gunnar's dead body breaks into song, as uplifting:

> Men said that he was chanting
> verses about honour
> and that four lights burned
>
> in corners of the chamber:
> which opened then, as he turned
> with a joyful face
> to look at the moon.

Harmon does want to read this optimistically, even though, in 'Njal's Saga', as he himself actually points out, Gunnar's singing has a negative effect: "Gunnar sang about honour in battle, about prefer-ring to die than to submit, and by his words drove his son and followers to his death."[36] It says something about the pressure to read Heaney positively, as a purveyor of model conflict solutions, that Harmon simply ignores the implication of Gunnar's song. But if Harmon does not want to develop the implications of the song, then we can do it for him. Both 'Berck-Plage' and 'Funeral Rites' end with people (children in the former) turning to look at something (the moon in one case, "a hole in the sky" in the other) which they consider to be wonderful but which the speaker regards as extremely sinister. Read in this light, 'Funeral Rites' would be as pessimistic as many other poems in *North* and would chime with the last line of 'Berck-Plage': "There is no hope. It is given up."

Given the claim which this essay is making for Plath's influence on him, why would the extensive criticism of Heaney, and of the Bog

poems in particular, not have identified and explored the connection
already? Heaney's own essay on Plath is not a record of his indebt-
edness, even if the closeness of his scrutiny suggests a deep level of
engagement with her canon. To take the last point first, Heaney's
essays are usually not point-by-point accounts of indebtedness. The
essay on Auden in *The Government of the Tongue* does not suggest a
deep influence either, even though the influence of the Englishman
on Heaney is significant. Furthermore, to the extent that he has
constructed his own 'literary family-tree', Heaney has tended to
identify himself with heterosexual, male, "priapic" poets who are, in
effect, national bards (Lowell, Yeats, Hughes, Kavanagh). This may
have inhibited an explicit identification with Auden and Plath. The
reasons why other critics have overlooked Plath's influence are more
tangled.

On a simple level, it is surprisingly hard to conceive of Heaney
under the influence of a female poet. Heaney has been associated with
an exclusively male group of poets (Derek Mahon, Michael Longley,
James Simmons) and all of the well-acknowledged influences on his
work are men. Indeed, when Helen Vendler lists the major influences
on Heaney's work they are all male.[37] Another inhibiting factor is
Heaney's relationship – poetic and personal – to Ted Hughes, which
may have discouraged him from laying excessive emphasis in the
account of his own poetic progress on the work of Hughes's first wife.
A further point is that critical debates about Heaney which centre on
his poetry of conflict are usually bound up with his relation to Irish
society, politics, and history – narratives where Plath's presence does
not 'fit'.

In her own study of Heaney's poetry, Helen Vendler glances at a
link between Plath and 'Bog Queen'. As she points out, the end of the
poem, with its "final rising … owes something to Plath's 'Lady
Lazarus'".[38] But Vendler pursues this link no further. Plath is made
to seem like an accidental influence, one which had better be
mentioned, and then rapidly forgotten. Vendler goes on to discuss
some of the other Bog Poems in terms of Heaney's "ambivalence" as
a spectator of violence or of its results, a familiar critical move, which
the poems often seem to invite.[39] However, that ambivalence is
characterised as social and political, a matter of Heaney's attitudes as
a citizen in a difficult moment, rather than an ambivalence about his
poetic influences. As this familiar reading would have it, Heaney has
mixed feelings about the matter of Ireland which the poems flow forth
and embody, and they are not to be read within the kind of influence-

relation which Harold Bloom would presumably encourage.

We find a rather similar, if more detailed, instance of this critical pattern in Neil Corcoran's study of the poet. Corcoran is alert to the connection between 'Bog Queen' and 'Lady Lazarus' and in a footnote he helpfully suggests a further connection between Plath's poem and Heaney's 'Come to the Bower', a link which turns on the fact that both poems identify a corpse with red hair.[40] At a separate point in the book, Corcoran briefly discusses Plath's influence on a poem in which Heaney touches on marital difficulties, 'Summer Home', noting that Plath's influence is "unexpected".[41] As with Vendler, Plath's influence is detected even when the critic is not searching for it and finds it hard to assimilate. Conspicuously, no attempt is made, in any of these cases, to weave Plath's influence into a larger critical narrative.

In *The Achievement of Seamus Heaney*, John Wilson Foster considers Heaney's decision to associate political conflict with gender. For Foster, this is, in the manner of its execution, an original and successful move. But Foster relates this manoeuvre to the traditional Irish nationalist trope of seeing Ireland as female. Despite a passing reference to Heaney's essay on Plath, he does not make the leap of seeing Plath behind *North*, even when he writes passages like this:

> ... it is implied [in *North*] that poetry is Ireland's form of redress. She actually survives by dint of those [colonial] misfortunes, for she has become, like her bogs, ineradicable because absorbent of aggression. The forms and even content of the various penetrations are preserved, but posthumously, on the terms of the ravaged goddess.[42]

To any alert reader of modern poetry the critical language which is being used here (note the echo of Alvarez's study of suicide and literature, *The Savage God*) is suggestive of the issues we associate with Plath's legacy.

To admit the considerable influence of Plath on Heaney would change how we think about his poetry's treatment of gender. As a disapproving essay by Patricia Coughlan illustrates, Heaney has written many poems which are vulnerable to feminist critique. Claiming that his poetry is "insistently and damagingly gendered", Coughlan's essay woodenly constructs Heaney as an unregenerate Catholic male unconsciously reproducing the most crude male-female stereotypes.[43] Emboldened by her theoretical framework, she concludes the essay in the most provocative critical language:

The integral self counted as so precious to the capacity for expression of these poets [Montague and Heaney] is won against a necessarily subordinated ground of merely potential, never actual feminine selves. In Lacanian terms, they seem to be stuck in the self/not-self dualism of the mirror stage, failing to arrive at an acknowledgement of the existence of an autonomous subjectivity in others: a structure common to sexism and racism.[44]

Coughlan's essay barely discusses any *poetic* influence on Heaney and is itself open to the charge of sexist construction since it does not credit Heaney with the open-mindedness to learn from female poets. If Coughlan had taken stock of Plath's influence, her argument would have to be complicated beyond the point of coherence. As is so often the case with publicly-oriented criticism of Heaney, a definite interest is served by not noticing Plath's influence – it would spoil too soon a neat critical agenda. When Edna Longley notes that the "female figures in the [Bog] poems, perhaps understandably, bear a family resemblance to one another ..." it is surprising that, for a critic with such a well-developed ear (and in a gendered context) the link to Plath's 'Lady Lazarus' is not made.[45] Again, it would change how we read the continuum of female figures in *North* if the prevalence of Plath's influence were admitted, because one could then read all those poems as, *to some extent*, embodying Plath's presence.

Let me draw some of the threads of this chapter together. Heaney writes about his own repression unconvincingly because his responsibility to others is always going to make reticence seem like a virtue. Heaney can never make his own repression widely understood because it is always apt to be misread. In the autobiographical parable from 'Mossbawn', he writes that, on hearing the approaching voices, "for no reason at all I began to weep." But, of course, there was every reason for him to weep; by those voices, the self's inwardness was decisively compromised.

Heaney's political relationship to violent conflict in *North* is mirrored by his literary relationship to Plath's *Ariel*. In both cases he is a conspicuous onlooker, a knowing bystander. In relation to Plath's controlling metaphor of the bell jar, for example, Heaney stands not on the inside (or, as it were, inwardly), but *just* outside (or, as it were, overcoming inwardness). His attitude is one of close proximity rather than complete identification. He is close enough to allow a sympathetic reading and a degree of imaginative projection but not close enough for 'union'. Heaney was attracted to the Plath myth – but not to the point of re-enacting it.

Repeatedly, Heaney, like Plath, hesitates between the sense of vision (disassociated, inward) and the sense of touch (associated, community-oriented) – or to put this another way the poems hesitate between the poles of involvement – emotional, social, physical – and of non-involvement. The child who is a spectator of dead relatives in 'Funeral Rites' abandons the role of onlooker by means of touch ("kissing"), a moment described by Heaney with mixed feelings of veneration and repulsion. Drawn to Plath by her withdrawal from community, Heaney eventually uses community to overcome her. I think that this is one of the key (implicit) messages of his essay in *The Government of the Tongue*. Like the proximate stance of his speakers to bog corpses – he succeeds (by living) whereas they, however gloriously or glamorously, have failed (by dying). Heaney admits that Plath's poetry is not "*poetically* flawed" but, his essay implies that, at a deeper level, at a level where she fails, he succeeds.

Notes:

1. Seamus Heaney, 'Mossbawn' in *Finders Keepers: Selected Prose 1971-2001* (London: Faber, 2002) pp. 3-13. p 3.

2. Robert Harbison, *Eccentric Spaces*, (Cambridge, Mass., M.I.T., 2000), p. 83.

3. Seamus Heaney, *Stepping Stones*, p. 31.

4. Ronald Hayman, *The Death and Life of Sylvia Plath* 1st ed. (London, Heinemann, 1991), 2nd ed. (Stroud: Sutton, 2003), p. 46.

5. Seamus Heaney, 'The Indefatigable Hoof-Taps: Sylvia Plath' in *The Government of the Tongue* (London: Faber, 1998), p. 168.

6. Seamus Heaney, *Opened Ground*, (London: Faber, 1988), p. 408.

7. *ibid.*, p. 268.

8. *ibid.*, p. 312.

9. W.H. Auden, "'The Truest Poetry is the Most Feigning'", *Collected Poems*, p. 621.

10. Seamus Heaney, *Finders Keepers*, p. 98.

11. *ibid.*, p. 99.

12. Seamus Heaney, 'On Ted Hughes's "Littleblood"', *ibid.*, pp. 407-409.

13. Alice Entwistle, 'Plath and contemporary British poetry' in Jo Gill ed. *The Cambridge Companion to Sylvia Plath* (Cambridge: CUP, 2006), pp. 63-8, p. 64.

14. Nathalie F. Anderson, 'Queasy Proximity: Seamus Heaney's Mythical Method' in Robert F. Garratt ed. *Critical Essays on Seamus Heaney* (London and New York: Prentice-Hall, 1995), pp. 139-150, p. 147.

15. Sylvia Plath, 'Lady Lazarus', *Collected Poems* (London: Faber, 1981), p. 244.

16. Seamus Heaney, 'The Grauballe Man', *North* (London: Faber, 1975) p. 28.
17. Sylvia Plath, 'Elm', *Collected Poems*, p. 192.
18. Sylvia Plath, 'Ariel', *ibid.*, p. 239.
19. Sylvia Plath, 'Edge', *ibid.*, p. 272.
20. Seamus Heaney, 'The Grauballe Man', *North*, p. 29.
21. Syvia Plath, 'Poem for a Birthday', *Collected Poems*, p. 136.
22. Seamus Heaney, 'Hercules and Antaeus', *North*, p. 47.
23. Sylvia Plath, 'The Burnt-Out Spa, *Collected Poems*, p. 138.
24. Seamus Heaney, 'Punishment', *North*, p. 30.
25. Sylvia Plath, 'Cut', *Collected Poems*, p. 235.
26. Sylvia Plath, 'Poem for a Birthday', *ibid.*, p. 133.
27. Seamus Heaney, 'Kinship', *North*, p. 36.
28. Seamus Heaney, ''Exposure', *ibid.*, p. 68.
29. Seamus Heaney, 'The Indefatigable Hoof-Taps: Sylvia Plath' in *The Government of the Tongue*, p. 162
30. Sylvia Plath, 'Nick and the Candlestick', *Collected Poems*, p. 240.
31. Sylvia Plath, 'Getting There', *ibid.*, p. 248.
32. Maurice Harmon, ' "We pine for ceremony": Ritual and Reality in the Poetry of Seamus Heaney, 1965-1975' in Elmer Andrews ed. *Seamus Heaney: A Collection of Critical Essays* (London: Macmillan, 1992), 67-86, p. 77.
33. Sylvia Plath, 'Berck-Plage', *Collected Poems*, p. 199.
34. Seamus Heaney, 'Funeral Rites', *North*, p. 7.
35. Edna Longley, ' "North": "Inner Émigré" or "Artful Voyeur"?' in Tony Curtis ed. *The Art of Seamus Heaney* 4th ed., 1st ed. 1982 (Bridgend: Seren, 2001) pp. 65-95, p. 85.
36. Harmon, ' "We pine for ceremony" ', p. 78.
37. Helen Vendler, *Seamus Heaney* (Cambridge, Mass.: Harvard University Press, 1998), p. 4.
38. *ibid.*, p. 45.
39. *ibid.*, p. 49.
40. Neil Corcoran, *The Poetry of Seamus Heaney: A Critical Study* (London: Faber, 1998), pp. 70-1
41. *ibid.*, p. 51.
42. John Wilson Foster, *The Achievement of Seamus Heaney,* (Dublin: Lilliput, 1995), p. 33.
43. Patricia Coughlan, ' "Bog Queens": The Representation of Women in the Poetry of John Montague and Seamus Heaney' in Michael Allen ed. *Seamus Heaney* (London: Macmillan, 1997), pp. 185-205, p. 200.
44. *ibid.*, p. 200.
45. Edna Longley, *op.cit.*, p. 79.

JOHN BURNSIDE: THE CORPSE AS THRESHOLD

The poems of this century and of the last are populated to an unusual degree by corpses. The standard way to account for this – to point to the literary impact of two world wars – is also a strong one. An explanatory thread can usefully be drawn – and has been drawn by such critics as Paul Fussell, Edna Longley, and Fran Brearton – from the poets of the first world war to those of the second. The same line can usefully be extended to laureates, reluctant or not, of other violent conflicts. More specifically, a loose literary genealogy may be traced in which poems like Keith Douglas's 'Vergissmeinnicht', Sylvia Plath's 'Lady Lazarus', Ted Hughes's 'View of a Pig', Seamus Heaney's 'The Grauballe Man' and Paul Muldoon's 'The More a Man Has the More a Man Wants' are helpfully related.

When pondering the legacy of past bloodshed, we might argue that corpses force their way in to literary structures, but, in truth, poets and their poems rarely offer resistance. The presence of a dead body in any art-work is always a convenient exploitation, a fact no less diminished by the feeling that it is the last thing one ought to exploit. For poets, the dead offer many advantages. Around a corpse it is possible to build an especially dramatic object-poem, in which the writer's gifts are centred on a single, immobile target. By prompting implicit questions about the afterlife, a corpse may serve, too, as a screen for the author's patterns of belief. In staging their metaphysical agonies, twentieth-century poets have gathered their share of cadaverous props. From a long list of examples, one could adduce Lowell's 'A Quaker Graveyard in Nantucket', Jarrell's 'The Death of the Ball-Turret Gunner', Berryman's 'Dream Song 384', Jorie Graham's 'At Luca Signorelli's Resurrection of the Body', and Auden's 'Musée des Beaux Arts'. In the last case, the double marginalisation, in painting and in poem, of Icarus descending may be taken to say that we humans too easily disregard suffering. That is a reasonable reading, of course. But another way to read the conclusion is as a commentary on the exploitation, by art, of suffering. Auden may be hinting that on the margins of an artwork is not a bad place for corpses to be.

In this chapter, where I explore the uses to which corpses are put in the poetry of John Burnside, many of the above considerations are echoed and illustrated. As any reading of the Scottish poet's canon is bound to conclude, the trajectory of his writing has been towards ever more ambitious, ever more public, modes of significance. Like many other writers in this book, Burnside, as his career has prospered and borne fruit, has felt a pressure to accommodate himself towards the public sphere. With some determination, his work has sought to locate itself on a public map of significance, dutifully behaving in a manner which we expect from canonical writing. His treatment of dead bodies – animal as well as human – may be read against a quest for what can only be called 'importance'.

We encounter a typical Burnside corpse in 'Wrong', a poetic sequence which explores, in somewhat dislocated fashion, the growth from childhood of a psychopath. In the third section, the speaker reflects on a discovery made, presumably by his parents or by workmen, in an obscure part of the family home:

> that substance they found one winter, tucked in the flue,
> all shinbone and whiskers, and nothing they could have named
> with its winglike arms and a blue, almost questioning face,
> a stitchwork of horsehair and mortar to hold it together,
> mislaid all its life in a gap between snowfall and cinders.[1]

Discoveries of this sort recur in his poetry. As is usual in such cases, the entity has an air of incompleteness, and the speaker, by contemplating it, offers an implicit self-commentary. The voice, seemingly on the brink of trailing off, is consistent with the resigned, near-liturgical tone which the poet favours. The compound nouns evoke a being which is held together by little more than words, suggesting that the lines themselves are its last hope of resurrection. Meanwhile, the author takes the opportunity provided by this find – well, *of what* exactly? – for some sonorous description. As I intend to show later, we are not far from those pressing metaphysical questions of identity in Heaney's 'The Grauballe Man': "Who will say 'corpse'/ to his vivid cast?/Who will say 'body'/ to his opaque repose?"[2]

The propulsion behind Burnside's writing derives from a damaged early family life, which, as his autobiography vividly describes, was variously afflicted by drink, poverty, the death of a sister, and the cruelty of a deeply inadequate father. It is not too much of a leap to conclude (Burnside all but concludes it himself) that these formative pressures are loosely translated by the poems into a set of

linked obsessions with the skin, 'the soul', language and violence. The
body, to this poet, is a precarious thing, and his writing is sensitive to
what we might call, 'the swirl beneath the skin'. Typical in this respect
is 'Vanishing Twin', in which the speaker attempts to re-imagine (or
to re-incarnate) his missing sibling:

> She bled away. But sometimes I wake in the dark
> and feel her with me, breathing through the sheets,
> or I turn in the shimmer of day
> and catch her out:
>
> my opposite, though still identical,
> she's reaching down to haul me from a web
> of birthmarks, age lines, scars beneath the skin.[3]

Burnside, who is generally in favour of all kinds of continuity,
asserts the ongoing presence of the dead through a kind of continuum
of the skin. In his poetry, the flesh is soft, mobile, uncontrollable –
always sliding away to those other shapes it might have assumed,
towards those other people we might have been. In a literary culture
which is used to stressing concepts of otherness and difference,
Burnside's poetry makes an odd plea for oneness and identity, for
same as finale of seem.

Burnside has published eleven collections of poetry, as well as
eight novels, a very high rate of activity for a middle-aged poet. With
his sibling's death (real and re-imagined) at its centre, his canon, like
Plath's or Berryman's, has the air of something produced urgently,
compulsively – as if it were an exorcism. While the level of industry
is formidable, it may also be misleading. Burnside is not a wide-
ranging poet, indeed his artistic 'comfort zone' is relatively small.
Many of his poems seem like drafts of one another, or like the drafts
of some remote master-poem which we never get to see. For example,
in *A Normal Skin*, an altogether representative collection, one poem
describes "a black light, angelic and cold". Twenty pages later,
another contains the phrase, "The light is angelic and black" – and
then the whole formula is repeated a few lines later.[4] Partly because
of such conspicuous repetition and partly because Burnside has
published so much within a relatively short space of time, it is hard
to divide his poetry into finely defined phases. Some of the poems in
his first book, *The Hoop*, would not be out of place in *The Hunt in the
Forest* and vice versa. Nevertheless, in this chapter, I do want to make
a broad distinction between his early and late work, a distinction

which will largely turn on how Burnside comes to universalise his
private experiences.

Burnside's autobiographical account of his troubled upbringing,
A Lie about My Father, provides a valuable, if severe, background for
a reading of his poetry. Burnside grew up in a working-class family
in Cowdenbeath. His father, the memoir's dominant figure, was a
sometimes violent alcoholic, a brickie's assistant, who liked to obscure
his personal failures with extravagant fantasies in the manner of
Walter Mitty. By contrast, Burnside's mother was a sensitive, long-
suffering woman who did what she could to soften the impact of her
husband's dysfunction. Escaping his unhappy life at home, the young
Burnside took refuge in his imagination. Throughout his autobiog-
raphy, (which, we are warned, contains elements of fiction) the
writer's creative powers are shown coming under unbearable
pressure, both to shield the author from a malignant parent and to
provide a forlorn substitute for everything he feels to be missing. In
the same way that his father, a foundling (an abandoned child who
was passed around different families as he grew up) had to cope with
the physical absence of his parents, Burnside's childhood was haunted
by the early death of his sister, Elizabeth. The boy's suffering was
increased by his father's habit of wishing aloud that Elizabeth, rather
than her brother, had survived. So accustomed did the young
Burnside become to the cruel sting of this taunt, that he evolved a
counter-narrative which, on such occasions, he would silently artic-
ulate to himself. When interpreted against this tragic background it
is not hard to understand why the writer's mind gave birth to an
imaginary brother. This is the act of creation which Burnside refers
to as 'the myth of the twin' (it forms the title of one of his collections):

> In one form or another, I would keep him by me all my life, my soul-
> friend, my other self. He would continue where I left off, and I would live
> for him, tuned in to the rhythm of an otherworld that nobody else could
> hear; a whole kingdom of ghost brothers, hidden in the dark.[5]

The title of one Burnside poem – 'Everything Is Explained By
Something That Happened In Childhood' – states one presumption
which they share. It also suggests another: that everything can be
explained by the perspective of a child. Reflecting the conflicts in his
own family, Burnside's early work records a kind of one-sided 'War
against the Grown-ups' and, as a consequence, divides between two
worlds. The first of these worlds, which is much less prominent, is
roughly coterminous with an adult sensibility, while the second world,

which almost completely dominates the first and in which most of
the poems dwell, is roughly associated with the imaginative life of
boyhood. The first world is hazily populated by a 'we' while the
second is squarely occupied by an 'I'. Both worlds are static and are
often evoked by verbless descriptions. Within them the range of action
portrayed is mainly of a habitual nature, which, in the first, a matter
of tedious routine, and in the second, is a matter of thrilling ritual.

Cyclical, obsessive, full of repetitions and returns, Burnside's
canon can be described, with only a slight risk of over-statement, as
one giant poem choosing to reveal itself in slightly different ways.
Such a convergence is consistent with the poet's unashamed Platon-
ism. In the ur-Burnside poem, his monism makes itself known
through a multitude of signs, but principally through the bodies of
the dead. As with discarded bottles, batteries, birds' nests and swing-
tyres (the bric-a-brac of the exploring child), so with bone, hair,
ligaments, and teeth. All the iron filings of incidental detail are myste-
riously magnetised towards the One. The relevant ontological arrows
are not, however, visible at all places or all times. The speaker of the
ur-poem perceives them only intermittently, as he travels through his
favoured liminal zones, – allotments, side-roads, abandoned build-
ings, river-banks, out-of-season resorts. Violence, as in the poetry of
Ted Hughes, is a handmaid to heightened perception and, in the ur-
poem, glows with an ambiguous benevolence, always with the
implication that to break the skin of another may open a path to a
higher reality.

A good candidate for the ur-Burnside poem is 'A Stolen Child',
which appears in what may be his most pivotal book, *Swimming in
the Flood* (1995):

My father would say
I belonged to someone else:
the fairies had come in the night, invading his house
with spells, and the mouse-smell of hemlock.

And I would go out at dusk
to the edge of the world,
finding the snow-flavoured gaps
in the swimming barley
and searching for the palace of the king

who might be disguised as a tramp, in an old black coat,
bobbing for mice and hedgehogs in the weeds
and changing them into the semblance

of children, to fill his house
with pockets of warmth, games for the cold to enjoy.[6]

This displays many of the Scottish poet's most characteristic touches. Framed by the sharp, if inexplicable, hostility between the father and the child, the second, corrective part of the poem retreats into an imagined world, which, in its way, is as mesmerizingly dangerous as the Yeatsian escape to "the waters and the wild." With an air of disassociated intimacy, the poem's flatness is itself a sign of withdrawal – what the child articulates is not so much a way of thinking as it is a way of coping. The mutability of the body is a source of vital fascination and substitutes, in a softly terrifying way, the corpse for the child. Another typical feature, too, is the blank description of the boy's home – it hangs on, just about, in the middle distance – compared with the carefully specific description of the liminal area. In the final phrases, there is a tang of cruelty, a flavour which appears to capture, in displaced fashion, the violence of the father's disregard. Overall, the poem is a quest, an impossible search for a king who could serve as an alternative father. But where the quest ends, and what the boy at the end of the poem actually finds, is a deadly, indifferent life-force which is ultimately inseparable from the personalised 'cold' of the final line.

Children often explore corporeal limits – plucking the wings off butterflies and the like – but throughout this poem, and others of its kind, the obsession with mutilation and mortality is altogether more keen. Childhood, here, is not only bound up with corpses, it is itself changed into a kind of corpse. Novalis once had it that chaos, in the work of art, should shimmer behind the veil of order. In Burnside's variation on this, the body is a veil behind which an uncertain order shimmers. Spurred on by the chaos of his circumstances, the poet's childhood self seeks out those punctured bodies from which a kind of order seeps. Because the bloodjet, for him, is poetry, so the world is more full of weeping than he can understand. Or, as Burnside, in 'A Normal Skin', would put it sharply:

What we desire in pain
is order, the impression of a life
that cannot be destroyed, only dismantled.[7]

In the rest of this chapter, I propose to chart Burnside's career, and in particular to make what I hope is a useful distinction between his early and late work. Partly, that division is centred on a gradual convergence of the two worlds of his early poetry. After all, it is hard to maintain a War against the Grown-Ups, the longer that you are one. As his writing developed, Burnside made ever more serious attempts to escape from the claustrophobic, if fascinating, privacy of his early work.

§

In his debut book, *The Hoop*, the world of adults was evoked by a prematurely aged, exhausted voice which roughly derived from the Movement: "We live against the silence of/ imagined bears...", "We have been lost/ in our own house for years... ".[8] In reducing the adult world to a tedious, even repellent, form of make-believe, the book is conventional. Much post-war, post-imperial British poetry has regarded the society by which it is surrounded as a creative drawback – all the more so when thinking of the 'opportunities' for poets elsewhere, in Northern Ireland, say, or in Eastern Europe. In *The Society of the Poem*, Jonathan Raban has written about this curiously torpid phase in British poetry, arguing that, in the wake of the Movement, a significant number of poets accepted the daily rituals of the post-war world as nearly sufficient for the inner life:

> The imprints of the same mass images, the same commuting time-schemes, the same communal hopes and neuroses, have given our lives so many shared versions of order and metaphor that the poet's work is almost done for them.[9]

Because Burnside's early work, like that of Ted Hughes, was a sharp reaction to such acceptance, he allowed his private secondary world – with its fantasies of boyhood and adolescence – to overrun the supposedly sensible public domain of adults. An early example of childhood sovereignty appears in 'The Game of Finding'. Alone and at home, the young speaker is on alert for elusive presences in empty rooms:

> That game of finding someone in the house,
> of stopping dead and listening for steps
> behind a door. Only a game,
> until the make-believe insinuates
> a form. Or I pretend
> something has just melted from the room
> when I walk in, sensing the pinprick chill
> of kindred skin.[10]

Childhood, here, is animal, irrational, and instinctual. Poems of this type frequently try to give their readers "verbal gooseflesh" (to borrow a phrase from Seamus Heaney.) There is often an appeal to a sixth sense, (the sense we have of someone looking at us when our back is turned, or of registering a special moment which will stay with us). Subverting the adult world by such means does not, however, mean that the speaker is in control. By the end of the poem, his gothic projections acquire an ominous solidity, "fast becoming teeth and eyes." This reminds us that, at heart, the speaker's condition is one of powerlessness. Lacking poise and self-possession, he opposes the public world not with bursts of youthful energy but with the lonely excitement of his own erasure.

In *A Lie about My Father*, Burnside persuades us that his own grinding descent into substance abuse was an attempt to block out unbearable experiences[11]. Such a process of 'blocking out' is matched in his poems by a kind of widely applied, almost indiscriminate, blindness. Employment of this mobile, thoroughly flexible screen is curiously balanced by the kind of highly focussed close-ups which initially attract the reader. Although the setting of the poems is nearly always contemporary, vast areas of life as we know it are kept firmly out of view. While piling up a series of symbols – angels, mermaids, corpses – the meanings of which are implacably private, his second world attempts to blot out the mass images to which we are half-addicted. But it is not just the background hum of the media which his work moves to suppress. Other "shared versions of order and metaphor" which derive from the Land of the Grown-Ups – pub-quizzes, weddings, elections, and tax returns – are either completely excluded or else quietly drained of all significance.

Because of the rich link between landscape and adventure, children's books – *Watership Down, The Lord of the Rings, Swallows and Amazons* – often place their faith in maps. It is tempting to imagine Burnside's secondary childhood world, which, in its insular grotesqueries has some kinship to *Lord of the Flies*, as if drawn on parchment. In reading the poems we have the impression, however haphazard, of a guided tour: here, on the left is My House, there on the right is the Wall of the Angel, behind the trees is the Ivy Gargoyle, and across the bridge is the Corpse of the Weasel. The various symbolic points, like home-made pylons, are arranged within humming distance of each other. This system of mapping is crucial because it verifies the child's alternative order, enlarging the occasional arbitrary secret into a firm pattern of significance.

Moreover, the child's habit of cultivating a psychic geography is a way of confirming himself in the face of the world. In his autobiography, Burnside reflects on this:

> In those days, being a child was all about navigation. At eight years of age, my entire body was a map, a nerve chart of dogs and fruit trees, and the places where bottles might be found, to be rinsed out later and redeemed at Brewster's for a penny or two. My homeward routes were records of the movements of bullies, of teachers and priests, of beautiful strangers.[12]

As with 'the parochial eye' of Glyn Maxwell's poetry, such a survey of the local and secret is critically defined by where it stops. Although hoarding all that is prized by the child, the map is, at the same time, intended to exclude. Everything lying beyond its boundaries is enthusiastically shrouded. Hence nearly all Burnside's early poems have a curious mixture of sharp definition and strategic vagueness. Lifting their eyes from yet another childhood revelation, readers are faced with the melting turbulence of an Impressionist landscape – such phrases as "a cold rain fuzzing the trees", "ghost rain fuzzing the leaves", "the midsummer distance where towns dissolve", "this washed infinity", "the blur/ of bricks and glass", "this blur of heat".[13]

Mainly because of his father's compulsive fantasising, Burnside's memoir presses itself against a network of falsehoods. Epistemologically troubled, by what we know and don't know, the drama of *A Lie about My Father* is always hinged on recognition and realisation. At the verbal level, this is reflected by the repetition of some closely-related formulae. The opening sentence is an example: "My father told lies all his life and, because I knew no better, I repeated them."[14] At one of the key moments in the book, while his mother lies dying in hospital, the young man confronts his father at home:

> 'Does she know?' I asked.
> He shook his head, 'No' he said 'And she's not going to know, either.'

As this conversation goes on, the father attends to the dishes in a strange manner, washing and drying each one in turn. When Burnside remarks that it would be quicker to wash the lot and then to dry them, the father, with pointed satisfaction, replies, "Do you think I don't know that?"[15] A further example of the motif occurs earlier in the book. The fifteen-year old Burnside encounters a barfly in the local pub. This man, who will later get into a brawl with

Burnside's father, attempts to forewarn the son. Unable to grasp the point of the exchange, the boy naively offers to buy him a drink:

> He almost smiled. I was fifteen years old, and he knew it. I had no idea what I was doing, but I was putting on the most convincing act I could manage, and he knew that too. Trouble was, he was doing the same thing – and, at that moment, I knew that too.[16]

As the book unfolds, passages which turn on the concept of knowledge grow more numerous: "We knew enough to know that it wasn't the usual game played by boys and girls ...", "All the time, I knew something else was there, waiting to arrive and touch me." "My mother knew, at some level, what was going on, but she had no way of putting it into words; or if she did, my father would pretend he didn't understand."[17] Perhaps the most dramatic of all the moments in the book is the one of aborted parricide. Having determined to kill his father in an ambush, Burnside arms himself with a knife and lurks in the darkness:

> To know that I wanted to do it, even if I couldn't see it through – that mattered. I knew I hated him, and I knew I was too sensible, or too much of a coward to act. But it still mattered. It was a piece of knowledge I needed to possess.[18]

Knowledge is then a useful category to bear in mind when reading Burnside's work, although it is better regarded from a psychological, rather than a philosophical, point of view. This is because its presence in the poems has more to do with control than it does with understanding. The motif also helps to explain Burnside's occasional dabbling with the rhetoric of science. Rather than the tedium of observing and recording, what excites him most about scientific endeavour is the part with the greatest emotional pay-off: the act of discovery. In Burnside's aesthetic, every can is full of worms, every box contains a Jack.

Hovering between the physical and the metaphysical, the intellectual drift of the Scottish poet's work could be described as an attempt to look behind life, in the way that one might open a clock-face and scrutinise the quietly wriggling mechanisms. In this regard, the poems often depict curiously literal attempts to see and touch Life Itself. The seventh part of the sequence 'A Process of Separation', for instance, deals with the poet's typical fascination for an animal corpse, as a knacker takes it apart:

I've watched him skin a carcass in the yard:
skilful and unrepentant, drenched in blood,
he scattered the wet remains across the earth
and entered them, becoming what he killed.
Once I reached in and touched the smoking lungs,
the barrel of the ribs, the cooling heart.[19]

The perspective adopted here may remind the reader of some of Seamus Heaney's work – the mix of sensuousness and fear in 'Death of A Naturalist', for example, or the ambiguous mode of reflection in 'Strange Fruit'. Confronted by a scene which might ordinarily be expected to cause repulsion, the author's pattern of thought unexpectedly shifts into involvement. Such evidence of influence in Burnside's work is not unusual. Quite often, individual lines, stanzas, whole sections of his poems strongly remind the reader of other writers – in particular Hughes, Heaney, Longley and Hill. Nevertheless, his poems tend to redeem themselves with the idiosyncrasy of their underlying vision – locally derivative, yes, but globally original.

In 'A Process of Separation', as in other poems, the physical activity of working with a corpse is implicitly equated with the literary activity of describing one. To dissect, to inter, to butcher, to embalm – such procedures, which are celebrated as technical accomplishments, are set down beside what the poet's technique accomplishes. In *The Hunt in the Forest*, a poem about a dead badger, 'Uley Blue', is immediately followed by 'Poppy Day', a poem describing the work of a butcher. In the latter, it is notable how the speaker regards the cutting up of a carcass through the prism of the butcher's technical mastery. The poet's own technical capacity is thereby linked to an activity which, from at least some points of view, is morally questionable:

Out on the kill floor, veiled in a butterslick
circumflex of marrowfat and bone,
he rinses off the knife and goes to work,
his voice so sweet, the children come to hear

the beauty of it, ...[20]

In the introduction to this chapter I offered a few reasons for the prevalence of corpses in 20th century poetry. Burnside's technical treatment of corpses brings to mind another of these, one which encourages me to use a critical metaphor from the work of Richard Rorty – that of 're-description'.

In his philosophical writing, especially *Contingency, Irony and Solidarity*, Rorty associates the activity of re-description with a developing phase of modernity in the nineteenth century. In his view our increasing ability to speak of the same thing in different ways had the effect of undermining various meta-narratives, discouraging us from thinking that there could be one ultimate description of everything:

> ... it somehow became possible toward the end of the nineteenth century, to take the activity of redescription more lightly than it had ever been take before. It became possible to juggle several descriptions of the same event without asking which one was right – to see redescription as a tool rather than a claim to have discovered essence. It thereby became possible to see a new vocabulary not as something which was supposed to replace all other vocabularies, something which claimed to represent reality, but simply as one more vocabulary, one more human project, one's person's chosen metaphoric.[21]

Naturally, when the clash of descriptions concerns a dead body the stakes are raised. Hence we can read the questions asked by Heaney's speaker in 'The Grauballe Man' as drawing attention to just such an issue. Similarly, we can read the collision of world-views, of disciplines, of languages, in various well-known poetic descriptions of corpses – one thinks, for example, of Keith Douglas's 'Vergissmeinnicht' where the technical accomplishment of the British sniper is opposed to the emotional attachment of a German girl:

> Look. Here in the gunpit spoil
> the dishonoured picture of his girl
> who has put: *Steffi*. Vergissmeinnicht
> in a copybook gothic script.[22]

And this kind of tonal opposition may be traced back further, for example, to the clinical detachment which has been so much remarked in Auden's earliest poetry ("Brought in now,/ Love lies at surgical extremity;/ Gauze pressed over the mouth, a breathed surrender.")[23]

Burnside's use of re-description has a special flavour because it reverses the logic of Rorty's argument. Rather than cancelling the need for a meta-narrative, the facility of re-description, for the Scottish poet, seems to require the consolation of one. Because intellectual coherence is, for a poem, merely an effect (and a thoroughly dispensable one) his poetry can tolerate the fizz and glow of this seeming contradiction. Indeed the tension created by this pattern of

thinking helped to sustain his fifth book, *Swimming In The Flood*.
There one finds much of his strongest work: the title-poem, 'Science',
the first and last parts of the sequence 'Burning A Woman', 'Parousia',
and 'Hypothesis'. The latter poem concludes with some of his most
memorable and mysterious lines:

> ... waking will sometimes resemble
> the sudden precision of gunshots out in the field,
> when the woods are immersed
> in a clear and improbable dawn,
>
> and traces everywhere of what is risen:
> bonemeal and horsehair, a fingerprint etched in the dust,
> whatever it is that fades when we enter a room,
> leaves only the glitter of brass, and the gloved noise of water.[24]

In that weirdly effective final cadence, "the gloved noise of water",
Burnside captures his obsession with containers (like the body), with
hidden but active presences (water in a pipe), and with the scientific
handling of objects (scientists in gloves). Through this kind of privi-
leged epiphany, we are fleetingly aware of an underlying, receding
oneness, even as it its apparent agent, the water's voice, is muffled.

At once pointing to his forays into the novel, and anticipating his
later poetic style, *Swimming in the Flood* is notable for its use of
dramatic characters. Often these characters are difficult to distinguish
from each other and make themselves known through hazy but
menacing monologues. The main benefit of this technical expansion
is that the poems are allowed to inhabit new, more adult areas. Thanks
to these extra poetic tools, Burnside is able to extend the 'play-acting'
of childhood into unexpected areas. Poems which benefit from this
treatment often pair narrative uncertainty with sudden close-ups of
sinister action. Into the resulting expository vagueness there flow such
elements as causality, psychology, and history, while into the various
close-ups (clearly favoured by the writer) swim such elements as
surface-texture, sensuality, and technical prowess. The back and forth
between these two modes has a spotted effect, making some of the
poems seem wooden and vital by turns.

We find a fairly typical example of these inconsistencies in
'Wrong', a poem divided into sections, which appears to be distrib-
uted amongst different speaking voices. In its first section we are
introduced to an individual who appears to be a psychopath, while
in the second section, at a seemingly later date, we encounter someone

who may have been his victim. The first monologue is relatively focused, while the second is more fluid, uncertainly reflecting on the violent crime. The resulting effect might be contrasted with Heaney's 'Strange Fruit', where the Irish poet manufactures a moral 'turn'. In that poem the speaker remonstrates with himself for enjoying the appearance of a corpse, even though it is the language of enjoyment which gives the writing its charge. When Heaney switches to the language of self-reproof, it comes across as an unhappy, and mechanical, compromise. Burnside's poem, likewise, has its mechanical moments. For instance, the poem seems to begin more than once:

A swallowed nail. A trick with razor blades.

Round the allotments, four in the afternoon,
October: I was gouging out a face,
A jack-a-lantern's grin of candlelight, ...[25]

Here, one might guess that the first, startling line, verblessly set apart, represents a separate stage in the process of composition. The second and third lines contain most of the 'boring' exposition – they 'have to' be there – but since they would make for a dull beginning, Burnside supplies a startling one-line preamble. Although the verbless sentences appear to invite some kind of psychological interpretation, the poem is actually keen to show where understanding fails, gesturing towards mental states which the writer cannot penetrate. The switchblade, in this case, is mightier than the pen. The poem's evident fascination with death is also a fascination with the possible end of words and this is the point, paradoxically, where the language most comes alive. When the miscreant describes his lair, the diction starts to sparkle, suggesting that, in his case, the end of art is psychosis:

– that was my shed, my bunker, that smell of grease
and sacking, shrivelled tubers, rows of shrouded jars,
permethrin and flowers of sulphur,
phoxim and derris, rat poison's prussic blues, ...[26]

Reading these lines one can immediately sense that the writer is on home turf. As the use of a necrophiliac vocabulary becomes ecstatically technical, the diction celebrates the self's omnipotence in a territory which it has made its own. After this early climax, the second section of the poem loses pressure. The monologue accorded to the victim appears to provide 'moral cover' for the poet, as though to say, psychopathic behaviour may make for some intriguing lines of verse, but we mustn't forget the moral consequences of what may follow. The exposition becomes perfunctory. The victim strays into a public festival involving bands, clowns, and dancing – a child's version of the public world – and, after the damaging, but non-fatal, attack the section ends with a typical Burnside blur.

The gravitational pull of violence, felt throughout Burnside's work, is more than just an enlivening literary trope. *A Lie About My Father* goes a long way to explaining the recurrence of this theme. At various points in his memoir the author portrays himself as dangerously anti-social – for example during a phase where he experimented with arson. Encouragement was provided by one of his peers:

> Like me, he'd grown tired of the little fires we'd been making, and gone out on his own, riding around on a bike looking for things to burn. Once he'd found a disused hut next to an old railway line; after he'd set it alight, he'd taken photographs of the blaze with his mother's camera. He showed me the pictures. They weren't expert, but they were moving.[27]

We might contrast Burnside's poetic deployments of psychosis with another contemporary example: Carol Ann Duffy's well-known poem, 'Psychopath' ("One thump did it, then I was on her,/ giving her everything I had. Jack the Lad, Ladies Man.")[28] In both cases popular clichés about these near-ubiquitous cultural icons – we are never far from the cinematic territory of *A Clockwork Orange*, say, or *Friday the 13th* – are forced uneasily through dramatic monologues. The major difference between the two approaches is that Duffy leaves the reader in no doubt about what she finally thinks – her psychopath is damaged and his behaviour is wrong. Burnside, by contrast, leaves a reader to wonder what he really thinks.

The figure of the psychopath is also represented in Burnside's fiction, a particularly sharp example being provided by his novel, *The Dumb House*. Most of the book's drawbacks, in terms of plot, characterisation, and dialogue, can be traced to the artificially insulated world which Burnside wants to create. *The Dumb House* is a first-person narrative told by Luke, an intelligent but antisocial young man, who is strangely dominated by his mother, and obsessed by the way language is, or is not, acquired. He is especially fascinated by mute individuals. After his obsessions draw him into the orbit of several maladjusted characters, he meets a homeless girl called Lillian, with whom he has an affair. Lillian bears twins – and then conveniently dies. This gives Luke, who becomes increasingly detached from social norms, the opportunity to perform a perverse experiment whereby the twins are raised in an environment sealed off from human speech.

Many of the main character's obsessions, with corpses, with language, with a fantasy landscape, are those which are pursued in Burnside's poems. Although Luke, who shows himself capable of murder and torture, evidently cares little for moral norms, he is surprisingly zealous about promoting one cultural norm: the cause of science. It is with respect to this subject that the narrator sounds at his least convincing, lapsing every so often into Mad Scientist mode: "Throughout history, the important discoveries were made by those who ventured upon the unspeakable." "... for a moment, I had looked into life itself, and I knew that, one day, I would discover its essence." Given that Burnside's sensibility is more taken by words than by sentences, it is little surprise that the novel has almost no memorable dialogue. Whereas Burnside's tone may often be conversational, he struggles in his writing to represent conversation. The novel, which is supposedly pursuing the subject of the acquisition of language seems oblivious to the fact that language largely reflects the existence, and history, of a wider community.

All the minor characters in *The Dumb House* are as rootless and untraceable as possible – vagrants, misfits who have no inconvenient relatives. This means that the plot does not have to detail a potentially complicated, and complicating, social background. Luke has no obvious trade or special skill and he seems entirely unbothered by this state of affairs. Whenever he wants to perform a technical task, he simply undertakes some research at the local library, so that, by the end of the book, he has read a sufficient number of medical textbooks to perform a laryngotomy. Everything, as in a dream, is somehow to hand: tape machines, video recorders, surgical masks – whatever the central character needs to further his experiment. Like any fantasy of control, the book becomes increasingly frictionless. This extends to the motif of long car-journeys (these always have a special status in Burnside's writing) which grant the driver a kind of existential elevation: "I managed to create an illusion of floating, of being detached from the human world a casual visitor, not necessarily of the same species." Although *The Dumb House* is supposed to work by demonstrating how close the author is to being a psychopath, it might have been improved by showing just how far he is from being one.

§

If Burnside's early work is an attempt to think and feel exclusively on his own terms, the change which gradually overtakes his writing, and which, roughly speaking, allows us to separate it into early and late phases, is marked by attempts to think and feel on terms which are not his own. This change may be discerned around the time of *A Normal Skin*, and its follow-up, *The Asylum Dance*. In those books, Burnside shows signs of engaging with the adult world in a more socialised manner. *A Normal Skin*, for example, contains a noticeable number of poems about neighbours, and there are some fragile portraits of a normal, Grown-Up life, In poems like 'Epithalamium', 'Agoraphobia', and 'Snake', Burnside's monism begins to extend itself from bodies which are dead or dying to those which have a viable pulse. A quotation from Plato placed at the beginning of the book seems apposite: "And if the soul, too, my dear Alcibiades, is to know itself, it must surely look into a soul."

We might think of the way Burnside came to handle the public world with the assistance of some of Harold Bloom's categories of poetic influence. If we replace the influence of a strong precursor, as laid out in Bloom's theory, with the influence of the public sphere, then Burnside's early poems seem to me good examples of the tropes of *clinamen* and *kenosis*. In order to achieve an isolate sufficiency, Burnside's early poems swerve away (clinamen) from the public sphere and empty it out (kenosis). His later poems, by contrast, seem to me good examples of the tropes of *tessera* and *apophrades*. With these motifs, Burnside attempts to complete the public sphere (tessera) or finds that he has been inside it all along (apophrades). Rather than isolating himself from the public sphere, Burnside, in his later work, imagines himself as its true embodiment. I think these Bloomean categories are all the more useful here because Burnside centres the Oedipal struggle within his own family on the tactic of the lie. His poetry illustrates well one of Bloom's points about the development of the poet in which troping is associated with lying:

> A trope is a willing error, a turn from literal meaning in which a word or phrase is used in an improper sense, wandering from its rightful place. A trope is therefore a kind of falsification, because every trope (like every defense, which is similarly a falsification) is necessarily an interpretation, and so a mistaking. Put another way, a trope resembles those errors about life that Nietzsche says are necessary for life.[29]

Throughout *The Asylum Dance*, the voice is resolutely adult – its modulated neutrality capable of sounding wistful, tense, exhausted – but now the poems have been converted to the religion which Burnside has made of his childhood experience. We find evidence for this in 'Blue', a nostalgic poem much-influenced by painting. Here childhood experience adheres to the remembered 'blueness' of towns, and shades off into an ambiguously evoked collective – a childhood which belongs to Burnside but perhaps to us as well:

> The way we found ourselves
> in waiting rooms and
> haberdashers' shops
> gone strange in the blue of it: fish-scaled with souls of ink;
> the way we stood for hours
> in the town museum,
> watching that bowl of cinquecento fruit
> the painter had sickened with rot ...[30]

These ink-coloured impressions of childhood, which are crossed with an evocation of decaying fur and rot, may slightly recall Heaney's 'Blackberry-Picking'. Belonging to the world of childhood, the evoked blue is inexplicable, Dionysian, and deeply attractive. It is linked to a thrilling perception of decay, a welcome disorder that may, in turn, be a higher kind of order. It is noticeable how quick Burnside is to separate these remembered perceptions of colour from the symbolism which we associate with organised religion:

> ... in snow-light, walking home from Mass
> we chose it over incense and the singing
> dizziness that made us think of God,
> stepping away from the crib and the noise of bells
> to feel the midnight darkness from the woods
> cooling our faces, pagan and undefiled.[31]

As a metaphysical scheme, this has a Lawrentian crudity which is unpersuasive. As a verbal performance, however, it is sustained by a powerful sense of atmosphere and a usefully murky logic. For the speaker of the poem, it is not so much a matter of choosing paganism over Christianity, or the gold of the fruit against the blue-black of the scabs, as it is a matter of accepting them both. The poem reconciles these apparently competing areas of experience as parts of an all-embracing principle. As the collective pronoun in 'Blue' indicates, the later Burnside likes to use a vague 'we', although it is generally unclear whether it stands for 'I', or for 'myself and the reader', or for 'my selves', or for human beings in general. What is clear, however, is that this 'we' is meant to be an instant unifier, a sign that we are One already, even if we do not know who 'we' are.

In later Burnside, the obsession with corpses is ever more explicitly an obsession with thresholds to the World Beyond. Usually, the poems are content to approach that otherworld through slow, funereal steps, and they always stop well short of arrival. Intriguingly, Burnside manages to reverse the usual spirit-science equation. Instead of the biological body – the body of flesh, blood, and DNA – undermining our belief in another world, the poems contrive to make it seem like a proof. Darwinism, here, is not so much a termination of the world of spirit as it is a point of access. Although Burnside is content to dispense with God he offers us instead a kind of supernatural materialism, where the world of colliding atoms is supplemented by dreams, souls, angels and all manner of categorical uplift.

As they have grown longer, Burnside's poems have grown slower. In seeking to embody the notion that All is One, they have little reason to admit change. Motion becomes ever more unnecessary. Omnipotence within a private sphere (the early poems) is replaced by omniscience within a public one (the later ones) – an exciting doer is replaced by an exhausted seer. The poems more and more seem to suggest that as long as our knowledge has been correctly tuned, as long as we have achieved the right state of mind, there is no need to make action urgent and its nature clear. Richly active foregrounds through which the speaker may pass are subordinated to hazy, static backgrounds. The poems try to swallow reality through serpentine lists which behave like parts of some longer, cosmic catalogue. In 'Surveyors', the second section of 'The Improvable Fact: A Tayside Inventory', we read a typical example:

> sunfish
>   and blue-stemmed grasses
> the tender
>   improbable gold
> of cottonwood
>   the thoughts of others
> music in the dark
>   the ultrasound
> of bats around a pool
> continuous
>   with sunlight on the firth

    the streaming roads
        to Perth or Invercasse
    birchwoods
        and miles of pasture in the rain
    come to a vivid standstill.[32]

Seeking external ratification, the late poems increasingly compare themselves explicitly or implicitly, with examples of other art-forms. In a book where a number of the poems refer to, or are described as being 'after', Edvard Munch, the composition of the above lines is painterly. The effect is strengthened by the use of contrasting colours and the careful flashing backwards and forwards from "sunfish" to "dark" to "sunlight on the firth". This is a good example of the speaker's omniscience. Intended to hint at an underlying unity, this list suggests that everything, however distant, is immediately, if vaguely perceptible. The modifiers for gold, "tender" and "improbable", could readily be applied to the other nouns in the list, for these words are signals as to how we should perceive, symptoms of the onset of all-knowledge. Even as we hear about "the thoughts of others" (without hearing what they are thinking), "music in the dark" (without hearing what is playing) and "the ultrasound of bats" (without knowing what is signalled), the slow pace of the exposition has the air of a medicated calm.

In their transmission of a deliberately willed peace Burnside's later poems seem ever more monastic. This institutionalisation of feeling is evident in the title-poem of *The Asylum Dance*. The poem is a slow narrative, a form perhaps encouraged by the author's ventures into prose. In relatively leisurely fashion, the poem's speaker describes how he liked to travel with his mother to "the asylum", to take part in an annual summer dance. The lack of hurry seems designed to fix the reader within the right state of contemplation:

    At one time, I looked forward to the dance:
    wandering back and forth in the quiet
    heat of an August morning,
    packing the car with cup cakes and lemonade,
    boxes of plums or cherries, petit-fours,
    nuts and spice cake, mousse and vol-au-vents.[33]

Lulled by the middle-class normality of these gentle arrangements, the poem gradually approaches the more uncertain environment of the asylum. The tone remains bright as the interactions between the

well-meaning visitors and the mental patients are described. These
eventually end in a dance. Rather than drawing individual characters,
the aim of the narrative is to combine the more-or-less habitual with
the more-or-less collective. Visitors and patients softly merge. The
continuum of the skin asserts itself in the speaker's closing perception
of the dance, where the force of the imagery suggests that the author
intends a portrait of humanity as a whole:

> ...wisps of movement on a lawn
> at sunset: faces muffled, bodies twined;
> the figures so close to the darkness, they might be
> apparitions, venturing on form,
> pinewoods above the lake, a suggestion of watchers,
> a gap between night and day, between light and shade,
> and faces melting, one into the next
> as if they were all one flesh, in a single dream
> and nothing to make them true, but space, and time.

One way to measure the evolution of Burnside's work is to
compare a fairly typical early work, *The Myth of the Twin*, with a later
more ambitious book, *Gift Songs*. In *The Myth of the Twin*, the poems
scarcely ever go over the page, and most are between ten and twenty
lines long. In *Gift Songs*, however, many of the poems, which are
several pages long, are divided into numbered sections and the book
is split into parts with impressive-sounding names. Whereas *The Myth
of the Twin* has a modest appearance, *Gift Songs* positively burns with
a sense of its own importance – the first section of the latter, for
example, is entitled 'Responses to Augustine of Hippo' and its final
section is even more presumptuously entitled 'Four Quartets'.
Whereas his early poems existed comfortably within the limits of his
own territory, his later poems seem like anxious compromises with
the public sphere, as though the author had hastily concluded a series
of treaties with history, philosophy, and Art. It is true that his later
poetry still contains much attractive diction, but it is increasingly
weighed with categories like 'dream', 'beauty', 'space', and 'time', or
by words with a philosophical character like 'reality'. Whereas
Burnside's early work might bear the title of one of his poems, 'Every-
thing is Explained by Something That Happened in Childhood', the
later poetry might bear the title, 'Everything is Explained by
Something That Happened to John Burnside'.

Another of the presumptuously-titled sections in *Gift Songs* is
entitled 'Varieties of Religious Experience'. The nod to William James

appears to be part of Burnside's advocacy of what he calls a 'free religion', a religion of the present moment. But the peculiar aspect of this reference to the father of pragmatism is that Burnside appears to reverse the pragmatist emphasis on action and experience. Instead of stressing that which makes a difference in a concrete situation (and arranging our categories accordingly) Burnside takes every concrete moment as a chance to invoke the numinous. This pursuit of all-trumping abstractions is of the type which inspired William James, in *Pragmatism*, to one of his more poetic flights:

> Something to support the finite many, to tie it to, to unify and anchor it. Something unexposed to accident, something eternal and unalterable. The mutable in experience must be founded on immutability…. This is the resting deep. We live upon the stormy surface; but with this our anchor holds, for it grapples rocky bottom. This is Wordsworth's "central peace subsisting at the heart of endless agitation"…. This is Reality with the big R, reality that makes the timeless claim, reality to which defeat can't happen.[34]

We see this pursuit at work, for example, in 'Le Croisic', the third of Burnside's 'Four Quartets', its first section bearing the formidable title, 'Sacred'. The poem describes a pleasure port on the west coast of France, where the houses in winter are mostly boarded up. This eerie, out-of-season venue naturally appeals to Burnside and he detects within it an angelic presence, protecting the houses while their owners are away. While the poem has some good concrete moments, it is swallowed by a reality to which defeat can't happen. This occurs when one of the owners returns to his house:

> Nobody sees the angel face to face,
> its mostly induction, a reading of clues and signs
> as, after the fact, he remembers the sea as it was
> on a specified morning, two or three seasons ago:
>
> how something was there, all along,
> in the afternoon light,
> the path leading down to the inlet spotted with vetch
> and orchids, the flex of the sacred
>
> as faint as a faraway voice
> on the shimmering water,
> though all that matters now, in this quiet arrival,
> is learning to live as a guest in the house he inherits;[35]

These lines are not all bad. The concluding idea of being a guest in one's own house is apt, and the phrase "flex of the sacred" has an attractive surprise. But in order to enjoy such moments we are forced to pass through a succession of clichés or near-clichés. To apprehend divinity while staring out to sea is, after all, as void and predictable as hearing the "faraway voice/ on the shimmering water".

By the time of *The Hunt in the Forest*, the slackening of Burnside's style is most apparent.[36] Increasingly, the poems are glazed with respectability, as though finally being frozen by the middle-class, middle-aged values they had once set out to cancel. The collection's sense of purpose is dominated by the public imperative, causing it to appear sagacious, worldly, and learned. A minor sign of this is the prevalence of arty references to visual media. The reader is button-holed with phrases like "that shade of grey// you know from Super-8/ or Danish painting" ('Treatise on the Veil'), "pine trees/ like the trees in Chinese paintings" ('Amor Vincit Omnia'), "damp pinks and pioneer blues, from the age/ of Kodachrome" ('Trappist'), "Awake all night, as the lovers are awake/ in that Godard film where everyone runs forever," ('In Memoriam').[37]

While these forays into other art forms may widen his range of reference, they also constrict his style. Burnside may always have been a poet of corpses, but by *The Hunt in the Forest*, he has become a taxidermist on an industrial scale. A necrophiliac déjà vu settles over the poems. Given that the corpses have the familiarity of old friends, the collection is radiant with the cosiness of a regularly performed ritual, and completely drained of surprise. Having originally found vitality through the adult perspective on a child contemplating death, the poems begin to congeal into an adult perspective on that adult perspective. The opening of the title poem betrays the tiredness of the trope:

> How children think of death is how the shadows
> gather between the trees: a hiding-place
> for everything the grown-ups cannot name.[38]

Rather than playing down the evident similarities to Mahon's 'The Hunt by Night' (also about the Uccello painting, and also the title-poem of a collection) Burnside positively draws attention to it. Curiously, the poem he chooses to shadow is a tired ekphrastic exercise, one which has itself fallen victim to literariness. This makes Burnside's poem seem all the more pallid, a marginal note on a marginal note. It is tempting to read it as a memory, a description of the kind of reward which the hunt for words once afforded the poet, an experience which now takes place at second- or third-hand.

Many years ago I read a newspaper story about a young man who sought attention for a stomach-pain. When the hospital doctors opened him up, they found to their shock a foetus, seven inches long. This quasi-corpse was the man's twin, 'absorbed' long ago in the womb and still surviving off the body of his brother. One detail was particularly grotesque: the entity bore the teeth of a sixteen-year old. Falling squarely into the macabre atmosphere which Burnside favours, this episode might serve as an emblem for his work. Indeed it finds an echo at various points in his canon: The prose-poem, 'Aphasia in Childhood', for example, deals, in part, with Burnside's exploration of woods as a boy and there we come across the following passage:

> ... I was sure, if I dug a few inches deeper, I would find a being which resembled me in every way, except that it would be white and etiolated, like a finger of bindweed growing under stone.[39]

Like some of the best moments in his work, the image has an almost biblical suggestiveness. 'Aphasia in Childhood' well illustrates, amongst other things, how the corpse may be used as a vehicle for self-control, or self-assertion. Here, in his embattled imagination, the young Burnside finds an opportunity to play God with a weaker version of himself. Live, large, and potent, the boy contrasts starkly, and meaningfully, with the discovered creature. I think this is an image which can help us to frame Burnside's work as a whole. In his 'purer' early poems, it is the creative gift, his poetic ability, which allows Burnside to swap his damaged childhood (the corpse) for a position of omnipotence (the imaginative boy). In this context, the poetic gift has a corrective power – it is an effective vehicle for self-transformation. By the time of Burnside's later work, however, the desire to be adult and respectable has, from the point of view of the poetry, succeeded too well. In feeding off each other, the roles of the poet and his poetry are reversed. While the powerful, mature adult poet is now in the position of the living boy, it is the poetry which has become increasingly white and etiolated.

Notes:

1. John Burnside, 'Wrong', *Swimming in the Flood* (London: Cape, 1995), p. 8.
2. Seamus Heaney, 'The Grauballe Man', *Opened Ground* (London: Faber, 1988), p. 116.
3. John Burnside, 'Vanishing Twin', *A Normal Skin,* (London: Cape, 1997) p. 29.
4. John Burnside, 'Agoraphobia', *ibid.*, p. 30.
   John Burnside, 'The House by the Sea', *ibid.*, p. 54.
5. John Burnside, *A Lie About My Father* (London: Vintage, 2007), p. 133.
6. John Burnside, 'A Stolen Child', *Swimming in the Flood,* (London: Cape, 1995), p. 35.
7. John Burnside, 'A Normal Skin', *A Normal Skin*, p. 1.
8. John Burnside, 'Ursa Major' *The Hoop* (Manchester: Carcanet, 1988), p. 32.
   John Burnside, 'Runners' *ibid.*, 30.
9. Jonathan Raban, *The Society of the Poem* (London: Harrap, 1971), p. 70.
10. John Burnside, ''The game of finding', *The Hoop*, p. 14.
11. A sequel to his autobiography, *Waking up in Toytown* was published in 2010. It documents his mid-life struggles with alcoholism and mental illness.
12. John Burnside, *A Lie About My Father*, p. 42.
13. John Burnside, 'Scavenger', *A Normal Skin*, p. 8
   John Burnside, 'Muddy Road by Adam Johnson's House', *ibid.*, p. 16.
   John Burnside, 'The Man who was Answered by his own Self', *ibid.*, p. 19.
   John Burnside, 'Agoraphobia', *ibid.*, p. 30.
   John Burnside, 'Floating', *ibid.*, p. 43.
   John Burnside, 'Heimweh', *ibid.*, p. 46.
14. John Burnside, *A Lie About My Father*, p. 17.
15. John Burnside, *ibid.*, p. 209, p. 210.
16. John Burnside, *ibid.*, p. 156.
17. John Burnside, *ibid.*, p. 54, p. 41, p. 72.
18. John Burnside, *ibid.*, p. 200.
19. John Burnside, 'A Process of Separation', *A Normal Skin*, p. 13.
20. John Burnside, 'Poppy Day', *The Hunt in the Forest,* (London: Cape, 2009), p. 30.
21. Richard Rorty, *Contingency, Irony, and Solidarity,* (Cambridge, CUP, 1989), p. 39.
22. Keith Douglas, 'Vergissmeinnicht, *The Complete Poems* 1st ed. 1978, 3rd ed. (London: Faber, 2000), p. 118.
23. W.H. Auden, 'Because sap fell away', *The English Auden,* (London: Faber, 1986), p. 441.
24. John Burnside, 'Hypothesis', *Swimming in the Flood*, p. 15.
25. John Burnside, 'Wrong', *ibid.*, p. 5.
26. *ibid.*.
27. John Burnside, *A Lie About My Father*, p. 148.
28. Carol Ann Duffy, 'Psychopath', *Selling Manhattan* (London: Anvil, 1987), p. 29.

29. Harold Bloom, *A Map of Misreading*, (Oxford: OUP, 1975) p. 93.

30. John Burnside, 'Blue', *The Asylum Dance*, p. 45.

31. *ibid.*.

32. John Burnside, 'The Unprovable Fact: A Tayside Inventory', *The Asylum Dance*, p. 67.

33. John Burnside, 'The Asylum Dance', *The Asylum Dance*, (London: Cape, 2009), p. 31.

34. William James, *Pragmatism* (New York: Cosimo Inc, 2008) p. 117.

35. John Burnside, 'Le Croisic' *Gift Songs*, (London: Cape, 2007),p. 69.

36. Burnside published another collection of poems, *Black Cat Bone* (London: Cape) in 2011.

37. John Burnside, 'Treatise on the Veil', 'Amor Vincit Omnia', 'Trappist', 'In Memoriam', *The Hunt in the Forest*, p. 45, p. 42. p. 33, p. 2.

38. John Burnside, 'The Hunt in the Forest', *The Hunt in the Forest*, p. 2.

39. John Burnside, 'Aphasia in Childhood', *Feast Days* (London: Secker & Warburg, 1992). p. 8.

BRUSHING AGAINST PUBLIC NARRATIVES:
THE POETRY OF VONA GROARKE

In autumn 2006 a group of academics descended upon the sunny tax-haven of Monaco to explore the theme of 'Irish poetry after feminism'. Anyone familiar with such events (particularly with those which decorate the world of Irish Studies) would find the proceedings, as captured in hard covers, to be about par for the course. Elegantly edited by Justin Quinn, the essays range over topics like 'the poetry of misogyny' and 'post-feminist spaces'. Critical attention falls on an uncontroversial spectrum of poets, including such names as Eavan Boland, Medbh McGuckian, and Derek Mahon. Reading through the essays, one gathers that the conference must have been fractious, and if that is not exactly what one would expect nor is it exactly a surprise. Animosity is not unknown in Irish Studies.

The one unusual aspect of the book is the nature of the fractiousness on display, which has about it an old-fashioned bitterness, strangely redolent of the 1970s. It is true that since those more ideological times a few things have changed. Rather than questioning the validity of feminism as a discourse, for instance, it is noticeable that the participants accept it more or less as a given. One searches in vain for an explicit divide between pro-feminists and anti-feminists. Instead we discover a jagged fault-line between those critics who choose to emphasise formal qualities and those critics who are more theoretically motivated. Against those participants who hold that feminist analysis is more of less irrelevant to the reading of a 'well-made poem', others maintain that a direct engagement with feminism is vitally relevant to the well-being of poetry. One of the latter is Moynagh Sullivan. In line with the tense mood of the proceedings, her essay accuses some "Irish and artistic groups" of invoking, "a lexicon of aesthetic defence that is steeped in a fascination with, and deep fear of, woman."[1] In reply, Peter McDonald, loosely associated with some of the groups under fire, complains that the nature of her assertions is a hindrance to debate:

> ... I cannot imagine a direct response to [Sullivan's] essay which does not have truck with such things as aesthetic standards and poetic value. And for me, there are in fact such things; but I am effectively denied these

terms by Sullivan who believes that cultural and gender studies have seen through them long ago.[2]

I do not intend to arbitrate between Sullivan and MacDonald. The global validity, or otherwise, of feminism and of feminist literary criticism is not the focus of this chapter. But, before passing on, I note that these two opponents agree on at least one thing: that in the application of feminist critique to contemporary poetry, there is a great deal at stake. Feminism may have been broadly accepted into the public sphere, but there remains an ongoing, and sometimes bitter, battle about how much it should influence the reading of literature.

What this chapter explores is the relevance of public-oriented readings, especially those with an explicit feminist purpose, to the Irish poet, Vona Groarke. It also dwells on the critical *expectation* that readings of this sort should have some kind of traction; Groarke's poems, with a certain shrewdness, feed off that expectation. Throughout this chapter I have used some of the submissions to the conference in Monaco as handy critical mooring-points. The one from which this chapter sets out is also the one to which, after a voyage through Groarke's poetic career, it returns. Groake is one of the most respected of the younger Irish poets and, at the time of the conference, her fourth collection, *Juniper Street*, had just been published. That helps to explain her prominence in the proceedings, a prominence which encouraged the following analysis.[3]

The spotlight which fell on Groarke's work during Monaco was directed by two critics, Lucy Collins and Selina Guinness. Some years before, the latter had described Groarke as, "a senior figure" in the new tranche of Irish poets, and in line with this favourable estimate, she devotes her entire essay in this volume to Groarke's poem, 'The Annotated House'.[4] As well as appearing in the afore-mentioned *Juniper Street*, this poem, according to Guinness, had been the subject of a workshop discussion at Monaco (a discussion to which we will have cause to return.) Guinness uses 'The Annotated House' as a kind of critical wind-tunnel, to test the strength and mobility of her ideas, and I have followed her example. Accordingly, a large portion of this chapter is given over to a reading of this one poem.

Since both Collins and Guinness are unambiguously in favour of a close relationship between reading poetry and feminist analysis, one might expect that an exploration of 'The Annotated House' and of Groake's work in general, would bolster their case. Whether or not this is so is the pivotal question of this chapter. Here, then, is the poem:

The Annotated House

The window is flush with words but my page
hangs limps as the snow cloud slouching over
Carlo's house. I am killing time between lines
I have written in dust on the sill. Sometime
before evening, I will shift in this chair, shake out
my stockinged feet, put down my book and ask
the porch screen something pointed but oblique.

Or else, I will take myself off to lie in a bed
silken with usage, beneath a cover laced
with verbs for getting on. In truth, there is
nowhere to go from here. The treads and risers
of every line return me to a carpet scheming
with print. One wrong foot, and there's
no telling what months heaped in the basement –
like laundry thinned by colour – will reveal.

A sequence of breath cuts a dash in the hall.
In the kitchen, the evening bucks its rhythm
and lull. Even the grammar of branches
can't be pinned down. As the smoke flirts
with meaning and falls back into disarray
above the clean, straight-talking roofs,
so my pen, scratching through loose leaves,
comes to a dead stop at the very moment when
the boiler downstairs, like breaking news,
shunts the here and now into one full clause.[5]

I will reserve my own reading of this poem for the conclusion of
this chapter but, in the meantime, I want to focus on the critical
scaffolding with which Guinness surrounds it. I begin with her own
tale of what happened when the poem was passed around for
comment at Monaco. As she remembers it, 'The Annotated House'
provoked a striking interpretive consensus, one which may come as
something of a surprise:

> It took an embarrassingly long time for a room full of close readers
> (myself included) to register the scene of female masturbation that
> climaxes at the end of the third stanza, and once pointed out (by
> Moynagh Sullivan), discussion closed down as if the text had been
> 'solved'.

In returning to that apparent 'solution', her essay goes on to offer a much more elaborate interpretation of 'The Annotated House'. As the identity of the poem's speaker is not in doubt, Guinness's reference here to "female masturbation" – and not, simply, 'masturbation' – signals that her essay will be emphatically gendered. This is indeed how it turns out. As Guinness portrays it, any difficulty a reader might have in detecting an auto-erotic event is no accident. The burden of her feminist analysis is devoted to how concealment of the act has been effectively forced on the poet by patriarchal pressures.

This provocative, and memorable, strand of Guinness's argument is woven around with less controversial threads which trace the allusive intertextuality of 'The Annotated House'. Adducing a set of persuasive examples, she builds up an image of a poem anxious about its place in relation to earlier texts, and anxious, too, about the author's position in the established canon. By casting these anxieties in a strongly gendered light Guinness makes the analytical choice which most defines her essay. Arguing that male and female qualities are ranged against each other in the poem, she finds that this reflects a wider, ongoing struggle, one into which any female poet, by entering a field dominated by men, must plunge. Her gendering of the poem is extensive. As well as finding in 'The Annotated House' an association – in itself unremarkable – between the pen and the phallus, Guinness thinks that the poem equates the world outside the speaker's window with a hostile masculinity. Against these disagreeable forces, the poem, in her account, launches a counter-strike which relies on the *jouissance* of female auto-eroticism and the fertile domestic space of the house:

> The task of writing is sexualised as impotently male ('my page/ hangs limp'), sterile ('lines/ I have written in dust on the sill') and violent ('even the grammar of branches/ can't be pinned down'). Opposed to this, the details of the house are feminised ('the window is flush with words'), eroticised ('A cover laced/ with verbs for getting on') and frustratingly available if a more indirect approach were taken ('As the smoke flirts/ with meaning and falls back into disarray/ above the clean, straight-talking roofs ...')[6]

Thus, just as the conference itself was a battle between two relatively well-defined points of view, Guinness's essay manages to divide the poem between two loosely antagonistic 'constellations', as abstract as they are concrete, composed of objects, moods, and situations. Since it bears sharply on my feelings about how much or how little public interpretation should be applied to most poems, I am going to return to her argument later in the essay. But first I want to remove this poem, temporarily, from the microscope and to reflect on how Groarke's work has evolved up to *Juniper Street*. 'The Annotated House' is quite typical of her writing and underlines, if nothing else, its thematic consistency.

'Where does the mind end and the rest of the world begin?' If Groarke was to tackle this beguiling question (posed by the cognitive philosopher, Andy Clark) she might answer with the word 'house'. As will become abundantly clear, Groarke's imagination has always tilted towards the architectural. This same word concludes the first line in her first book, *Shale*, and is strikingly repeated in the titles of her second book, *Other People's Houses*.[7] While the motif of the dwelling-space is central to all of her collections, Groarke treats it from the beginning as an existential question rather than a material fact, as a framework for what we might be as well as an index of what we are. In describing a house she likes to tone down physical detail allowing latent symbolic properties to come to the fore. In *Shale* most of the poems about architectural spaces shy away from documentary catalogues, preferring to exploit enclosed spaces for their psychological charge.

Shale's play with matters of identity takes place against a wavering formal backdrop. Typical of many first collections, the poems seem to hesitate between formal options, as though the writer was herself an edifice under construction. Sprinkled through the collection, and contributing to its air of instability, are different types of object, ranging from the obviously poetic (moon, fire, river) to the simply domestic (bed, lamp, door.) At times, the poems are so balladic and lilting that they recall Dylan Thomas or Louis MacNeice – one might think of them as casting a range of musical spells to ward off the outside world. David Wheatley has commented usefully on this aspect of the collection:

> [*Shale's*] elementally fresh and simple imagery recalls the American poet Louise Glück. In 'What Becomes the River?' a few key terms (river, stone, sea) are repeated with incantatory force, as Groarke's syntax creates a musical balance between movement, pause, transformation and sameness.[8]

In a similar vein, Justin Quinn has ventured that the tone of *Shale* moves between, "the incantatory and the discursive".[9] In 'The Riverbed', for example, we see an example of a relatively ecstatic mode which the poet would later discard:

> There is sun in the mirror, my head in the trees.
> There is sun in the mirror without me.
> I am lying face up on the riverbed.
> My lover is swimming above me.[10]

In these lines, the balladic energy and surreal juxtapositions seem to herald the arrival of something urgent and novel, although by the end of the poem the reader is left with a curious feeling of having been sidestepped. As the images slide by with the dazzle of cut-glass, the speaker's dream-like game of hide-and-seek hovers between embodied and disembodied states, between presence and absence. The poem's drama resides in the repeatedly dissolving speaker attempting to establish herself against the apparently solid "floor" and "bed" of the river. 'High-value' words like "sun", "mirror", "trees", "river", and "lover" radiate with the pleasure of experiment rather than, as in some of her later work, with the force of a settled view. In a pattern we shall repeatedly see, the drama of poetic self-realisation is blended with surprise. The poet seems to hijack the well-worn poetic accessories of 'sun', 'mirror' and 'river' with a kind of stunned pleasure that they are actually at her disposal.

While the above represents one of the striking exceptions in her debut collection, Groarke's poetry is generally static. Her poems are wary of vigour. To sketch a condition, to capture a place, to define an object, are the kinds of achievement which they find sufficient and in the afterglow of which they are prone to bask. This underlying conservatism is matched by her tone which is generally sombre and guarded. Within her work there are no bohemian adventures, no sprawling canvases, no reckless questions. In the same way that Marianne Moore likes to disappear behind her armoured animals, Groarke likes to linger in her defensive shelters. But this deep-seated desire to keep the outside out is far from a guarantee of safety.

Born in Edgeworthstown in County Longford, Groarke is linked – by an accident of birth if nothing else – to one of the first Irish novelists, Maria Edgeworth. She has also noted, in an autobiographical essay, the proximity of Lissoy, the townland where she grew up, to the parsonage associated with Oliver Goldsmith. Auspicious as these connections may be, we are not asked to read them as stable existential foundations. When the speaker in 'Patronage' declares, "I was born in the ballroom of Maria Edgeworth's house,"[11] this fact is

offered as a further complication, as another obstacle on the crooked
road of self-knowledge. Wary of the sense of entitlement displayed by
others, Groarke's work is careful not to seem presumptuous. The facts
of her birthplace are not equated with a birthright. Tracing a deliber-
ate tangent to the past, 'Patronage' ends in a manner which looks
forward to the blurred habitats of her mature work:

> I have never returned to Maria Edgeworth's house,
> but I've passed behind it on the Longford train
> and seen them sitting out in the garden.
> I've noticed how they turn towards us as they pass,
> how their faces are lost in the shadow of the house.[12]

As the house is seen as a decisive existential boundary, these
various transactions between outside and inside may be read as trans-
actions between public and private spheres. But the exchanges are
not equal. Privacy is always privileged. As the poems recoil from the
materialistic clichés of public discourse, from the bland priorities of
auctioneers and estate agents they find refuge in more private uses
of language. Only when they are woven through dreams, memories,
and conversations do her houses take on reality (or become the reality
which is taken on). In her work, a dwelling exists, not by deed or
covenant, and not according to some public map, but by virtue of our
emotional and psychological exertions. In *Shale*, for example, the title
of 'The History of my Father's House' seems to promise some kind
of verifiable, documentary account of a family space but the poem
itself is a wash of impressions, dead ends, and mis-directions:

> I am trying to find out the year this house –
> my father's house – was built.
> You are remembering not by year,
>
> but by keepsake and event.
> You tell me there is a photograph
> of him in the pram on the avenue.
> But this house has no avenue
>
> and is only as you decide it to be.[13]

Significantly, details which could 'stand up in court', like the refer-
ence, here, to the year and the photograph, are viewed with suspicion,
while those fragments torn from the nets of private discourse are
emphatically prized. We find a similar tension in 'Sunday's Well':

I've been dreaming again of an unlit room
where everything is clean and orderly:
a bed in the corner, a row of books,
a lover's photograph, clothes on a chair.
It needs only a woman to enter and say,
'I know this room. This room is mine.'[14]

Groarke's approach to exposition leaves her writing hard to pin down. Her characters are often un-named and their standing in the world is uncertain. In this poem, we never find out who the 'I' and the 'you' represent. She approaches what John Mole, in describing some 1980s poetry (including some of Groarke's influences), called, "the current aesthetic of being 'none the wiser'".[15] The speaker's passive state is balanced, here, by an airy sense of potential which settles on those objects by which she is surrounded. Contemplating a room of her own, the speaker seems to flirt with the language, if not the outlook, of feminism. In opposition to the self-possessed domesticity of her dream, she places the chaotic silence of the city, a kind of anonymous version of the public world in which she fears that she might be lost. Some critics might read this as a drama of a woman struggling to define herself against a stultifying patriarchy. As in many of her late poems, however, this kind of public narrative flashes into view only to disappear again.

Generally, the poems in *Shale* evade the public world in favour of vaguer, aestheticised spaces, rarely containing more than a handful of people. Within these private retreats, small, local activities may be undertaken, but no world-implicating project appears to be available. Large-scale processes – capitalism, democracy, the European Union – sharply recede, and are emphatically closed to critical inspection. This deflation of the public sphere is not an accident. Given the ambition and monumentality to which most Irish poets – from Yeats to Heaney – have aspired, to make one's way through an Irish poetic landscape without meeting any grand narratives might be compared to wandering the Earth after the extinction of the dinosaurs. The novelty value is high. Working on the reader's sense that something is missing, Groarke's better poems are purposefully quietistic. They turn the radio dial to frequencies which can scarcely be heard, to those moods which are generally anchored in a personal relationship, and which have no obvious public context.

Cultivating privacy, the narrator, throughout *Shale*, casts the public world as a distant planet, entirely indifferent to her fate. We might describe this condition as one of 'alienation', if that did not suggest levels of hostility and involvement that are absent. Rather than disaffection we find detachment. At the end of 'Trousseau', for example, the speaker, who is travelling by train on her honeymoon, grandly divests herself of her wedding garments. The comic conclusion of the poem constructs a kind of alternative 'wedding-train' as a line of underwear which is left trailing on the tracks. While the surrealism of that image is worth remarking, what is more important is the explicit lesson which the speaker draws:

> Not even the final blaze of ice
> seen from the westbound Oslo train
> was as lavish, as immediate as this:
> our wedding gift to a world
> that wanted nothing, held nothing of us.[16]

The last line serves to crystallise an attitude which, much of the time, lies just below the surface of her work – the suspicion that, merely by existing, we are excluded. Here, the geographical context provides a cue for the feeling – the speaker after all is not Norwegian – but as a statement of marital intent, the ending of the poem implies that it is only to the private and familial that the poet owes any allegiance.

As with poets like Patrick Kavanagh and Seamus Heaney, this feeling of marginalisation may owe something to the geography of her upbringing. We should mention, too, that this melody of un-belonging is also sounded in the poems of her husband, Conor O'Callaghan, himself an Irish poet with a considerable reputation. Justin Quinn has observed that, somewhat in the manner of Hughes and Plath, the writings of Groarke and O'Callaghan might profitably be read as a developing, intra-poetic conversation. Certainly both poets are devoted to obliquity and understatement and both are hostile to the urge – perennially tempting to many – to romanticise Irish environments. O'Callaghan has written with warmly vehement defensiveness about the life of small-town Ireland, suggesting a desire to withdraw - in social and literary terms at least – from the ambience of the capital:

> … give me a dreary eastern town that isn't vaguely romantic,
> where moon and stars are lost in the lights of the greyhound track
> and cheering comes to nothing and a flurry of misplaced bets
> blanketing the stands at dawn is about as spiritual as it gets.[17]

Although the rhythm and propulsion of this has an aggression which we do not find in Groarke, its psychological landscape – de-peopled, unglamorous, humdrum – is the same one that she occupies. Significant action is relegated to what Raymond Chandler used to call, "the country behind the hill". What we see onstage seems to vibrate with an awareness of something more significant which is only just offstage.

How Groarke evaluates the social status of her Irish Midlands background – and the matching blankness of her poetic landscapes – is closely bound up with her general assessment of the poet's role. In her writing, the atmosphere of the disregarded margins seeps from the site of her upbringing to the habits of her chosen vocation. To put it another way, Groarke locates Irish poets in a kind of Midlands of the mind, as becomes clear in her autobiographical essay:

> Poetry wasn't something we [Groarke's family] held in very high regard. But then, who does? I can think of no Irish poet who talks of growing up in a family where poetry mattered a whit. I wasn't unusual, amn't unusual: my coming to it was as tricky and devious a process as it surely ought to be. Like every other poet, I discovered my subjects and my voice almost by stealth: by reading; by noticing what I was supposed to be writing: and by learning by writing that, and then eventually, not quite that.[18]

Although this statement is emphatically phrased, it does leave itself open to question. Is the development of every poet – or even every Irish poet – necessarily "tricky and devious"? The phrasing appears to elevate an idiosyncratic self-description to the status of a universal condition. It also underlines the fact that Groarke sees poetry as a marginal activity, a sort of half-forgotten side-road with little traffic. That attitude is faithfully reflected in the poetry's downbeat and desultory air, and in its undramatic landscapes.

We should also note Groarke's attitude to the question of influence. She asserts, convincingly enough, that a poet begins by imitation and develops by gradual variation: a Bloomean model which matches observable practice. Her emphasis on a process of tricky evasion is, however, more contentiously specific and, had it not been for the example of Paul Muldoon, might not seem like such a natural thing for an Irish poet to say. This is useful to bear in mind when we are confronted with the poker-faced obliquity of 'The Annotated House', a poem which in significant ways is a self-conscious demonstration of poetic influence.

On the face of it, the title of Groarke's second book, *Other People's Houses*, promised a more socially-oriented collection. The family likeness of the collection's titles – 'House Rules', 'House Contents',

'House Viewing', 'House Plan' – bluntly announced a controlling theme. Many of the poems featured symmetrical formal arrange-ments – large, regular, stanzaic blocks – which were suggestive of architectural order. The dominant impression of the book was of an author finding her subject, which proved to be neither people nor houses but one's apartness from others. Just as in the prosperous Ireland of the period one measured one's status by the relative size and location of one's property, so the controlling voice in *Other People's Houses* seemed to measure her distance from her fellow citizens with a survey of their dwellings. The feeling of exclusion, which was mildly noticeable in *Shale*, was keener in this book and, from poem to poem, was made more disturbing because its origin was hard to locate.

As hinted above, a publicly-oriented reading of this collection might explain these feelings of exclusion with reference to a specific Irish economic context. David Wheatley has pointed out that, *Other People's Houses*, "was written against the backdrop of the economic upturn of the late 1990s and its spiralling property prices."[19] Can we plausibly give these poems the kind of publicly-oriented reading which we have seen Guinness attempt to supply for 'The Annotated House'? I think not, but it is crucial to our experience of reading these poems that we *almost* can. The way in which Groarke allows her poems to brush against seemingly relevant public narratives gives them a necessary, extra charge. So let me move on, in this portion of my argument, to showing how one of those significant public narra-tives, the iniquity of Celtic Tiger Ireland, *almost* becomes central to our reading of *Other People's Houses*.

In the period in which Groarke's second book was written, the Republic of Ireland was experiencing a lengthy and unprecedented boom with an economic growth rate which regularly exceeded five percent. In that context many of the old stereotypes about Ireland - that, for example, it was a relatively poor, church-dominated society which forced its young to emigrate – were bound to dissolve. By way of compensation, new sources of anxiety emerged, mostly in relation to the accelerating materialism. Perhaps the most keenly perceived vice was an obsession with property. In relation to this Terence Brown has noted the size and scale of the associated urban development:

[Between 1996 and 2002] … in the province of Leinster with Dublin as its lodestar, the population exceeded two million. Accordingly many commuter towns within range of fifty or so miles of the capital saw large increases in population, when rocketing house prices in Dublin put a home beyond the reach of many first-time buyers.[20]

These developments therefore were most significantly felt in areas which were in commuting distance of Dublin, towns like Athlone, near where Groarke grew up, and Dundalk, to which she moved. One might guess that, for a poet with a background in Longford, the kind of literary anxiety one might ordinarily feel about one's relationship to the Irish capital would, in this period, be intensified by these fresh socio-economic factors. That Groarke has felt the ambiguous magnetism of the east coast has been confirmed by the autobiographical essay which she published in 2001. Growing up in the Midlands, as she describes it, a journey was typically defined by its orientation to or from the capital:

> The real road …runs east to west ….the whole point of that road was to take you to Dublin, past Uisneach, if you truly knew where you were for. In the midlands, north and south are not political distinctions. A journey in either direction is likely to bring you nowhere: at best it could be a deviation, at worst a dead end. True journeys must be either with or against the sun: only in this path does anything visibly change.[21]

During the years of the Celtic Tiger, the helter-skelter development of existing towns and the creation of new estates gave to the car – quite apart from its traditional role as a status symbol – an elevated status. Hence Groarke's point about the 'real road' running by her house is underpinned by a growing economic reality. *Other People's Houses* is substantially defined by what Robert Puttnam has called 'drive-by relationships', the characteristically thin social bonds which obtain in societies organised around electronic communication and mechanised transport.[22] We see these at work, for example, in the poem 'Lighthouses', a mild play on Yeats's famous epitaph, where the dominant voice urges the speaker/reader not to pass by on horseback but to *drive* on in their automobile. Like the earlier 'Patronage', 'Lighthouses gives us a fleeting view of other existences from the perspective of mechanised transport, invoking the kind of frail travelling coincidence which is no sooner established than it is lost. Here is how the poem ends:

> Living rooms with lamps
> and stoked-up fires; mirrors above them that catch
> a glimpse of us; windows flecked with Christmas trees
> and flicking bulbs that are telling us
> to notice this … Don't notice this. Drive on.[23]

This poem passes through dwelling-spaces which are haunted not by their missing inhabitants but by their inhabitants' possessions. To this materialistic flotsam and jetsam, where the glory of escutcheoned doors gives way to the Argos catalogue, the speaker brings a knowing theatrical scrutiny, as though that which it surveys has already been seen elsewhere. This is a 1990s 'sea of disappointment' not so different from the dystopic vision of Kinsella's 'Nightwalker'. Groarke wields the plural pronoun with a strategic vagueness. While we might picture this collective as a couple travelling together, gazing at the urban development that slides by in the windscreen, we might also read it as standing for a more general group – Irish people, say, or modern consumers. Both of these possibilities – it is true – flirt with social relevance but not insistently so. The possibility of a publicly useful reading seems like one more house-light vanishing in the windscreen, as the poem, rather than choosing to tackle the social conditions it has evoked, prefers to glance off them. Adding another emotional layer, the contrasting injunctions to notice and not to notice might be heard as issuing from the poem itself, as it toys with the prospect of its own eventual disregard. Confronted by a philistine reality in which poetry has no obvious foothold, the poem appears resigned to its fate.

Groarke's depiction of the poet's wider role also helps us to understand a particular pattern in her poems which I am going to label the 'Marie Celeste effect'. By this I mean a general evocation of spaces which seem freshly deserted, where the disposition of what remains – a lit fire, a steaming kettle, a broken window – implies proximate human action. As a motif which may be put to diverse ends – creating, for example, degrees of mystery, detachment, and impersonality – it is also an implicit challenge to the reader to 'join the dots' and to project something appropriate into the scene. In a related fashion, the art critic Peter Campbell, writing about paintings, has reflected on the image of the empty room. This he regards as a "late subject" about which he concludes:

> Pictures of empty rooms ...suggest private places, but ones which, because they are empty, you are tempted to enter ....Sometimes, finding yourself alone in a room, if only, fictively, you wonder what kind of life is, or could be, lived there.[24]

Campbell captures well the curious mixture of uncertainty and intrigue which a deserted room can engender. The relative lateness of the subject in painting and, perhaps, in poetry, may owe something to a post-Enlightenment model of the universe where man is no longer at the centre. Of course, there are more obvious literary precedents for Groarke's practice: the postmodern fictions of Robbe-Grillet and Barthelme, the minimalist interiors of the early Abbey Theatre and, later, Beckett, and, most proximately of all, the abandoned poetic locations favoured by Derek Mahon.

Despite drifting by the materialistic reefs we associate with the Celtic Tiger, Groarke chooses not to moralise. Here and elsewhere she avoids any denunciation of those who fumble in greasy tills – a literary choice which, I guess, is the default one for her generation. This is *quite the reverse*, however, of the generally moralistic and highly judgemental public discourse which was prevalent at the time and which any casual inspection will find. Take, as an example, Kieran Allen's acid commentary on the sudden rise in Irish house-prices.

> In 1994 at the start of the boom, the ratio of house prices in Dublin to the average industrial wage was 4.3:1. Four years later this had doubled to 8.2:1. The price of property did not increase because of any major escalation in the cost of raw materials. It was driven purely by the anarchy and chaos of a market that rose with the lure of profit in a booming economy.[25]

The absence of that kind of argumentative righteousness in Groarke's work lends it a peculiar spin.

One of the prevailing public anxieties in this period was how to ensure that Ireland's newfound prosperity would benefit those groups – among them the elderly and the illiterate – which had over many years received poor treatment from the state. It was feared that rather than erasing inequality the country's material success might ensure, in the words of the political economist Peadar Kirby, a "growing social polarisation between those who are benefiting from it [the boom] and those being marginalised by it."[26] One of the groups which assumed a kind of centrality in the associated debates was that of the travelling community. Fintan O'Toole, a well-known cultural commentator, gave a passionate assessment of their plight which in its vehement righteousness was typical of the time:

> The failure, during a period of abundant resources, to better the lot of a relatively small community (24,000 people or 0.6 percent of the population) that has suffered naked exclusion is perhaps the most damning indictment of boom-time Ireland.[27]

Similarly, the senior Irish poet, Paul Durcan, addressing the Irish people in his weekly radio slot, diagnosed a sickness in the relationship between the two communities:

> The so-called Traveller Problem in Ireland is as much a settled community problem .... we need urgently to find our Traveller roots – to go back to our original Traveller feelings and let go of our property mania and all the collected and related manias.[28]

Because travellers, came to be seen as a kind of litmus test of the liberal and humanitarian pretensions of the Celtic Tiger economy, Groarke's prose-poem, 'House Fire' usefully tests her relationship to the public sphere of the time. Although none of the actors in this prose-poem are explicitly identified, it appears to portray – in the manner of a flattened-out short-story – a dark incident involving members of the travelling community. The piece is set in the classic 'non-space' of a car-park, and the title refers, with a certain troubling irony, to the caravan of a recently deceased old lady which has been mysteriously set alight. 'House Fire' immediately follows 'Lighthouses' and brings to mind the same theme of fraying social bonds:

> Lately, a fire in the car park that sparked loose talk of bombs and broken faith. In the morning, it got out. After her death, they had burned her caravan, fittings, furniture, the lot.[29]

While the general dereliction of the environment might remind us of many poems by Groarke's major influence, Derek Mahon, the subject-matter encourages a particular comparison with his apparently anti-bourgeois poem, 'Gipsies'. There are, however, instructive differences. Not only does the speaker of Mahon's poem demonstrate affection for the gipsies, he also appears to identify with them ("the fate you have so long/ endured is ours also.")[30] Groarke's speaker by contrast treats the departed woman with warmth but her attitude to the travellers is blankly non-committal. Her poem deliberately flaunts major gaps in its exposition, causing the travellers to appear and disappear with the casual arbitrariness of the natural element to which they are compared:

> One day there was a camp of them spilling out like rainwater stopped in saucepans on the footpath and the bonnets of half-broken cars. Then they were gone, moved on.

The reference to saucepans and broken-down cars may remind us of activities which are traditionally associated with members of the travelling community, and tends to reinforce the secondary nature of their relationship to the materialism of the settled community. I am reminded here of Michael Cronin's suggestion that we think of the Traveller lifestyle as representing an alternative form of nomadicism, one which is in a kind of ironic competition with the more 'accepted' rootlessness of urban elites.[31] Rather than judge one community at the expense of the other, the poem gives an impression of global dysfunction.

Shorn of a controlling context, the possible interpretations of 'House Fire' proliferate – the relevant public narratives remain just offstage. In an Irish context, the reference to "bombs", for example, carries negative paramilitary associations, while the phrase "broken faith" may encourage the reader to detect references to a post-Catholic ethos. A reader who forms an image of burning witches might even see the poem as a '*Crucible*-like' allegory of social judgement. Here is how the prose-poem describes the aftermath of the fire:

> In their wake, a ring of blackened saplings, indelible shadows on the lock-up wall, the tarmac scorched for good. And a shattered hull that still rests in the dead end of the old car park.[32]

The unhappy details resonate with a "strange poetry of decay".[33] Like the scene which confronted those boarding the Marie Celeste such an aftermath is hypnotising because it seems to offer if not an easeful death then certainly a better alternative to life. It is an afterlife free of rivals and responsibilities, lacking drama or interruption, prolonging its sensation by keeping life invisible but teasingly proximate. Although the social significance of these marks must be negative there is also, in the speaker's stance, a measure of satisfaction in being able to contemplate them. The act of recording the marks has about it a rhetorical certainty, as though the poem in its grudging motion indicates that, "What's done is done". Temporarily lowering itself into a dramatically alien landscape, the narrator's voice quickly manages, by dint of its composure and restraint, to rise above it. Standing apart, the narrator transcends not only the local disaster but also the society by which it was fostered. As we will see in 'The Annotated House', these brushes with public narrative continue to qualify the author's privacy, giving it a mysteriously troubled flavour. Gesturing towards the possibility of a publicly-oriented reading, which they know is likely to appear on the reader's agenda, they attain much of their force in that expectation's denial.

It may be that Groarke chose not to persist with the upbeat, 'ecstatic' approach of some of the poems in *Shale* because it was inconsistent with the kind of landscape mapped out by poems like 'House Fire'. Her developing poetic stance is that of a latecomer, forlorn and beyond change. Such a belated mood, for example, permeates the short poem, 'The Big House', where the 'Marie Celeste effect' gives the impression of entering a scene long after decisive activities have been concluded:

I took it for another ancient ruin
with gaping windows and the roof all in.
But as we drove up underneath its bulk
I saw that what was darkening our truck
was not the shadow of a burnt-out pile
but a stack of tightly-packed hay-bales
built up like bricks, its facade high
and monumental, latticed to the sky.[34]

As in 'Lighthouses' and 'Patronage' the poem places in question what forms of mechanical transport allow us to see. The title casts a crafty glance at the Big House tradition in Irish literature, one that reached its high watermark in the poems of Yeats, and one which is occasionally revived, now, mainly for ironic effect, by contemporary writers. Like Patrick Kavanagh, Groarke invokes this tradition only to refuse it, asserting a contrasting set of unillusioned, down-to-earth priorities. The formidable shadow of literary tradition appears to fall across the speaker, sending the reader in search of signs of influence. Here, the principal precursor it seems to me is Larkin, whose most famous poem of mechanised transport, 'The Whitsun Weddings', shifts in the background. While Groarke's tightly packed hay-bales are suggestive of Larkin's "squares of wheat", his eye can also be sensed in the imposing height of the structure. This dominating image brings to mind poems like 'High Windows', 'Days', and 'Cut Grass' where the speaker's focus on an elevated point is associated with a kind of powerlessness. According to this pattern, the passive speaker is as helplessly separated from what he apprehends as he is impressed by it.

Read in this manner, 'The Big House' moves from the romantic to the numbly prosaic, a trajectory typical of her work. Again, the reader is encouraged to expect a particular destination which the poem narrowly misses. The anticipated presence of Yeats, as signalled by the 'ancient ruin,' swerves away into the suburban English anonymity of Larkin. By aligning the hay-tower's monumentality with the formidable peaks of her literary heritage, the speaker indicates an achievement which can scarcely be matched and creations which cannot be undone. The conditions for the poet's being are determined by that which preceded her, and realising her helplessness only deepens her melancholy. Once more we find that self-identity, in Bloomean fashion, is densely entangled with questions of literary influence. The poem makes a choice (or at any rate has a choice made for it) about its relationship to one aspect of Irish literary tradition and this, in turn, determines the kind of person the speaker must be.

Perhaps encouraged by the success of *Other People's Houses*, Groarke's third book, *Flight*, is more self-assertive. If her second collection had carved out a poetic subject, then her third is an attempt to broaden her methods. *Flight* represents a 'linguistic turn'. Instead of signalling human presence and absence through the mysterious arrangement of domestic spaces she increasingly relies on a self-conscious play with idiomatic phrases. Justin Quinn interprets the book's title in the following way:

[Re Flight] The 'flight' of the title resonates on several levels: first, it is the flight from one's parents and one's hometown into adulthood; second, it is the occasional flight from one's own responsibilities and the blankness of middle age; and third, it is the unalloyed joy in the flight of the imagination at the height of its powers.[35]

If the phrase, 'unalloyed joy', is a little over the top, Quinn has a point that *Flight* is Groarke's most playful collection. The ludic habits on display do not, however, always succeed. The book's general flavour is well-captured in 'The Verb "to herringbone"', a slight poem which is, in a self-reflexive manner, about slightness. Selecting a minor motif, the poem elaborates it in such a minimal manner that it seems not to go anywhere, content with the limited ripples it causes on the linguistic surface. Here is the first stanza:

Something beginning with slightness
and possibly taken from there.
As though unheard of, inauspicious,
the way a pheasant or a wood-pidgeon
will find a point of no return, on a lorryless
side-road or on the lee side of an air.
Something begun and veering off at once […][36]

The grammatical uncertainty caused by the lack of a main verb reflects the masked intentions of the speaker. Like 'House Fire' and 'The Big House' the poem circles a perhaps non-existent centre, but this time the orbit is more verbal than physical. In *Flight*, a Larkinesque use of negative adjectives is especially noticeable – a partial list includes "uncut", "unlit", "unruffled", "unstooped", "untallied", "uninscribed", "unearmarked", "unsworn", and "unfathomable". Taken together with her repeated use of "nothing" ("It was something of nothing", "the measure of nothing", "In those days nothing came of anything"), and her playing on unheard melodies ("a promise almost made", "what was never said", "what's possible/ elsewhere") *Flight* builds its nest in negative space.

Preparing us for the knowing, self-conscious quality of 'The Annotated House', *Flight* is densely allusive. Groarke may not mean the opening line of 'Thistle' ("It's hard to get away from hay these days") as a playful nod to Paul Muldoon's influence, but he is certainly present in individual poems like 'Currency' and 'White Noise', and more generally in the widespread use of renewed colloquialism ("Something begun and veering off at once// as though to double back would be the point of it").

Muldoon's influence also allows us to feel the presence of Frost. The latter is strongly evident in the use of what Richard Poirier, in his work on Frost, describes as "vague conjecturals", idiomatic turns of phrase which, to return to Groarke's description of the developing poet as "tricky and devious", are deployed for their cunning elusiveness. Such turns-of-phrase have been extensively mapped by critics of Irish poetry in recent years for example by Rachel Buxton. Indeed their use has become so widespread that a reader might be reminded of the bureaucratised use of the definite article in British poetry of the 1930s. These two examples are representative:

> It was what do you call it and what is its name
> and how does it go when it comes to be gone?[37]

>   Whatever had been on the tip
> of the tongue, that never slipped; a misremembered
> name; a choked-back curse; a promise almost made;[38]

Perhaps the most eye-catching poem in the book is 'Or to Come', which recalls not only Mahon's handling of Yeatsian big stanzas in 'A Disused Shed in Co. Wexford', it borrows that poem's tone and subject-matter. Extending the territory of 'House Fire', the poem also brings to mind Kavanagh's 'Loch Derg' and Tom French's 'Pity the Bastards':

> There are always unvisited corners
> where the only sound is the turn taken by dandelions
> or a robin rustling in the aftergrass nearby.

By placing 'The Verb "to herringbone"' first in the book, Groarke over-rates the stylistic developments which it serves to introduce. The book is weighed down by its influences – its playfulness is too anxious to be convincing. It would seem that Groarke needed the stimulus of new territory and this was provided by her move to America. The resultant *Juniper Street* is a much stronger book, one which agreeably blends the approaches of her first three collections.

§

I have embarked on this long detour through Groarke's canon in order to support the argument which follows about 'The Annotated House'. There are many poems within her books to which it bears a strong resemblance and this must colour how we read it. Guinness's essay is quite persuasive on matters of influence – the chart of echoes which she abstracts from its sonic landscape is helpful and sensitive. She is right, for example, to hear traces of Louis MacNeice and Ciarán Carson in its spacious acoustics. Like the hay-bales in 'The Big House', the poem's pointed intertextuality reminds us of the compromising shadows cast by other writers. In this sense the poem is territorial, a battle for possession of the literary domain. Given Guinness's alertness to signs of influence, it would have been useful for her essay to have aligned the poem with the rest of Groarke's canon. That she does not do so is understandable – 'The Annotated House' is, after all, chosen by her principally to illustrate an argument about the efficacy of one kind of analysis. Nevertheless the absence of such a context skews her interpretation of the poem.

So in returning to examine Guinness's argument, let's start with her most arresting claim: is 'The Annotated House' a poem about female masturbation? I am inclined to say 'no', although I do not think that a libidinous reading is entirely misplaced. The poem undeniably contains the kind of vague masturbatory dimension that exists, say, in 'A Disused Shed in Co. Wexford', but identifying that dimension with a specific act carried out by the speaker seems unjustified. The aura of eroticism in Groarke's poem appears to emanate from the house itself and serves the purpose of providing an ironic contrast with its sole inhabitant. In mimicking the often anguished daydreams of the creative mind, 'The Annotated House' constructs a mosaic of active and passive elements and, within that chaotic mixture, the dwelling's 'virility' appears to balance the speaker's 'sterility'. The personification of the house which this process involves is quite in accord with those other poems by Groarke – especially in *Other People's Houses* – where the speaker's life-force is mysteriously displaced and then absorbed by her immediate environment. As a general rule, her speakers are lugubriously confined to a continuum of writing, daydreaming, observing, and listening and, consistent with this, the speaker in 'The Annotated House' is, like a female Oblomov, busy doing nothing. Even the choice between chatting with the porch screen or lying down in bed proves to be too much. In this sleepy context, the proposed act of auto-eroticism would be better assigned to the zestful house rather than the resting speaker.

Guinness proposes that the final verse takes place in the bedroom, where, as she reads it, the surreptitious act of masturbation ought to be nearing its conclusion. But, as I see it, the possibility of retiring to the bedroom is only raised by the speaker in the second stanza, and this internally voiced suggestion is immediately followed by the phrase, "In truth, there is nowhere to go from here." Perhaps the poem is telling it slant, but to me this simply signals that the speaker has decided to stay put. Furthermore, if the speaker were lying down in bed for the duration of stanza two, why would she refer to walking on the carpet as well as to the potential danger of placing 'one wrong foot'? We do well to remember that going to the bedroom is figured as an option, one of two, and that both of these are couched in the future tense. Having mulled these choices over the rest of the poem reverts to the present tense, underlining the fact that the speaker has never shifted from her chair.

Whether or not the act of masturbation occurs in the poem, it is certainly not explicit. For Guinness this is a point in favour of her argument. As she sees it the female speaker is oppressed by patriarchal forces, and therefore not fully able to articulate her sexual self. Intriguingly, Groarke's autobiographical essay of 2001 averted to the possibility of writing about the female orgasm. The conclusion which she reached, however, is hard to square with Guinness's point:

> ... if you want to write poems about the female orgasm or Class A drugs,

you're unlikely to have to brush the chips of too many Irish poets, male
or female, off your shoulder before you begin. But maybe if you live in
Ballymacargy and haven't been to too many raves down there, you might
not know exactly where to begin …[39]

In other words, writing about the female orgasm is made easier,
in Groarke's eyes, precisely because it is not situated on territory
where there is a well-established set of grumbles. Rather than being
shut down by an oppressive patriarchy, such territory might be hard
to reach for other reasons, for example, thanks to the provincial
ambience for which 'Ballymacargy' has been chosen here to stand.

Whatever the reader concludes about the poem's masturbatory
subtext, my main disagreement with Guinness lies elsewhere. Our
ways decisively part where her more sharply feminist analysis begins.
As I see it, her reading of the poem is forced into a series of contor-
tions, especially where it relies on a sharp contrast between male and
female elements. For example, this is how she finishes her essay:

> While the poem ['The Annotated House'] celebrates the fact that female
> jouissance can find full articulation, it suggests that critical and poetic
> decorum prevents it here from recording that sound. That this decon-
> structive reading is so tightly pitted against the poem's formal graces
> shows Groarke at her most skilful and intellectually controlled. However,
> if I have read the poem plausibly, the self-defeat this end entails proves
> the need in Irish literary culture for a continued awareness that real bodies
> shape critical and poetic dialogues and that their presence, and the forms
> they take, require precisely the sort of analysis feminism affords.[40]

In this reading "critical and poetic decorum", which stands in for
a literary establishment traditionally dominated by men, prevents the
full realisation of the speaker's possibilities, narrows her life-chances.
The genders are unhappily opposed and their opposition assumes
physical expression in the speaker's environment. But in mapping
sexual antagonism across this suburban scene, Guinness goes beyond
ingenuity and engages in a form of critical wishful thinking. As I read
it, there are no traces of gender *opposition* whatsoever in the poem.
Let us look at some examples, two minor and one major: (1)
Guinness asserts the presence of male violence in the poem with only
the slightest of evidence, making much of an attempt (which does
not anyway succeed) to pin down "the grammar of branches". But
this can be read – with more innocence and less strain – as a good
description of a daydreaming poet who is watching trees move in the
window. There is nothing in the language to suggest that this activity

is either male or violent.

(2) Guinness tries to read the masturbatory activity as potentially liberating – a surreptitious blow against patriarchy. But it confuses matters more than a little that the apparent instrument of liberation is a pen. As well as putting us in mind of Heaney's (not very feminist) poem, 'Digging', the pen is an obvious phallic symbol. To square the argumentative circle, Guinness, concedes the 'maleness' of the pen, but identifies it as *potentially* female. Naturally, this is unpersuasive – the apparent instrument of liberation has yet to be liberated.

(3) A more complicated example of contortion is bound up with the poem's movement between outside and inside. Broadly speaking, what lies outside the house is read, by Guinness, as male, and what lies inside is read as female. Even so, she identifies the smoke, which is *outside*, above the roofs, as a part of female domestic space. Perhaps this apparent contradiction might matter less is she did not also alter the equation with which 'The Annotated House' concludes. The last verse makes a parallel between two conflicts: *as* the smoke falls back *so* the poet's pen comes to a stop, *as* the roofs talk straight *so* the boiler starts up. Unfortunately, for Guinness, this parallelism shuffles her configuration of male/outside versus female/inside in 'the wrong way'. So she offers an alternative pairing:

> Where it would be possible to turn the 'scratching through loose-leaves' into an image of female masturbatory pleasure, the pen refuses to comply because it is already structured by the 'clean' (non-bodily), 'straight-talking' (unambiguous) lines of literary tradition where patriarchal prejudice has been seen to shelter.[41]

Arguing that the pen impedes the flow of *ecriture feminine*, she aligns it vaguely with the external patriarchal forces which are consolidated in the horizon's architecture. But I think this is a misreading. It is clear from the syntax that the pen and the smoke are allies not enemies – being 'poetic', 'interesting', and ineffectual, both fail in a similar fashion. Therefore rather than a conflict taking place between a male outside and a female inside in the poem, it is better to accept that conflicts are occurring *both* inside *and* outside. In a battle between practical action and creative speculation, the pen and the smoke are overcome by the blunt functional efficiency of the roofs and the boiler. In this alignment of the poem's forces, the accessories to the speaker's daydreaming are brought up short by the disobliging there-ness of the world.

Perhaps the most serious objection to Guinness's reading is that objects and situations are gendered male and female according to how it suits the argument. As the following example shows, domestic space, which is supposedly female, is consigned to the male realm when the verbal context turns negative.

> While the bedroom setting supplies (courtesy of Marvin Gaye) the ghost of a groovy 'it' to 'getting on', this is tagged to the primary meaning of getting on in the world, the participle's dependence on 'laced' again connecting the idea of writing, male sexuality and ambition with unreliability or treachery.[42]

To persuade us that male sexuality appears at this point in the poem I think Guinness needs more that a speculative glance at Marvin Gaye. Admittedly, she faces a problem. While the vocabulary in these lines is slightly negative, this is for her the site of female masturbation. Since she does not want to equate female sexual activity with negativity, her solution is to identify male sexuality as the rogue element. So the word 'laced', which if anything has more female associations, gets press-ganged into a negative male verbal constellation. One is reminded of the once well-observed habit of British newsreaders who would describe certain sport stars, when they were prospering, as 'British' and, when they were not, as 'Irish', Welsh or 'Scottish'. Simply put, for Guinness, any point in the poem is 'male' when the surrounding context seems negative, and is 'female' when the surrounding context seems positive.

In offering my own reading of the poem, I want to suggest that it is held open to a quite different set of pressures. Let us start by observing that the poem depends on the same motif of interrupted consciousness which animated the most important poems of Derek Mahon. The house is *almost* silent, which makes any noise a candidate for interrupting the author's stream of thought. When the boiler comes on it specifically interrupts the act of writing but it also more generally disrupts the narrator's solipsism. Far from representing the rarefied possibilities of an *ecriture feminine* the boiler is a reminder of those blank workaday tasks which interfere with the time to write. In quest of some form of imaginative sovereignty, the poem figures the various noises off as 'rivals' to that potential state. Indeed the poem is more explicit about its underlying concerns than equivalent poems by Mahon – one thinks of 'A Disused Shed' and 'Leaves'. Groarke's speaker is unambiguously worried by her temporary writer's block.

It is a weakness of Guinness's case that she does not discuss the American situation of the poem, a context which is heavily advertised by the book's title-poem and elsewhere. Justin Quinn has noted that *Juniper Street*, "takes its name from a street in Philadelphia (the city where she [Groarke] lived in 2004)."[43] I think this is a better background against which to read her reflections on the 'clean-straight-talking roofs' since this phrase is likely a measure of Irish fascination at American efficiency and practicality (Groarke's mother was American and, according to her essay in the *Dublin Review*, something of a workaholic, so references to energetic knowhow may have an extra personal charge.) In the volume *Juniper Street*, 'The Annotated House' is immediately preceded both by the title-poem and 'Glaze' – two poems which are explicitly bound up with the poet's new, unfamiliar living conditions. All three poems dwell on the coldness of the poet's new environment and in each case there is a kind of existential taking-stock, as though the speaker is doing a double-take with respect to her situation. Recovering some of the novelty and surprise of *Shale*, there is in 'Juniper Street', a fascination with how everyday life has been translated into a fresh range of objects, and how those objects, with their reminders of cultural differ-ence, exert a hold on the speaker. As in 'The Annotated House', the female speaker in 'Juniper Street' is at something of a loose end ("I am queen of the morning: nothing to do but to fiddle/ words or quote the gilt-edge of our neighbour's forsythia")[44] To be thus becalmed, one could argue, increases the speaker's sense of being a fish out of water. This is an American house with an Irish poet in it. The porch screen and the snow cloud are minor manifestations of the foreign, firm reminders of a mildly alien world which outside the window unnervingly goes on with its business. This world challenges any migrant (or visiting writer) with the question, 'where do you belong?' This is all the public narrative the poem needs.

By being attached to exhaustion, to the exhausted melancholy which, in the work of younger poets, so often vibrates with a sense of their belatedness, Groarke follows Mahon, her primary precursor. I suggest that 'The Annotated House' is one of the summits of her exhaustion. Its effect is as if to say, 'so much has happened', 'we have come so far', 'we have lived so many lives'. At the same time, the poem is, in an effort of self-assertion, anxious about priority – anxious not so much for a room of one's own, as for elbow room of one's own. We saw the same climate of feeling, manifested with unusual intensity, in Mahon's poetry. 'A Disused Shed in Co. Wexford' establishes much of its special tone with its first two words, "Even now". There too the opening verbal gambit suggests something decisive has already happened off-stage in some dramatically unknowable fore-time and that the poem is, at best, a superior kind of afterthought. As in Yeats's early poetry, the effect is also to marginalise action as vulgar and unnecessary. Groarke, too, likes the phrase "even now" and in her poem 'Transatlantic', it has the final line to itself:

an awkward
dawn that is
rounding
on you
and your swansong
even now.

It may be that Groarke had in mind another notable use of the word by Michael Longley at the beginning of 'Swans Mating', "Even now I wish that you had been there/ Sitting beside me on the river-bank."[45] Whether or not a reference is intended does not matter so much as the world of feeling into which the reader is thrown. Groarke uses the little phrase again in 'Slow Set', an intensely nostalgic poem, in which, thinking back on the dances of one's youth, the speaker refers to "the most beautiful boy/ in the room who is walking towards you even now." Because the American context gives her the opportunity to take stock of her life up to that point, using a 'how-did-I-end-up-here?' tone, so flashbacks to youth are woven into a general air of exhausted valediction. The atmosphere of *Juniper Street* is accordingly deepened. As a reminder of this mood, the word 'even' frequently appears in the book: "The rug also is withering and even the view is slinking off." "Even the roses are borrowed from someone else's room." ('Terms and Conditions' – this poem, like 'The Annotated House' seems to refer to MacNeice's 'Snow'); "... even in January, with our snow-boots lined up" ('Juniper Street'); "even the cypress tree inside the wall" ('Chinese Lacquer'); "When it steals inside an offhand dusk, not even I/ will muster a send-off ..." ('We Had Words'); "Even your hand stops as I unhook the gate" ('The Return').

In Mahon's 'A Disused Shed' the opening phrase is intimately connected to the last – 'Even now' and 'in vain' are sonic cousins which both speak for a world of deep, but inscrutable, regret. Similarly the word 'even' which appears in the last stanza of 'The Annotated House' is consistent with much else in Groarke's work in evoking a kind of free-floating helplessness, an existential sorrow which is at once not to be helped and consolingly distinctive. In Groarke's poem, the sonic cousins of 'even' are the twice-repeated 'evening' as well as 'leaves' and 'reveal'. Indeed to the web of inter-textuality which Guinness draws for the poem one might reasonably add Mahon's 'Leaves' and 'The Snow Party'. To say this poem is about the boundaries of the self is another way of saying that it is about poetry.

Groarke's mature phase as a writer begins, I think, with *Other People's Houses*, where she links the theme of imaginative sovereignty to the eclipse of publicly-oriented narratives. 'The Annotated House' is a pillar in a long-term project of self-construction which is taking place in a kind of metaphysical void. Hers is a quest for definition mainly conducted inside webs of literary influence – an individual struggle which takes place in an unpeopled, anonymous landscape. In relation to this struggle the public sphere has only the most limited relevance, teasing us, at best, with reminders of its absence. It may be that these "tricky and devious" reminders are what tempted Guinness to read her in politically feminist terms. But, as I have shown, there are alternatives to Monaco.

Notes:

1. Moynagh Sullivan, 'Irish Poetry after Feminism: In Search of "Male Poets"' in Justin Quinn ed. *Irish Poetry after Feminism: A Collection of Critical Essays* (Gerrard's Cross: Colin Smythe, 2008), pp. 14-34, p. 16.
2. Peter McDonald, 'The Touch of a Blind Man: Forms, Origins, and "Hermeneutics" in Poetry' in Justin Quinn ed. *op. cit*, pp. 35-44, pp. 35-6.
3. A fifth collection, *Spindrift*, was published in 2009 (Oldcastle: Gallery Press), after this chapter had been written.
4. Selina Guinness ed., *The New Irish Poets* (Newcastle: Bloodaxe, 2004), p. 129.
5. Vona Groarke, 'The Annotated House', *Juniper Street* (Oldcastle, Gallery, 2006), p. 55.
6. Selina Guinness, 'The Annotated House: Feminism & Form' in Justin Quinn ed. *op.cit.*, pp. 69-79: p. 74.
7. Vona Groarke, 'Shale', *Shale* (Oldcastle: Gallery, 1994), p. 11.
8. David Wheatley, 'Irish Poetry into the Twenty-First Century' in Matthew Campbell ed. *The Cambridge Companion to Contemporary Irish Poetry* (Cambridge: CUP, 2003), pp. 250-267: p. 261.
9. Justin Quinn, *The Cambridge Introduction to Modern Irish Poetry, 1800-2000* (Cambridge: Cambridge University Press, 2008), p. 207

10. Vona Groarke, 'The Riverbed, *Shale*, p. 14.

11. Vona Groarke, 'Patronage', *ibid.*, p. 23.

12. Vona Groarke, 'Patronage', *ibid.*, p. 23.

13. Vona Groarke, 'The History of my Father's House', *ibid.*, p. 26.

14. Vona Groarke, 'Sunday's Well', *ibid.*, p. 15.

15. John Mole, *Passing Judgements: Poetry in the eighties: Essays from Encounter* (Bristol: Bristol Classical Press, 1989), p. 96.

16. Groarke, 'Trousseau', *Shale*, p. 56.

17. Conor O'Callaghan, *Seatown*, (Winston-Salem: Wake Forest University Press, 2000), p. 42.

18. Vona Groarke, 'A few acres, a few ditches, some mist' *The Dublin Review* 5 Winter 2001-2, pp. 21-31: p.29.

19. David Wheatley, *op. cit.*, pp. 250-267: p. 262.

20. Terence Brown, *Ireland: A Social and Cultural History 1922-2002* (London: Harper Perennial, 2004), p. 384.

21. Vona Groarke, 'A few acres, a few ditches, some mist' *op. cit.*, pp. 21-31: p. 24.

22. Robert D. Putnam *Bowling Alone: The Collapse and Revival of American Community* (New York: Simon and Schuster, 2000), p. 177.

23. Vona Groarke, 'Lighthouses', *Other People's Houses,* (Oldcastle: Gallery Press, 1999), p. 36.

43. Peter Campbell, 'In an Empty Room', *London Review of Books* July 9 2009, p. 29.

25. Kieran Allen, *The Celtic Tiger: The myth of social partnership in Ireland* (Manchester and New York: Manchester University Press, 2000), p. 94.

26. Peadar Kirby, *The Celtic Tiger in Distress: Growth with Inequality in Ireland* (Basingstoke and New York: Palgrave, 2002), p. 5.

27. Fintan O'Toole, *After the Ball* (Dublin: New Island, 2003), p. 101.

28. Paul Durcan, *Paul Durcan's Diary* (Dublin: New Island, 2003), p. 24.

29. Vona Groarke, 'House Fire', *Other People's Houses*, p. 37.

30. Derek Mahon, 'Gipsies', *Selected Poems,* (Middlesex: Penguin, 2000), p. 36.

31. Michael Cronin, 'Ireland, Globalisation, and the War against Time' in Kirby, Peadar, Gibbons, Luke, and Cronin, Michael, eds. *Reinventing Ireland: Culture, Society and the Global Economy* (London: Pluto Press, 2002), p. 59.

32. Groarke, 'House Fire', *Other People's Houses*, p. 37.

33. Derek Mahon, 'The Sea in Winter', *Selected Poems*, p. 81.

43. Groarke, 'The Big House', *Other People's Houses*, p. 39.

35. Justin Quinn, *The Cambridge Introduction to Modern Irish Poetry, 1800-2000*, p. 208

36. Vona Groarke, 'The Verb "to herringbone" ', *Flight*, (Oldcastle: Gallery Press, 2006), p. 13.

37. Vona Groarke, *ibid.*, p. 47.

38. Vona Groarke, 'Pop', *ibid.*, p. 72.

39. Vona Groarke, 'A few acres, a few ditches, some mist' *op. cit.*, pp. 21-31: p. 29.

40. Selina Guinness, *op. cit.*, pp. 69-79: p. 78.

41. *ibid.*, pp. 77-78.

42. *ibid.*, p. 76.

43. Justin Quinn, *The Cambridge Introduction to Modern Irish Poetry, 1800-2000*, p. 209

44. Vona Groarke, 'Juniper Street', *Juniper Street* (Oldcastle: Gallery Press, 2002), p. 53.

45. Michael Longley, 'Swans Mating', *Collected Poems* (London: Jonathan Cape, 2006), p. 47.

DAVID JONES AND W.S. GRAHAM

One way in which public narratives distort the relationship between poetry and its readers is by encouraging the wrong kinds of attention, placing critical emphases where they are not due. Such narratives also contrive to take attention away from those writers who are more deserving, particularly in the case of poets like David Jones and W.S. Graham – the subjects of this chapter – who are considered to be modest or 'quiet'. While Jones and Graham, are not generally regarded as a pair, there are, to my mind, large similarities in their careers. Both were deeply damaged people, who lived idiosyncratic, ramshackle lives. Both were deeply uncomfortable with their working-class backgrounds, and depended on others for money. Both, under the influence of Eliot, wrote long religious poems based on the sea. Both operated at a distance from any national poetic project and from any real centre of literary power. Both shied away from the 'action', and thus managed to marginalise themselves. Their reputations have consequently suffered.

A recent essay in *New Welsh Review* spoke of David Jones as "unknown, misunderstood, misrepresented." It is hard to quarrel with this judgement. Even now, Graham could be assessed in similar terms. Are such outcomes simply the luck of the draw? While a poet's reputation depends, naturally enough, on the excellence of their work, it can be enhanced significantly by a range of extra-poetic factors. These include a sensational private life, celebrity (or proximity to it), attachment to a national or international literary project, convergence with the aims of a powerful or fashionable minority group, and close identification with an issue of some public urgency. It is impossible to argue with the judgement that Yeats and Hughes were excellent poets, but it is possible to argue that, because every one of the above factors worked in their favour, they are better known than they might have been. And it is possible to argue, in the cases of Jones and Graham, that because not one of the above factors worked in their favour, they are much less well-known than they might have been. One of the elements which draws us to these poets now is what initially kept some reader away: their distance from literary power. Both projected a self-effacing modesty which, on closer inspection, turns out to be something much more compromised and interesting.

As a recent study of the poet demonstrates, David Jones, who spent much of his life in therapy, is a subject unusually suited to psychological readings – sexually repressed, mother-orientated, chronically passive (or passive-aggressive), traumatised by war, agoraphobic, uncomfortably class-conscious, in short so over-supplied with neuroses it is a wonder he wrote at all.[1] Like the male figure in his painting, 'The Garden Enclosed', Jones is so far to the edge of his own picture that he is in danger of falling out of it. In his 'Autobiographical Talk' (collected in *Epoch* and *Artist*), Jones stressed the accidental character of his being what he is. The 'accidental' Jones was portrayed as the outcome of any number of contingent decisions from the victory in battle of Owain Gwynedd in 1149 to the decision of Jones's parents to encourage his drawing. The impulse to frame himself in this way was characteristically modest but it seemed to issue from something even deeper, more pathological, than modesty. While Jones wanted to be a small part of the story, or small parts in numerous stories, the effort of this was not to downgrade the small part but to elevate, to focus appropriate attention on, the larger whole.

Does a poet-painter, a London-Welshman fascinated by Roman Britain, who fought in and wrote about the First World War, and who saw world-history in religious terms, still speak to us now? Despite enlisting with the British Army to fight in the First World War (and wanting to enlist with King Arthur) Jones ended up without natural allies. Too awkward for any literary squad, his reputation has depended, and continues to depend, on the goodwill of individuals, mostly acting without coordination: endorsements from giants like Eliot and Auden; championing by critics like Thomas Dilworth and Neil Corcoran. While Jones's supporters emerge occasionally, they have no point of focus, no obvious leverage, for their campaign.

Jones's modesty is part of his charm – how novel to find a modernist poet who does not engage in distasteful breast-beating! I want to suggest, however, that the figure of the modest, self-erasing, 'accidental' Jones is something which comes between us and more useful readings of his work. Prospective readers may also be put off by the fact that is all too readily tugged into academic discussions. This is a little unfair. *In Parenthesis*, his prose-poem about the First World War, was densely-textured but rarely obscure. For all his modernist association with difficulty, Jones could be a very straightforward writer. Here is an example which arises early in his startling debut:

Some like tight belts and some like loose belts – trussed-up pockets –
cigarettes in ammunition pouches – rifle-bolts, webbing, buckles and rain
– gotta light mate – give us a match chum. How cold the morning is and
blue, and how mysterious in cupped hands glow the match-lights of a
concourse of men, moving so early in the morning.[2]

At this early stage of the poem, Jones allows himself to dwell on
the beauty of the military spectacle, framing the scene with his
painterly eye. Several signatures of his style are on display here: an
unusual attention to the materiality of things, especially those
manmade objects which have a precise technical function; a fondness
for pooling a set of almost interchangeable voices; and an enjoyment
of spectacle, the thrill of a large organised group moving across a
landscape.

Nor is the texture of his work always dense. Throughout *In Paren-
thesis*, especially, we find passages which are spare and uncluttered.
Often these are passages which, by virtue of their frequent lineation,
are more obviously 'poetic'. Here is an example of one of Jones's
experiments with a kind of centreless polyphony, as he allows a range
of voices to rise from the difficult stumbling of soldiers in the dark:

The repeated passing back of aidful messages assumes a cadence.
Mind the hole
mind the hole
mind the hole to left
hole right
step over
keep left, left
One grovelling, precipitated, with his gear tangled, struggled to feet again:
Left be buggered
Sorry mate – you all right china? – lift us yer rifle – an' don't take on so
     Honey – but rather, mind
the wire here
mind the wire
mind the wire
mind the wire
Extricate with some care that taut strand – it may well be you'll sweat on
    its unbrokenness.[3]

Compared with the first-quoted passage, this has an almost
Beckettian sparseness. As in *Waiting for Godot*, individual voices merge
with each other, as though sinking into and rising out of a deeper
communal voice, and the effect is oddly reinforced by a levelling

moment of slapstick – it could be you or me in that hole. One might add that these are just the kind of minimal, sinister props – hole, wire – which Beckett might have used, as is the whole impression of voices moving in an indistinct, emptied-out and stage-like landscape. One stresses this to indicate one of Jones's great strengths: stylistic variety.

A passive personality, Jones was said to have believed that the best way to get a cat to sit in your lap was *not* to stroke its back. It is hard to know what someone like this would make of being in a war, even if he does his best to tell us. One notices how in his inscriptions, or in his reproduced letters, Jones's writing would often leave the horizontal, curving around the edge of the page, proceeding upside-down and at right-angles, enclosing the text in a kind of embrace. Jones instinctively wanted to protect and to look after things – he had a maternal quality, something which must surely have appealed to Seamus Heaney, a poet who has felt his influence.

Jones's outlook was inclusive rather than conclusive. He was not a decisive artist. His poems, like his paintings, were curiously crowded because he wanted to leave nothing out, while suggesting that there was always more that could be put in. He tended to frame his visual material so that it could accommodate a hectic swirl of activity 'onstage', while at the same time, suggesting that even more exciting things were happening immediately 'offstage'. It was not for nothing that so many of his paintings contained open windows. In his writing, every footnote was a kind of open window. Everything he explained seemed to call for even further explanation, way led on to way. At the same time as the footnotes demonstrated how anxious Jones was to connect, each one created even more loose ends. So it was not so surprising that Jones's most ambitious poem, which would have greatly exceeded even *The Anathemata* in complexity and length, remained unfinished, and was probably unfinishable.

Jones's many-angled, gently inclusive imagination had little use for standard ideas of good and evil. Throughout his work, battles were won and lost, civilisations rose and fell, but in these dramas traditional categories like right and wrong played roles which are slight to vanishing. The war which *In Parenthesis* chronicled, was a matter for its soldiers to endure, a cosmic play into which they had stumbled. It was not a matter of ascribing blame. Like much else in his work, the war was simply not to be helped. It would have been redundant, then, for Jones's poetry to promote, or to appear to promote, any kind of political program. We sympathise with the soldiers of *In Parenthesis* as they live out their sacrifice, they are never allowed to be mere figures. Despite the book's large cast of characters, an aura of individuality settles over all who come into view. In this respect, a comparison with the work of Yeats, Eliot and Pound, works to Jones's advantage. He was rarely dismissive of other people. At the same time, Jones's characters never seem able to *effect* anything – to achieve, for example, an end to the war. Their operational efficiency, so admired by the narrator, ironically highlighted their cosmic helplessness.

Indeed, the soldiers endure their sacrifice much as Jones endured his poetic calling – as a vocation which must be played out to the end. His contract as a writer contained no escape-clause. His Catholicism, with its tragic focus on the Cross, is no doubt relevant here (Jones conceived of *The Anathemata* as a poem with the Cross, the axis of history, at its centre). He did not foresee practical solutions to historical problems. History, for Jones, was not a problem to be solved – and this was not a stance likely to endear him to politically-minded critics and readers.

Jones's self-erasing qualities must be placed in a careful context. Though contemporaries would describe him as mild, even 'hopeless', others noted a fanatical look in his eyes. One should not forget the single-minded nature of his project. Only someone with complete self-directedness, with a powerful inwardness, prepared to set his face against the world could possibly approach Jones's achievement. And this leads us to a tension in the work which is characteristic of much modern poetry. Jones's project was performative. We are left to admire the display, even though the work's ethos is implicitly hostile to attention-seeking.

In *The Performing Self*, Richard Poirier remarks that rickety, large-scale fictions, like God, principally move us now only in one way: by inspiring in us a nostalgia for the sense of completeness and reassurance which they once provided and, in turn, provoking us to create large-scale fictions which will replace such feelings:

> Creation follows on the discovery of waste. Fictions with the semblance and stimulus of reality, like God, become exposed by the pressure of time as no more than feeble fictions. They are strong enough only to promote nostalgia for the power they once exerted and excited, and to produce, in reaction to waste and loss, the desire to create new fictions, the excuse for new performances, new assertions of life.[4]

Poirier's suggestion that the imagination moves from waste to excess via performance is useful for thinking about Jones and his work because some of the ambitious qualities of the Welshman's work may distract us from its performative life.

When Jones says something like, "it is on account of the anthropic sign-making that we first suspect that anthropos has some part in a without-endness," we might think that he has it the wrong way around, that the idea of a without-endness arises from our ability to make signs.[5] And we might go on to say that it was not God who gave us writing and the wheel, but, as Régis Debray has it, writing and the wheel which gave us God. Poirier reminds us not only to look at what Jones, in his excessive way, concluded about God, but also how he reached that conclusion.

One of Jones's most appealing qualities was his desire to be fair. At no point reading *In Parenthesis*, do we feel that Jones was hostile to the German soldiers. A slight hostility to higher-ups in the British Army may be detected, but the overall impression is of a collective suffering which is common to all sides. Indeed this is clear from the book's dedication which concludes: "… to the enemy's front-fighters who shared our pains against whom we found ourselves by misadventure." The author's scrupulous fairness allows the psychology of the battle to be convincingly rendered. At one moment, Jones's protagonist, John Ball enters a wood where he engages in a grenade duel with a German soldier. In the aftermath of the battle (which he wins), Ball's attention comes to rest on odd little details:

> You scramble forward and pretend not to see,
> but ruby drops from young beech-sprigs –
> are bright your hands and face.
> And the other one cries from the breaking-buckthorn.
> He calls for Elsa, for Manuela
> for the parish-priest of Burkersdorf in Saxe Altenburg.
> You grab his dropt stick-bomb as you go, but somehow you don't fancy it and anyway you forget how it works. You definitely like the coloured label on the handle, you throw it to the tall weeds.
> So double detonations, back and fro like well-played-up-to-service at a net, mark left and right the forcing of the groves.

Jones supplies a footnote for his mention of the handle. The commentary is typical of his attitude:

> I cannot recall what it was, either stamped or labelled on the handle of a German stick-bomb, but I know the sight of it gave me pleasure–just as one likes any foreign manufacture, I suppose.

In the midst of all these horrors, he makes time to mention the design of the grenades. There is something oddly fitting in this. One rather doubts that every British soldier felt the same way about German stick-bombs, even though the way Jones tell it, one would think that this was a feeling widely shared. Incidentally, this illustrates how Jones was really only comfortable using 'I' in footnotes, usually with a kind of half-apologetic tone.

Jones's best book was his first. Like Flann O'Brien, another wildly idiosyncratic explorer of Celtic myth, Jones found himself early. The later books were impressive but – using the first achieved book as a benchmark – they were glittering signposts to what might have been. One thinks of *In Parenthesis* as a book which Jones felt compelled to write, and of *The Anathemata* as a book he felt he ought to write. It even seems significant that *In Parenthesis* used end-notes while *The Anathemata* uses footnotes. In the former one can choose to ignore the notes, in the latter this option is not really available. The difference is not trivial.

While it seems highly doubtful that he will be taken up by a general readership in the way that Joyce and Beckett are, his reputation is not in real danger. It is rather like worrying that not enough people read *The Mabinogion* or *The Tain* – Jones will surely outlast us. But I suggest that we read his work a little more perversely, not so much as pointing away from Jones as pointing right at him. We do better to read Jones as a weaver of his own fictions, as a self-creator. First and foremost, his books were a tremendous performance. Although not a vain poet he was, finally, self-assertive. I am not suggesting that we ignore the versions of the world to which he drew attention, but am suggesting that we dwell a little more on that from which he draws our attention, the performer and his performance.

*

In a century when many readers approach poets and other artists via the label of a group or movement, W.S. Graham had no label. In a period when writing was often politicised, by writers or critics, he was not political. Self-conscious about the working-class parts of his make-up, he wrote poems which were self-conscious about being made up. He lived his life – and to some degree chose to live it – at the margins of different, though ultimately interweaving, kinds of power.

The location of Greenock, his hometown, had a considerable influence on his poetry. During the period when it styled itself as the second city of the British Empire, Glasgow owed much of its economic prosperity to the river Clyde. Deepwater ships, arriving from the west, were not always able to navigate the whole length of the river (widened and deepened through various points in its history) and would sometimes deliver their cargo at more accessible locations. Greenock, downriver of Glasgow to the west, is located at the point where the Clyde widens dramatically into its Firth (or fjord), before flowing into the sea proper. Easily in reach of deepwater shipping, it was a place of traditional, labour-intensive industries, of fishing and shipbuilding, as well as being decidedly secondary in relation to the major city which it served. In sum it was a place through which traffic was always passing, a 'threshold', to use one of Graham's favourite words, between Glasgow and the sea.

Graham also lived at the periphery. Like Greenock he existed 'downstream' of the Big City, whether that city was Glasgow, London, or New York. While he could stay in any given metropolis for a short period of time he could never put down roots. Most of his life was lived in the relative seclusion of Cornwall, in the southwest corner of England, far removed from Scotland. His early years, like the ships and cargoes passing through Greenock, had an itinerant, provisional quality, as he moved about, always unsettled, and sometimes unsettling to others. His working-class background remained an issue – as he once said, jokingly: "Am I a poet? Or am I just a boy from Greenock?"

Graham's family lived on the top floor of a tenement building, which overlooked the "winches and steel giants" of the dockyards. As the son of a journeyman engineer, he left school at the age of fourteen, becoming a draughtsman's apprentice with a Glasgow engineering firm. Reading his work we sense the same link which is perceptible in Jones's poetry between class discomfort and an emphasis on technical capability. Partly that is because an emphasis on manual labour, on engineering knowhow (however widely or narrowly defined) is a nod to what – given the social and cultural patterns – one might have been, if one had not become a poet. A further point is that an emphasis on technology has a welcome levelling function – a complicated piece of machinery responds to you on the basis of your ability to operate it, not according to your accent.

As with Jones it is not necessary to take Graham at his own modest self-estimation. Even in the face of the simplest natural events, like the opening lines of 'Enter a Cloud', his poems generate force by being struck almost dumb. In this poem we encounter a very simple situation – a man lies on a hill and regards the sky. While the poem's diction is also simple, the sophistication of its syntax and line-breaks manages a dizzying depth out of seemingly nothing:

Gently disintegrate me
Said nothing at all.

Is there still time to say
Said I myself lying
In a bower of bramble
Into which I have fallen.

Look through my eyes up
At blue with not anything
We could have ever arranged
Slowly taking place.[6]

Attractively ineffectual, the speaking voice is constructed on the basis of its own marginalisation. The poem is, on the face of it, a plea not to be noticed, but as with Jones's work, this turns out to be a complicated form of self-display.

Most of Graham's life was lived in conditions which dipped in and out of poverty, and he was always dependent, to a greater or lesser extent, on the benevolence of others. From his teenage years, however, it was clear that he wished to improve himself, at least in a non-materialistic way. To the consternation of his traditionally-minded parents, he took some evening classes in Art appreciation and Literature at Glasgow University, and then, in 1938, began a year of study at an adult education institution, Newbattle Abbey College. Unusually progressive for the time, Newbattle modelled itself on an Oxford College, and was open to working students who were not from prosperous backgrounds. There Graham embarked on a mixed program of arts subjects, mainly concentrating on arts and philosophy. It was at this point that he gained a reputation among his classmates for writing poetry, as well as for being something of a 'character' or, more unkindly, a poseur.

These contacts also led further afield to London, and Graham moved south from Scotland to stay there in 1944. He became associated with the wartime literary community, especially the 'Fitzrovia' scene, which was based around pubs in Soho in the centre of London. In late 1944, Graham moved to Cornwall with Nessie Dunsmuir and initially they lived a very spartan existence in a pair of caravans.

Financially, they were not secure. Graham is said to have worked as
a casual labourer and fisherman during the early part of his residence
while his wife supplemented their income with some seasonal work
for a local hotel.

What is clear is that, except with very close personal friends,
Graham found communication stressful. In order to counteract this
difficulty, he would fuel himself with alcohol and treat each meeting
as a performance, even a high-wire act. Thus a reading, an interview
or the most casual encounter could easily become an adventure.
However jovially this was done, it tended to put his listeners, inter-
locutors and, indeed, readers on edge – or as he might see it, made
them aware that the edge was where they had been all along. A pattern
emerged, for example, of the poet turning his interviewers into inter-
viewees. Edwin Morgan, in his essay 'W.S. Graham and "Voice"',
records a typically amusing example taken from Graham's 1978
interview with Penelope Mortimer. It illustrates well the poet's
confrontational sense of humour:

> PM: Tell me about your parents.
> WSG: My dear. You must ask me something very small. Like 'Why do
> you put capitals at the beginning of the lines of your verse?'
> PM. Why do you put capitals at the beginning of the lines of your verse?
> WSG: To make people realize it's poetry.[7]

The advent of Graham's publishing career was not much appreciated
by his family. David Wright records one of Graham's more rueful,
and probably very painful memories, regarding the fate of *Cage
Without Grievance*:

> My father gave 5 dozen copies away to the paper salvage people about 4
> years ago. He just handed out the two packages which were unopened,
> straight from the printers. I had left them in the house when I went to
> Cornwall – thinking "well I'll always have those safe anyhow" – but there
> you are![8]

In an obvious point of comparison with Jones, Graham developed
relationships with many of the painters based around St Ives in
Cornwall. The setting was very agreeable to him. St Ives combined a
traditional (if declining) fishing community with the bohemian
atmosphere created by an influx of painters. Because of the Blitz
many were keen to escape London. Cornwall, where property was
cheap, had many attractions to painters: the chance to buy studio

space, the congenial presence of their peers, and the quality of the light. Graham met and made friends with many who would prove important to the history of postwar British painting like Peter Lanyon, Roger Hilton, and Bryan Wynter, writing poems about all of them.

The subject and methods of Graham's approach to writing found echoes in the attitudes of these painters. The style of the 'primitive' painter Alfred Wallis, for example, was a major influence on the St Ives painters, emphasising an existential approach to their art, blurring the border between subject and object. To this way of thinking, the painting (or the poem) was not so much as a commentary on life as an extension of it. Since the St Ives scene represented a mingling of Abstract Expressionism with British painting, Graham's position could be compared with those American poets like Frank O'Hara and John Ashbery, of the so-called 'New York School' who were coming to terms with Abstract Expressionism around the same time.

As a consequence of Graham's friendship with so many painters, his first book bore illustrations by Benjamin Crème and Robert Frame. Several poetic influences were at work on Graham in this collection: Hopkins, Dylan Thomas, and W.H. Auden – writers to which many in his generation responded. From Hopkins, Graham took the headlong rhythms, the compulsion to coin new words ("wildernight") and the packing of stresses in alliterative clusters ("garden day frames government"). From Auden he took the familiar psychologised landscape of 1930s British poetry, with its often sinister combination of pastoral and industrial images. From Thomas, however, he took the most. In his essay, 'W.S. Graham: Professor of Silence', Denis O'Driscoll draws attention to features of Dylan Thomas's style identified by John Berryman, the same features with which O'Driscoll notes Graham's poems become saturated:

> … unusual epithets, compound words, notions of dichotomy, marine imagery. Graham seemed to seize on all of them without allowing words the breathing space which Thomas did.[9]

Thomas's poems characteristically place a hazily-identified speaker, a kind of supercharged ego, within a network of conflicting and very powerful associations: love, grief, guilt, spring, summer. In this vein, Graham's first poem mysteriously touches on "jealous agonies" and "funnels of fever". The poem makes a sort of song or hymn out of this drama, which functions, often, as a measure of powerful, but entirely vague, states of feeling. The 'action' of the poem usually has a markedly surreal colouring and rarely lingers to describe any specific, recognisable state like a man walking down a street or a casual conversation. These poems depend on the inclusion of powerful ingredients, and when they fail, as they often do, it is usually through the inclusion of too many, rather than too few, of these ingredients.

Although Graham's poetry changed profoundly over the course of his writing career – deliriously lush at the beginning, quietly spare at the end – one feature of his aesthetic remained constant. Each poem was treated as what we might call an existential field. That is to the say the poem were not presented as commentaries on life, removed to one side. Each poem advertised its inseparability from life, and they became ever more self-conscious about this.

In Graham's second book he advanced a metaphor which remained with him throughout his career: the journey. The seven journeys of the title are related to the reader in the same breathless Thomasesque rhetoric of those in *Cage Without Grievance*. The general point of these is to declare personal independence, to show that the speaker is not dependent on external forces, like institutional religion. This is perhaps best illustrated by 'The Sixth Journey' in the course of which the speaker declares "the ocean my faith" and where he asks:

Who times my deity, defines my walking sin
In curfew inches on a chain of printed chimes?
What text is my breath on resurrected reefs
Where west records my teething bliss of helms?[10]

Even in this passage where the sense is (slightly) clearer than usual, most of the nouns are accompanied by unlikely and provocative adjectives. The passage seems to suggest that there is neither a law not an institution which can anticipate the experience of any moment. Each moment is a new experience, and the definition of its spirituality remains open.

In *2nd Poems*, a relatively short book, the 'I' of these poems was fractionally less impersonal and less supercharged than in the earlier work. Graham settled there on a recognisable Northern coastal landscape, which influenced his next book, *The White Threshold*. This was a significant transitional volume, which was also his first to be published by the preeminent British poetry firm, Faber and Faber. The book was accepted for publication by T.S. Eliot, and thus brought Graham into regular contact with the great man.

An important feature of *The White Threshold* was Graham's adoption of the three-stress line, a tempo which suited his contemplative style. Graham was reported to have trained himself in this form by using it to record every entry in one of his journals, an indication both of his ambitious formalism and of his single-mindedness. It was not just the three-stress line, however, which indicated his growing attention to form. The poems in *The White Threshold* were carefully shaped in a variety of ways with regular stanza forms, including ballad forms, tercets, quatrains, Yeatsian nine-line stanzas, and stanzas with patterned alterations of their line-lengths. There were a vast number of compounds in this book based on the word 'sea': 'seawind', 'sea-lamb', 'sea-tombs', 'seagreat', 'seachanged', 'sea-martyrdom', 'seabraes' and 'seabent' – a list which could readily be extended. The influence of the sea could also be felt in the titles like: 'Men Sign the Sea', 'Night's Fall Unlocks the Dirge of the Sea', 'Three Poems of Drowning' and 'The Voyages of Alfred Wallis' (the latter significantly drew a parallel between voyaging and painting).

The use of adjectives becomes markedly restrained, making descriptions crisper, and the diction becomes more harsh and clipped. This more measured style allows individual lines to stand out in a way which they could never have in his earliest work, as in the last stanza of 'Shian Bay':

> Last gale washed five into the bay's stretched arms,
> Four drowned men and a boy drowned into shelter.
> The stones roll out to shelter in the sea.[11]

The dignified finality of that last line, charged by the disturbing ambiguity of the word 'shelter' marks a new more powerful kind of effect in his work. The diction is unforced and simple, and the effects are gained precisely by the use of sombre understatement.

Attempting self-definition, *The White Threshold* (the title also refers to the sea), was an analysis of the poet's environment, the geographical and social factors which had shaped himself and his community. As such, it was the closest that Graham came to the mainstream of post-war British poetry. The style of the Movement called for restrained diction, careful observations and description and, more negatively, avoidance of grandiose poses and statements, or mystification of any kind. Since Graham was writing *The White Threshold* in the years before the Movement became established, he could not be said to be adhering to any program. Nevertheless the book demonstrated a temporary convergence with the cultural aims of some of his contemporaries, aims which would then sharply diverge.

The Nightfishing, his first really significant work, was dominated by two sequences, the title-poem and 'Seven Letters'. The epistolary sequence, 'Seven Letters' (an echo of *The Seven Journeys*), marked a significant advance in his technique. The letters were addressed to Graham's wife and inhabited a densely metaphorical landscape – recognisable features included the loch, the moor, the shore, and a pub called 'Mooney's' – combined with an increasingly self-reflexive focus on language:

> My love my love anywhere
> Drifted away, listen.
> From the dark rush under
> Us comes our end. Endure
> Each word as it breaks at last
> To become our home here.
> Who hears us now? Suddenly
> In a stark flash the nerves
> Of language broke. The sea
> Cried out loud under the keel.
> Listen. Now as I fall.[12]

'The Nightfishing' opens with a sound rather than a voice: the striking of a bell. The sound has qualities of command and strangeness, a solemnity which announces the process of change. That choice of opening reminds us of Graham's knowledge of, and love for, music. As a young man he was an enthusiast for choirs and singers, and travelled into Glasgow whenever he could to hear the best of them. 'The Nightfishing' too has a strikingly musical form, opening with a slow, dignified movement and gradually accelerating into the sonic storm of the long third section, until calming again towards its conclusion. As his friend Edwin Morgan testified, Graham's attitude to the reading of this poem (and others) was very much to perform like a cross between an opera singer and a stage-actor:

> I have his own copy of the programme he used for a reading at the Institute of Contemporary Arts in London on 26 November 1957, and the margins are spattered with handwritten commands to himself, almost in the manner of musical annotation, indicating exactly how particular lines are (or are not!) to be delivered. He writes: 'as clearly enunciated as possible', 'as formal and mechanical as possible', slow easy conversational', 'shock', 'take it easy', 'these words slow and separate', 'don't ham this', 'almost casual', 'slay them'.[13]

The opening of 'The Nightfishing' is also a kind of calling to attention, reminding us of Graham's uneasy desire to make a connection with a listener. At poetry readings, he treated the poem as a tour-de-force, and he would begin slowly, recognising the dramatic value of understatement.

> Very gently struck
> The quay night bell.

The opening illustrates the syntactical ambiguity which enlivens nearly all of Graham's poetry. Is the bell striking or is it being struck? Is it the object or the subject? The low-key invitation to listen which the poem extends to the reader remains at the heart of his work. An uncertainty about who or what is acting, or being acted upon, permeates the entire work.

There is, too, a synaesthetic aspect to Graham's work – that is to say, not only could he appreciate art forms other than poetry, he saturated himself in them. His poetry readings often became a dialogue between different kinds of art. Before a performance he would decorate a room with his own paintings and hangings, light the area with candles, and play appropriate music by Bartok or Mozart. The audience would be encouraged to join in and make dramatic sounds (the noise of a storm perhaps), while different poems would then be read by different voices. The sheer exuberance of this was striking, as if Graham were a man who sought in any given moment the special heightening which art, any art, can afford. As he once wrote: "I happen to feel most alive when I am trying to write poetry."

Such combinations were also a part of his working methods. When composing a poem over a long period Graham would use a wall, rather as a painter would use a canvas, and pin up phrases which he found particularly resonant. His notebooks were often composed in different inks, with lettering of different sizes, sometimes painted over with a wash of colour. His letters too, could read like an excerpt from Joyce's *Finnegan's Wake*, where a long list of puns and variations on words would unwind, creating a playful, intoxicating effect.

Although 'The Nightfishing' is presented as a journey out to sea, the reader is less conscious of where the speaker is going than of what he is undergoing. Whereas the poem may be based, in a ghostly way, on the form of a quest, there is no decisive arrival. Rather than progress, we have a sense of rising and falling (particularly falling) within an ambiguous environment. In a sense, 'The Nightfishing' creates a poetics of the wave, where the nature of its odyssey is the oscillation. The poem's insistent music – itself rising and falling through the seven sections – might be said to allow movement but not progress. If there is progress then it is circular in nature, like Shakespeare's "waves which approach the pebbled shore,/each one changing place with that which went before."

When he was at college, Graham took part in a production of J.M. Synge's 'Riders To The Sea', a one-act tragedy which invokes the sea as a symbolic force, while at the same time depicting the actual appalling conditions for fishermen on the west coast of Ireland. In that play, Synge effectively evokes the death of one of the fishermen, and anticipates the death of another, through the clothes retrieved from a drowned body. Although none of the action actually takes place on the sea, that element figures as an immensely powerful offstage presence, with the islanders like prisoners encircled by its malevolence. The entire atmosphere is one of doom and foreboding. In 'The Nightfishing', the outlook is not as bleak as this, informed as it is by Graham's energetic melancholy. Nevertheless, Graham's poem uses clothing in a similar way to Synge's play. The sea is presented as an all-encompassing, all-penetrating entity, which even works its way in to what the speaker wears:

> Here we dress up in a new grave,
> The fish-boots with their herring-scales
> Inlaid as silver of a good week,
> The jersey knitted close as nerves[14]

This quote from section II of the poem follows the speaker's discussion of the material conditions in which he has grown up. Again, as in Synge, the encroaching symbolism of the sea as a force of nature is not allowed to obscure bald observations about how harsh living conditions are for the speaker. It is precisely this kind of concrete detail which was absent from Graham's first book, *Cage Without Grievance*. The use of clothing details is of a piece with the points of technical authenticity ("tethers and springropes", "corks/And bladders") sprinkled throughout the text, from which the poem greatly benefits.

If Graham's poem is not a depiction of physical death, as in 'Riders To The Sea', it nevertheless anticipates and conveys a metaphysical death undergone by the speaker. The experience of the sea, which becomes a metaphor for all life-changing experience, focuses on the death of identity through experience. In the third section, words are inadequate to convey what happens and need constantly to be renewed as:

> This mingling element
> Gives up myself. Words travel from what they once
> Passed silence with. Here, in this intricate death,
> He goes as fixed on silence as ever he'll be.[15]

One of the other points of connection between 'The Nightfishing' and 'Riders To The Sea' is the association of the grave with domestic space:

> I sat rested at the grave's table
> Saying his epitaph who shall
> After me to shout farewell.[16]

Other antecedents of the poem include Pound's 'The Seafarer', Nansen's *Far North*, and *Moby Dick*. It also bears comparison with the maritime imagery, and religious, or quasi-religious, existentialism in Robert Lowell's 'The Quaker Graveyard At Nantucket', T.S. Eliot's 'Little Gidding', and, of course, parts of *The Anathemata*.

Despite being well-received, Graham did not follow up *The Nightfishing* with a new collection for fifteen years, when *Malcolm Mooney's Land* was published in 1970. He seemed to disappear from the literary scene at the very moment when he should have been most visible. One of his significant patrons during this bleak period in his life was Professor Robin Skelton, who as well as interceding with publishers on his behalf, was interested in collecting his manuscripts. In his introduction to an edition of Graham's notebooks, *Aimed at Nobody*, Skelton noted the extent of the poet's disappearance: "When in the late sixties I asked Faber & Faber why they had not seen fit to bring out a new Graham book I was astonished to be told that they had lost touch with him and did not know he was still writing."[17]

Faber may have forgotten about Graham simply because he went out of fashion. Whereas the typical Movement poem was ironic, low-key, and featured a lyric self acting in recognisable contemporary situations, the typical Graham poem was sincere, contemplative, and featured a fragmented self in strange, psychologised landscapes. Philip Larkin's *The Less Deceived*, one of the popular triumphs if the Movement style was published in the same year as *The Nightfishing* and probably helped to overshadow it.

Before embarking on a reading tour of Canada in 1973, when he was promoting *Malcolm Mooney's Land*, Graham wrote to a lecturer

friend at Calgary School of Art. Inquiring after the best approach to
Canadian audiences, the letter anxiously throws light on how Graham
saw the relationship between his background and his poetry:

> About the class thing. What shall I do? I suppose I am lower working class.
> Shall I be superior or inferior? How shall I behave? What shall I wear?
> I'm coming anyhow and I'll have to make the best of it fuck them.

This aspect of his personality was reflected in the stance taken by
his poetry. Calvin Bedient speaks of Graham's style as, "having
gained the surprised ring of one who had never expected to hear
himself speak".[18] One might add that part of the pathos of his later
poetry in particular was the articulation of a voice which did not
assume it would be heard. In their varying ways, the more public
poets of the 1960s, like Robert Lowell and Allen Ginsberg, wrote in
a way which commanded attention, where an audience was readily
assumed to exist. But Graham never counted on an audience. The
neglect of his writing must have hurt, however, and it is exactly
mirrored by the startling isolation of the speakers in *Malcolm
Mooney's Land*. Graham could not be certain about his words once
they had been digested by his readers, and this is something which
troubles his later poetry.

Graham's alcoholism, which played a considerable role in his life,
also partly derived from a Clydeside background where hard drinking
was common, the one easily available release for men from lower-
class backgrounds. The pub, though, was more to Graham than a
place where he could easily indulge himself. The culture of the pub
was close to the centre of his work, and often featured in his later
poetry. The pub was, for Graham, a meeting-place where views could
be exchanged, roles tried out and tested, and it permitted a kind of
heightened and free-flowing use of language. He was, for instance,
fascinated by the pub scene in 'The Waste Land' which foregrounds
this kind of slangy, side-of-the-mouth conversation. David Wright,
his friend and fellow-writer, has recorded examples of Graham's
sometimes abrasive pubtalk. Once confronted by a literary bore,
Graham suddenly burst out:

> In three days I will begin the novel of my life with – "Unlike my brother,
> the Grand Duke Ferdinand …". There is no reply –You have to sit and
> be talked to – OK OK Reply reply if you dare. Well well eh? So what?
> You don't know eh? –Yeheeh – Alright?, lay cards on table – I thought so.
> No cards eh?[19]

Perhaps one of the most puzzling aspects of Graham's character was how someone who, in person, could be voluble and gregarious, could also write such delicate, quiet, almost self-erasing poems. This paradox was mirrored by some other poets from the periods – like Dylan Thomas and Patrick Kavanagh – where the desire to become a 'character', with the help of alcoholic inspiration, masked fundamental sensitivity and shyness. A Celtic, that is to say a Scottish, Welsh, or Irish, poet of the time could be expected, especially by an English audience, to play a 'bardic' role, to play up to the stereotype of the mercurial, verbose, extravagant clown. Of course this role was also a trap.

Malcolm Mooney's Land opens spectacularly with the title poem, which introduces us to the book's uniquely frigid landscape, a snowscape which in its emptiness is even more uncompromisingly metaphorical than his earlier seascapes. In the title poem, which is divided into five sections, we read, as if in a journal, the words of an arctic explorer who is trying to come to terms with extreme conditions. Here is the definitive Graham figure, a seeker thrown entirely on his own resources, desperate to connect with others, yet facing the obstacles of the definitive Graham landscape, the blinding, page-like whiteness of the snow. The seeker is surrounded by figures and memories which rise beguilingly out of the whiteness as if to mock him with their presence. From time to time, he hallucinates a surreal yet significant event:

> Enough
> Voices are with me here and more
> The further I go. Yesterday
> I heard the telephone ringing deep
> Down in a blue crevasse.
> I did not answer it and could
> Hardly bear to pass.[20]

Commenting on his own book for a Poetry Society Bulletin, Graham wrote that a poem was not like a telephone call because you can never hear a voice speaking back. Thus the unanswered imaginary telephone in the ice partly stands for a possibility which is closed to explorer and to poet.

Again indicating Graham's fondness for the epistolary form, the explorer in 'Malcolm Mooney's Land' sometimes writes his journal as if it were a letter which has been found, or which is about to be found, like a message in a bottle. He dreamily addresses two figures in particular (not to be confused with any actual people in Graham's life) who may be his loved ones, 'Elizabeth' (possibly his wife or lover) and 'the boy' (possibly his son). Speaking of his expedition, the explorer urges Elizabeth to let the boy understand it in the form of a story:

> Tell him I came across
> An old sulphur bear
> Sawing his log of sleep
> Loud beneath the snow.
> He puffed the powdered light
> Up on to the page
> And here his reek fell
> In splinters among
> These words.[21]

The attractive simplicity of these lines with their almost reassuring tones, relates them to other forms which we usually encounter in childhood, the fairytale, the beast fable and the cartoon. With its imaginary creatures and its puzzling rules of behaviour, the book's imaginary landscape often resembles the imaginary landscape of a child.

After the opening poem, the figure of the explorer is replaced by others who are engaged in similar existential struggles. These figures remain isolated, they are never seen as part of a cohesive group. Often, they are artists, though other figures also appear: the climber, the gambler, and the prisoner. There lonely struggles taken to an extreme, against conditions which they may never overcome, are meant to be seen as parallel.

Given that Graham had started to become self-conscious about their literary status, it was not surprising that other literary writings became prominent within them. One of the foremost presences in the book was Samuel Beckett, a writer with whom Graham admitted he was fascinated. Particularly in his novels, Beckett presented a solitary voice very similar to the one we find in *Malcolm Mooney's Land*. That voice fails to come to terms with its own existence, although it can see no alternative to the attempt. In his essay, 'Walls of glass: The Poetry of W.S. Graham', Damian Grant lists the features which Beckett's novels have in common with Graham's later poetry:

> The revolving obsession with identity, consciousness, and articulating the telling of stories to create the fiction of the self; the reliance on pun and illusion as a literary method; the deepening doubt (which this implies) as

to the possibility of communication with our kind, and the admission of loneliness as one's ultimate condition ...[22]

Although the poems in the book are self-conscious, that does not mean that they are overwhelmingly cerebral or abstract. Graham does not allow us to forget that words are spoken by creatures of flesh and blood, especially in those poems which adopt the form of a letter. Although the poems have a strong emotional tug, they remain very human appeals from one person to an imagined other, with the poet usually able to stop just the right side of sentimentality. These qualities are particularly sharply felt in 'The Thermal Stair', his elegy for a painter friend, Peter Lanyon:

Uneasy, lovable man, give me your painting
Hand to steady me taking the word-road home.
Lanyon, why is it you're earlier away?
Remember me wherever you listen from.[23]

Childhood again appears in 'The Dark Dialogues', a long poem at the centre of the book which Graham, towards the end of his life, thought was his most successful. Here the landscape of the snow shifts into a ghostly evocation of Graham's own childhood in which he daringly imagines being, and speaks in the voice of, his parents. This also involves a description of the Greenock flat where he grew up:

Here, this is the door
With the loud grain and the name
Unreadable in brass.
Knock, but a small knock,
The children are asleep.
I sit here at the fire
And the children are there
And in this poem I am,
Wherever elsewhere I am,
Their mother through his mother.[24]

Again, as in 'The Nightfishing', Graham's use of pronouns unsettles easy identity. When we read this passage for the first time, we are not aware that the 'I' here is not the 'I' of the poem's other sections, that it is meant to be Graham's mother who is speaking. The effect is disorientating. While the poet locates himself within his own mother, he is, in the following section a ghostly presence in his own father. At

the same time, the poem traces a dizzying circle where Graham's
mother regards the boy who, later on, will imagine himself in the same
position as his mother looking at him. Unlike his earliest work where
the poem was a kaleidoscopic field for any number of heterogeneous
impressions, most of which were not arranged in any satisfactory
relationship to each other, each poem in *Malcolm Mooney's Land* is a
field where the situations described, the memories revived, are all
completely integrated. The poems behave like close relatives.

Implements In Their Places also begins with a poem in sections –
'What Is The Language Using Us For?' In its first section this poem
reintroduces us to the familiar explorer striking out over the frozen
wastes: "What is the language using us for?/ Said Malcolm Mooney
moving away/ Slowly over the white language?"[25] This opening
question is echoed throughout the rest of the book. At a philosophical
level, the poems have come to a point where they distrust the relation-
ship between words and the realities to which they refer. The poems
puzzle over the gaps between what is said and what was intended to
be said:

> What is the language using us for?
> I don't know. Have the words ever
> Made anything of you, near a kind
> Of truth you thought you were? Me
> Neither.[26]

One of the words which Graham repeatedly uses in what became
his last book is 'flying'. Giving to the poetry an eerie valedictory air,
this word is used to describe woods in 'The Murdered Drinker' and
'How Are The Children Born', and is used of jungles in 'Language
Ah Now You Have Me'. In the final stanza of 'A Note To The Difficult
One', the poet finishes addressing a mysterious other (himself? a
friend? the reader?) who is trying to speak:

> This morning I am ready if you are
> To speak. The early quick rains
> Of spring are drenching the window-glass.
> Here in my words looking out
> I see your face speaking flying
> In a cloud wanting to say something.[27]

This pattern crops up again in the book's concluding elegy, 'Dear
Bryan Wynter', where it seems to change the scene into something
phantasmagorical: "The house and the whole moor/ Is flying in the

mist."[28] Even though there are repeated images of flying in Graham's work, the movement is often downwards, as if the words were swooping down from a great height. As in 'The Nightfishing', the sea was no longer the all-embracing element of the poetry, but journeying still took place without any progress. As one of the fragments (No. 68) in the big title poem puts it:

> The earth was flat. Always
> The mind or earth wanderer's choice
> Was up or down, a lonely vertical.[29]

The long title-poem marked something of a departure in Graham's work, a sequence which was more like a collection of small fragments (there are 74 of them) which had not been worked into an obvious shape. Like a version of one of his work-boards on to which a set of vaguely interrelated pieces had been pinned, this was the closest Graham came to a poetry of process. This is not to say that the poem was disorganised, merely that Graham had decided to explore the possibilities of finishing a poem without the polish of complete finish. The difference felt throughout the book was not just that he was writing about language but that he was writing, intermittently, about his own technique:

> Nouns are the very devil. Once
> When the good nicely chosen verb
> Came up which was to very do,
> The king noun took the huff and changed
> To represent another object.
> I was embarrassed but I said something
> Else and kept the extravert verb.[30]

The emphasis on technique, meant as more than just friendly advice, was given a much fuller treatment in 'Johann Joachim Quantz's Five Lessons', in which a teacher instructs his student on how to play the flute. This recurrent theme had philosophical roots, and the title poem, as Tony Lopez has pointed out, owed its origins to Heidegger – Graham's examination of how we come to know the world through our implements, and the techniques that we have for employing them, is a central concern of *Being and Time*.[31] Through his final book, Graham showed that the fragments out of which he made his world are also his implements.

While Graham, like Jones, is a writer who might have been more

widely read, the Scottish poet has, more recently, received an
enhanced level of attention. Ralph Pite and Hester Jones contend that
his work has, "if anything, gained in stature and extended its reader-
ship, particularly during the 1990s."[32] In the beginning, though,
Graham did not receive his due. He was never fully accepted by the
Scottish Renaissance movement, at its height between the years 1920
and 1945. Although Graham himself never stopped identifying with
his homeland, thanks to his literary style and to his Cornwall migra-
tion, he seemed to be, for some, insufficiently Scottish. In any case
his fundamental stance was one of solitude – he did not exist for
formal groups or alliances, and they did not exist for him. During
periods when it was fashionable to be explicitly political, he was
obviously not so. This, as much as anything else, contributed to his
early neglect.

Notes:

1. Jonathan Miles and Derek Shiel, *David Jones: The Maker Unmade* (Bridgend:
Seren, 1995).
2. David Jones, *In Parenthesis* (London: Faber, 1937), p. 5.
3. *ibid.*, p. 36.
4. Richard Poirier, *The Performing Self,* (Piscataway Township: Rutgers University
Press, 2006), p. 39.
5. David Jones, *Epoch and artist: selected writings by David Jones* edited by Harman
Grisewood, 1959 (London: Faber, 1973), p. 156.
6. W.S. Graham, 'Enter a Cloud', *Implements in Their Places* (London: Faber,
1977), p. 33.
7. Edwin Morgan, 'W.S. Graham and Voice' in Ronnie Duncan and Jonathan
Davidson eds. *The Constructed Space: A Celebration of W.S. Graham* (Lincoln:
Jackson's Arm, 1994), 76-82, p. 78.
8. David Wright, 'W.S. Graham in the Forties – Memoirs and Conversations'
Edinburgh Review 75 (1987): 49-56, p 54.
9. Dennis O'Driscoll, Troubled Thoughts, Majestic Dreams (Oldcastle: Gallery,
2001), pp. 255-56.
10. W.S. Graham, 'The Sixth Journey' *The Seven Journeys* (Glasgow: William
McLellan, 1944), no page number.
11. W.S. Graham 'Shian Bay' *The White Threshold* (London: Faber, 1949), p. 39.
12. W.S. Graham, 'Seven Letters', *The Nightfishing* (London: Faber, 1955) p.
62.
13. Edwin Morgan, *op. cit.*, pp. 76-7
14. W.S. Graham, 'The Nightfishing', *The Nightfishing*, p. 18.
15. *ibid.*, p. 27.

16. *ibid.*, p. 31.

17. Quoted in W.S. Graham, *Aimed at Nobody* (London: Faber, 1993), p. viii.

18. Calvin Bedient, *Eight Contemporary Poets* (London: OUP, 1974), p. 173.

19. David Wright, *op. cit.*, p. 52.

20. W.S. Graham, 'Malcolm Mooney's Land' *Malcolm Mooney's Land* (London: Faber, 1970), p. 12.

21. *ibid.*, p. 15.

22. Damian Grant, 'Walls of Glass: The Poetry of W.S. Graham', in Peter Jones and Michael Schmidt ed. *British Poetry since 1970* (Manchester: Carcanet, 1980), pp. 22-38, p. 28.

23. W.S. Graham, 'The Thermal Stair', *Malcolm Mooney's Land*, p. 27.

24. W.S. Graham, 'The Dark Dialogues' *ibid.*, p. 31

25. W. S. Graham, 'What is the Language Using Us For', *Implements in their Places* (London: Faber, 1977) p. 11.

26. *ibid.*, p. 15.

27. W.S. Graham, 'A Note to the Difficult One', *ibid.*, p. 20.

87. W. S. Graham, 'Dear Bryan Winter', *ibid.*, p. 84.

29. W.S. Graham, 'Implements in their Places', *ibid.*, p. 80.

30. *ibid.*, p. 69.

31. Tony Lopez, *The Poetry of W.S. Graham* (Edinburgh: Edinburgh University Press, 1989)

32. Ralph Pite and Hester Jones, *W.S. Graham: Speaking Towards You* (Liverpool: LUP: 2004), p. 1.

Acknowledgements

We are grateful for permission to quote from the work of the poets discussed by John Redmond.

To Random House for quotation from the following poems by John Burnside: 'Vanishing Twin', 'Agoraphobia'. 'Scavenger', Muddy Road', 'Floating', 'The Man Who Was Answered by Himself' and 'Heimweh' all from *A Normal Skin* (Jonathan Cape 1997); 'A Stolen Child'. 'Hypothesis' and 'Wrong' from *Swimming in the Flood* (Jonathan Cape, 1995); 'Blue', 'The Unprovable Fact' and 'The Asylum Dance' from *Asylum Dance* (2000); 'A Lie About My Father' from *A Lie About My Father* (Jonathan Cape, 2006).
To John Burnside for quotation from 'Le Croisic' from *Gift Songs* (Jonathan Cape, 2007), Copyright © John Burnside 2007. Reproduced by permission of the author c/o Rogers, Coleridge & White Ltd., 20 Powis Mews, London W11 1JN.

To Vona Groarke and The Gallery Press Oldcastle, County Meath, Ireland for quotation from 'The History of My Father's House' from *Shale* (1994), 'The Big House' from *Other People's Houses* (1999), and 'The Annotated House' from *Juniper Street* (2006).

To the Estate of David Jones and Faber & Faber for permission to quote from 'In Parenthesis' by David Jones (*In Parenthesis*, Faber ,1963)

To Derek Mahon and The Gallery Press Oldcastle, County Meath, Ireland for quotation from 'A Disused Shed', 'Lives', 'An Unborn Child' and ' The Snow Party' from *New Collected Poems* (2011).

To Carcanet Press Ltd for four poems by Robert Minhinnick from *After the Hurricane* (2002).

INDEX

SEREN

Well chosen words

Seren is an independent publisher with a wide-ranging list which includes poetry, fiction, biography, art, translation, criticism and history. Many of our books and authors have been shortlisted for – and won – major literary prizes, among them the Costa Award, the Man Booker, the Forward Prize and the T.S. Eliot Prize.

At the heart of our list is well crafted writing and an idea presented interestingly or provcatvely. Seren is international in authorship and readership though rooted in Wales ('seren' is the Welsh word for 'star') from where we prove that writers from small countries have a worldwide relevance.

Our aim is to publish work of the highest literary and artistic merit that also succeeds commercially in a competitive and fast-changing publishing and reading environment. Help us achieve our goal by reading ore of our books – available from good bookshops and increasingly as e-books. You can buy Seren titles from our website. Join the Seren Book Club there and get a 20% discount on al our titles, from prize-winning contemporary poets to rediscovered poets like Keidrych Rhys, from critical works like *Poet to Poet: Edward Thomas' Letters to Walter de la Mare* to Irish classics like Liam Carson's wonderful *Call Mother A Lonely Field*.

www.serenbooks.com